C000257178

Celebrating the Saving Work of God

Celebrating the Saving Work of God

The Collected Shorter Writings of J. I. Packer
Volume 1

James I. Packer

paternoster press

Copyright © 1998 James I. Packer

First published in 1998 by Paternoster Press

04 03 02 01 00 99 98   7 6 5 4 3 2 1

Paternoster Press is an imprint of Paternoster Publishing,
PO Box 300, Carlisle, Cumbria, CA3 0QS, UK
http://www.paternoster-publishing.com

The right of James I. Packer to be identified as the Author of this Work has been
asserted by him in accordance with Copyright, Designs and Patents Act 1988.

*All rights reserved. No part of this publication may be reproduced,
stored in a retrieval system, or transmitted in any form or by any
means, electronic, mechanical, photocopying, recording or otherwise,
without the prior permission of the publisher or a licence permitting
restricted copying. In the UK such licences are issued by the
Copyright Licensing Agency,
90 Tottenham Court Road, London W1P 9HE*

British Library Cataloguing in Publication Data
A catalogue record for this book is available from the British Library

ISBN 0-85364-496-4

Unless otherwise stated, Scripture quotations are taken from the
HOLY BIBLE, NEW INTERNATIONAL VERSION
Copyright © 1973, 1978, 1984 by the International Bible Society.
Used by permission of Hodder and Stoughton Limited. All rights reserved.
'NIV' is a registered trademark of the International Bible Society
UK trademark number 1448790

Cover Design by Forum, Newcastle-Upon-Tyne
Typeset by WestKey Ltd, Falmouth, Cornwall
Printed in Great Britain by
Caledonian International Book Manufacturing Ltd

Contents

Foreword

When Martin Luther wrote the Preface to the first collected edition of his many and various writings, he went to town explaining in detail that theology, which should always be based on the Scriptures, should be done according to the pattern modelled in Psalm 119. There, Luther declared, we see that three forms of activity and experience make the theologian. The first is prayer for light and understanding. The second is reflective thought (*meditatio*), meaning sustained study of the substance, thrust, and flow of the biblical text. The third is standing firm under pressure of various kinds (external opposition, inward conflict, and whatever else Satan can muster): pressures, that is, to abandon, suppress, recant, or otherwise decide not to live by, the truth God has shown from his Word. Luther expounded his point as one who knew what he was talking about, and his affirmation that sustained prayer, thought, and fidelity to truth whatever the cost, become the path along which theological wisdom is found is surely one of the profoundest utterances that the Christian world has yet heard.

In introducing this mass of fugitive pieces I would only say that behind each of them lies a conscious attempt over more than forty years to hew to Luther's line, in hope that by adhering to his theological wisdom I might arrive at substantive wisdom in and through the grace of our Lord Jesus Christ. How far I have attained my goal is something that readers must judge for themselves. In retrospect, writing this material does not seem to have been time wasted, and it is my prayer that no one who explores it will feel that their time has been wasted either.

I thank Jim Lyster, Isobel Stevenson, Tony Graham and the rest of the staff at Paternoster for all their hard work in putting this collection together.

Chapter 1

The Trinity and the Gospel

Jesus answered 'I tell you the truth, no one can enter the kingdom of God unless he is born of water and the Spirit.'

John 3:5

Why is it that so many churches, schools, and colleges bear the name Trinity? I once taught at a British school called Trinity, and some people thought that its name came from the fact that three colleges had united to form it. But that, though true, was not the reason. We took the name Trinity College because Trinity is the Christian word for describing the Christian God.

The English Prayer Book of 1662, on which I was brought up, linked liturgical direction with tutorial instruction on many matters, and the Trinity was one of them. Accordingly, it directed that on Trinity Sunday, seven days after Pentecost, the Athanasian Creed should replace the Apostles' Creed in morning worship. Now this was not a very bright idea. The Athanasian Creed, which is a five-minute-long technical statement about the Trinity, takes a lot of unpacking; and if not unpacked, it bewilders. It contains lines like 'the Father incomprehensible, the Son incomprehensible: and the Holy Ghost incomprehensible' – which once, it is said, goaded a chorister into hissing, 'And the whole thing incom - prehensible!' I doubt whether much save mystification ever resulted from these yearly recitations, and the Prayer Book's insistence on them was something for which I could only, at best, give two cheers; perhaps on reflection, only one. But the Prayer Book then made up for this leaden requirement by a stroke of real genius. It set as its Trinity Sunday Gospel Jesus' conversation with Nicodemus in John 3. Have you ever thought of that conversation as a revelation of what faith in the Trinity is all about? It is so, as we are going to see.

'But what do we mean by faith in the Trinity?' asks someone (and I do not blame anyone for asking; the fact is that most worshipers

THE TRINITY AND THE GOSPEL was originally published in *Good News for All Seasons: 26 Sermons for Special Days*, Richard Allen Bodey, ed. (Grand Rapids: Baker Book House, 1987), pp. 91–98. Reprinted by permission.

nowadays are far from sure). Well, as stated in the Athanasian Creed, if I may hark back to that for a moment, it is the belief that God is as truly three as he is one; that the unity of his being, his 'substance,' as the creed calls it, is tripersonal; that the Father, the Son, and the Holy Spirit are coequal and coeternal, uncreated and inseparable, undivided though distinguishable. This is a truth that becomes clear when Jesus in the Gospels indicates, on the one hand, that though he is divine and to be worshipped, he is not the same person as the Father, whose will he does and to whom he prays – and then indicates, on the other hand, that the Holy Spirit, who will come as his deputy, is a further divine person on the same footing as himself. It is this truth that the Athanasian Creed is spelling out.

'But why,' asks the inquirer, 'does it use such long-winded laborious language?'

For a very good reason indeed. The purpose of what the creed so carefully says about the coeternity and coequality of the three persons within a single substance is defensive. The aim is to rule out erroneous ideas, of which there are always many when the Trinity is under discussion. There is, for instance, the idea that God is like the late great Peter Sellers in *Dr. Strangelove*, one person playing several roles in a single story. We actually project that idea every time we tell a Sunday-school class that as each lump of sugar has six sides, so the one God has three faces and identities. How common an illustration that is – and how heretical! I once saw a cartoon of a moth-eaten clergyman (Anglican, of course) telling a congregation of two old ladies, 'I know what you're thinking – Sabellianism!' The caption was meant, of course, as a joke (you realized that? good). But Sabellianism is the historic name for the idea I have just mentioned, and it is, in fact, widespread.

Then there is the idea that Jesus and the Spirit are not personally divine, but are God's two top creatures doing top jobs. Jehovah's Witnesses think that. There is also the idea that the Father, the Son, and the Holy Spirit are three gods whose solidarity in action masks the fact that they are not one in being. Mormons think that. A further false idea is that the Son is God of a weaker strain than the Father and that the Spirit's divinity is weaker still. All these ideas had a run for their money in the early church before being condemned as heresies. All of them still pop up from time to time today.

What this shows is that the idea of the Trinity is one of the hardest thoughts round which the human mind has ever been asked to wrap itself. It is far easier to get it wrong than to get it right. So if it were proposed that the Athanasian Creed should be not just dropped from public worship, but removed from the Prayer Book entirely, I should vote against the motion. The Athanasian Creed is historically a classic witness against unbiblical distortions and denials of the triunity of our God, and such witnesses will always be needed.

When, however, we turn to what Jesus said to Nicodemus, we find faith in the Trinity presented in quite a different light – not now as the linchpin of orthodox belief (which nonetheless it is), but as, literally and precisely, the sinner's way of salvation. How does Jesus' teaching here do this? Let me show you how.

Thirty years ago, in a 90-degree heat wave, a student group led me to the top of a 3,000-foot mountain outside Vancouver. The climb was rugged and the sweat was copious, but the view was glorious. When afterwards I asked where we had been, I was told I had climbed the Squamish Chief. I climbed it, however, without knowing what it was or what to call it. That is my illustration of how John 3:1–15, which we rightly think of as a passage proclaiming the gospel, introduces us to the Trinity. As one learns the Christian gospel and enters by faith into the riches of fellowship with God that it holds forth, one is, in fact, mastering the mystery of the Triune God. We might say he is climbing the mountain called the Trinity all the time, whether he realizes it or not. Jesus' conversation with Nicodemus makes this very clear. Look at it with me now.

Nicodemus, a senior Jewish ruler and theologian, a man as eminent as an archbishop, a cardinal, or a distinguished professor today, has come to meet Jesus, the novice preacher from the Galilean back-woods, who is in Jerusalem, it seems, for the first time since his ministry started. Being older (he appears to call himself an old man in verse 4 and was probably twice Jesus' age), Nicodemus speaks first. His opening words are kind words, words of affirmation and welcome. 'Rabbi (teacher),' he says, giving the young preacher a title of honour straight away, 'we [that is, "my colleagues and I," Jerusalem's top people] know you are a teacher who has come from God. For no one could perform the miraculous signs you are doing if God were not with him' (v.2). As if to say: 'I am sure, Jesus, that you are wondering whether we of the religious establishment accept you and approve of what you are doing and regard you as one of us. Well now, I am here to tell you that we do, and we shall be happy to have you as a regular member of our discussion circle (the Jerusalem Theological Society, as we might call it). Come and join us!' Such was the burden of Nicodemus' speech.

Do you see, now, what Nicodemus was doing under all that polite - ness? By treating Jesus as a recruit for the Jewish establishment, he was patronizing the Son of God! But Jesus did not accept patronage from Nicodemus or anyone else while he was on earth, just as he will not accept your patronage or mine now that he reigns in heaven. It is for us to bow down before him, not to expect him to bow down before us, whoever we are. So Jesus does not respond by thanking Nicodemus for his kind words. He strikes a different note and tells his eminent visitor that without being born again, one cannot see the kingdom of God. When Nicodemus expresses bewilderment, Jesus amplifies his meaning in the words of our text: 'I tell you the truth, no one can enter the kingdom of God unless he is born of water and the Spirit.' Then he explains that natural and spiritual birth are two different things and concludes: 'You should not be surprised at my saying, "You [plural: "you, Nicodemus, and all those whom you represent"] must be born again' (v.7).

Three Persons

I ask you, now, to notice two things. The first is that *there are three persons* mentioned in verse 5, which is our text. There is the 'I' of 'I tell you the truth,' the speaker, Jesus himself – God's 'one and only Son,' as John, in 1:14, has already called him, and as the beloved verse 16 of this chapter will call him again. There is 'God,' the One whom Jesus called Father and taught his disciples to call Father – God whose kingdom Jesus is announcing. And there is the Holy Spirit, through whose power in new creation one must start life all over again, if one is ever to see and enter the kingdom. These are the three persons of the divine Trinity who are our special concern now. This is the first of a number of places in John's Gospel where all three are spoken of together.

Three Stages

The second thing I ask you to notice is that *there are three stages* in the flow of Jesus' response to Nicodemus. We may set them out as follows.

> *Do you want to see and enter the kingdom of God? Then you must be born again, of water and the Spirit* (vv.3–10).

What is the kingdom of God? The whole New Testament makes clear that it is not a territorial realm (unless you think of the human heart as a territory), but a personal relationship. The kingdom exists in any life where God is made King and Jesus the Saviour is acknowledged as Lord. The relationship brings salvation from sin and Satan and spiritual death. Jesus bestows forgiveness of sins, adoption into God's family, and the joy of eternal life on all who entrust their destiny to him and give him the love and loyalty of their hearts. To this new relationship, the path – the only path, as Jesus explains to Nicodemus – is new birth. 'You must be born again.' Without new birth one can neither see nor enter the kingdom of God.

What is this new birth? What does it mean to be 'born of water and the Spirit?' Briefly, and with due respect to other views (for the ground here is much fought over), I state what seems to me to be quite clear. All explanations of this key phrase that posit a contrast between 'water' (John's baptism, Christian baptism, or the waters of physical birth) and 'the Spirit' are on the wrong track. 'Water' and 'the Spirit' are two aspects of one reality: namely, God's renewal of the fallen and unresponsive human heart. Jesus is referring back to these two aspects, the purifying and the energizing aspects, just as they were set forth in God's promise to renew Israelite hearts in Ezekiel 36:25–27:

> I will sprinkle clean water on you . . . I will cleanse you from all your impurities and from all your idols. I will give you a new heart and put a new spirit in you . . . I will *put my Spirit* in you and move you to follow my decrees and be careful to keep my laws (italics mine).

Sinners who are naturally and habitually in rebellion against God, as were the Jews of Ezekiel's day and of Jesus' day – and as we are, too, with the rest of the human race – need an inward cleansing and a change of heart that only God can bring about. Of this inward transformation, 'new birth' is a two-word illustration – a parable, in fact. The change is so radical and drastic that it constitutes a totally fresh start to one's life. That is what makes the picture of being born again so fitting a way to describe it.

Why am I sure that Jesus' words about water and the Spirit look back to Ezekiel? Because of the way Jesus chides Nicodemus in verse 10. 'You are Israel's teacher,' he says 'and do you not understand these things?' Jesus is implying that such ignorance is shameful in a Jewish teacher. But the rebuke only has point if the things Nicodemus did not understand were things that the Jewish Scriptures clearly set forth.

Thus Jesus lays it down that only through new birth can Nicodemus, or you, or I, or anyone else, come into the kingdom of God. This leads to the second stage in his flow of thought.

Do you want to be born again? Then you must be willing to learn from Jesus Christ (vv.11–13).

You have met people whose behaviour leads you to say, 'You can't tell them anything.' In verse 11, Jesus says that Nicodemus and his peers are behaving that way towards him and his disciples: 'I tell you the truth, we speak of what we know, and we testify to what we have seen, but still you people do not accept our testimony'. By Nicodemus' own admission, the Jewish theologians did not know about the new birth and God's present kingdom, but they had not so far shown any willingness to accept teaching on these things from Jesus, the country preacher. Yet Jesus was in reality the Son of man – that is, the Messiah – who had come down from heaven, as verse 13 declares, in order to make these things known!

Before we condemn those Jewish leaders, however, we should ask ourselves if we are any wiser than they were at this point. Do we let Jesus teach us spiritual things? Have we let him teach us our own need of new birth? Will we let him teach us the way into God's kingdom? This is the topic to which he now moves on. Hear him well, then, as he utters his final challenging words about it.

Are you willing to learn from Jesus Christ? Then let him teach you to trust in him and his cross for your salvation (vv.14–15).

Once more Jesus refers to the Old Testament – this time to the story in Numbers 21:6–9, which tells how Israelites suffering snakebite were told to look at a brass snake that Moses, at God's command, had put up on a pole: and those who looked lived. 'Just as Moses lifted up the snake in the desert,' says Jesus 'so the Son of Man must be lifted up, that everyone who believes in him may have eternal life'. The final message to Nicodemus, and to us, is this: Believe in Jesus – that is, trust in him, rely on him, tell him that he is your only hope, embrace him as your Saviour – and your sins will be forgiven, your sickness of spirit healed, and your uncleanness before God washed away. Then you will know that you, too, have been born again.

The statement of verses 14 and 15, pointing as it does to Jesus' cross as the means of our salvation, is the purest gospel, as is the beloved sixteenth verse that follows it: 'For God so loved the world that he gave his one and only Son, that whoever believes in him shall not perish but have eternal life'. In learning the good news from these words, we are on familiar ground. But what I am asking you to notice now is that the entire conversation with Nicodemus presents us with profound teaching about the Trinity also, by setting before us the person and work both of God's Son and of God's Spirit. Jesus, we learn, is the God-sent, divine-human sin-bearer, who by his cross secured eternal life for us. The Spirit is the divine regenerator who by transforming our inner disposition, and in that sense changing our nature, enables us to experience the life of the kingdom of God. Without the Son and the Spirit there can be no salvation for anyone.

One Truth

What it amounts to, then, is that in this passage, as in many more throughout the New Testament, the truths of the Holy Trinity and of sovereign saving grace prove to be not two truths but one. The doctrine of salvation is the good news of the Father's giving us his Son to redeem us and his Spirit to renew us. The doctrine of the Trinity is the good news of three divine persons working together to raise us into spiritual life and bring us to the glory of God's kingdom. The Athanasian Creed guards this good news in the way that fences round a field guard growing crops from preying animals. Such fences are needed, but they do not have equal value with the crops they protect, and such value as they have derives from those crops themselves. Trinitarian orthodoxy, in other words, has value only as it sustains and safeguards evangelical faith.

Two conclusions follow for us, therefore.

First: Do not dismiss the doctrine of the Trinity as so much useless lumber for the mind. If the place of any of the three persons is miscon - ceived or denied, the gospel falls. Jehovah's Witnesses and Mormons, and those liberal Protestants for whom the personal deity of the Son and the Spirit is suspect, can never state the gospel rightly because they think of the Godhead wrongly. Clear confession of the Trinity is foundational. The gospel proclaims precisely the joint saving action of the three persons, and it is lost as soon as one's hold on their distinct divine personhood slackens.

Second: Let the doctrine of the Trinity keep your understanding of the gospel in good shape. Let it remind you to give equal emphasis in your thinking and your witness to the sovereign initiative of the Father who planned salvation, the atoning sacrifice of the Son who obtained salvation, and the mighty power of the Spirit who applies salvation. Let it prompt you to lay equal stress on the love of each in the work of grace. The late Dr. D. Martyn Lloyd-Jones used to tell how early in his ministry a senior pastor said to him that having listened to several of Lloyd-Jones' sermons, he could not make out whether 'the Doctor' was a Quaker or a hyper-Calvinist, because all the sermons centred on either the Spirit's work in the human heart or the sovereignty of God in salvation, and so little was said about the cross and faith in the crucified Saviour. 'The Doctor' quickly took the point! But there are many preachers today, and other Christians, too, who in their thinking and speaking either stress the cross all the time and say all too little about the Spirit, or stress God's saving plan or the Spirit's renewing work all the time and say all too little about the cross. Take care! False proportions in our doctrine are the beginning of false doctrine itself.

So let the truth of the Trinity keep you balanced at this point. Make it a matter of conscience to do full justice in your thought, your speech, and your worship, both in public and in private, to the love, wisdom, power, and achievement of each divine person separately, as well as of all three together. Then your theology will benefit, and your soul will prosper, and your whole life will express, as it should, the spirit of this old and precious doxology with which I close:

Glory be to the Father, and to the Son, and to the Holy Spirit; As it was in the beginning, is now, and ever shall be, world without end. Amen.

Chapter 2

On Covenant Theology

I

The name of Herman Wits (Witsius, 1636–1708) has been unjustly forgotten. He was a masterful Dutch Reformed theologian, learned, wise, mighty in the Scriptures, practical and 'experimental' (to use the Puritan label for that which furthers heart-religion). On paper he was calm, judicious, systematic, clear and free from personal oddities and animosi - ties. He was a man whose work stands comparison for substance and thrust with that of his younger British contemporary John Owen, and this writer, for one, knows no praise higher than that! To Witsius it was given, in the treatise here reprinted, to integrate and adjudicate explorations of covenant theology carried out by a long line of theological giants stretching back over more than century and a half to the earliest days of the Reformation. On this major matter Witsius's work has landmark status as summing up a whole era, which is why it is appropriate to reprint it today. However, in modern Christendom covenant theology has been unjustly forgotten, just as Witsius himself has, and it will not therefore be amiss to spend a little time reintroducing it, in order to prepare readers' minds for what is to come.

II

What is covenant theology? The straightforward, if provocative answer to that question is that it is what is nowadays called a hermeneutic – that is, a way of reading the whole Bible that is itself part of the overall interpretation of the Bible that it undergirds. A successful hermeneutic is

ON COVENANT THEOLOGY was originally published as the Introduction to Herman Witsius, *The Economy of the Covenants Between God and Man: Comprehending a Complete Body of Divinity*, tr., William Crookshank, (London, 1822; reprinted, Escondido, Calif. the Den Dulk Christian Foundation, 1990). Reprinted by permission.

a consistent interpretative procedure yielding a consistent understanding of Scripture that in turn confirms the propriety of the procedure itself. Covenant theology is a case in point. It is a hermeneutic that forces itself upon every thoughtful Bible-reader who gets to the place, *first*, of reading, hearing, and digesting Holy Scripture as didactic instruction given through human agents by God himself, in person; *second*, of recognizing that what the God who speaks the Scriptures tells us about in their pages is his own sustained sovereign action in creation, providence, and grace; *third*, of discerning that in our salvation by grace God stands revealed as Father, Son and Holy Spirit, executing in tri-personal unity a single co-operative enterprise of raising sinners from the gutter of spiritual destitution to share Christ's glory for ever; and, *fourth*, of seeing that God-centred thought and life, springing responsively from a God-wrought change of heart that expresses itself spontaneously in grateful praise, is the essence of true knowledge of God. Once Christians have got this far, the covenant theology of the Scriptures is something that they can hardly miss.

Yet in one sense they can miss it: that is, by failing to focus on it, even when in general terms they are aware of its reality. God's covenant of grace in Scripture is one of those things that are too big to be easily seen, particularly when one's mind is programmed to look at something smaller. If you are hunting on a map of the Pacific for a particular Polynesian island, your eye will catch dozens of island names, however small they are printed, but the chances are you will never notice the large letters spelling PACIFIC OCEAN that straddle the map completely. Similarly, we may, and I think often do, study such realities as God's promises; faith; the plan of salvation; Jesus Christ the God-man, our prophet, priest and king; the church in both testaments, along with circumcision, passover, baptism, the Lord's supper, the intricacies of Old Testament worship and the simplicities of its New Testament counterpart; the work of the Holy Spirit in believers; the nature and standards of Christian obedience in holiness and neighbour-love; prayer and communion with God; and many more such themes, without noticing that these relational realities are all covenantal in their very essence. As each Polynesian island is anchored in the Pacific, so each of the matters just mentioned is anchored in God's resolve to relate to his human creatures, and have us relate to him, in covenant – which means, in the final analysis, a way for man to relate to God that reflects facets of the fellowship of the Son and the Spirit with the Father in the unity of the Godhead. From this, perhaps, we can begin to see how big and significant a thing the covenantal category is both in biblical teaching and in real life.

'The distance between God and the creature is so great,' says the Westminster Confession (VII.i), 'that although reasonable creatures do owe obedience unto him as their Creator, yet they could never have any fruition of him as their blessedness and reward, but by some voluntary condescension on God's part, which he hath been pleased to express *by way of covenant.*' Exactly! So biblical doctrine, first to last, has to do with covenantal relationships between God and man; biblical ethics has to do with expressing God's covenantal relationship to us in covenantal rela - tionships between ourselves and others; and Christian religion has the nature of covenant life, in which God is the direct object of our faith, hope, love, worship, and service, all animated by gratitude for grace.

Our theme is the life-embracing bedrock reality of the covenant relationship between the Creator and Christians, and it is high time we defined exactly what we are talking about. A covenant relationship is a voluntary mutual commitment that binds each party to the other. Whether it is negotiated, like a modern business deal or a marriage contract, or unilaterally imposed, as all God's covenants are, is irrelevant to the commitment itself; the reality of the relationship depends simply on the fact that mutual obligations have been accepted and pledged on both sides. Luther is held to have said that Christianity is a matter of personal pronouns, in the sense that everything depends on knowing that Jesus died for *me*, to be *my* Saviour, and that his Father is *my* God and Father, personally committed to love, nurture, uphold, and glorify *me*. This already is covenant thinking, for this is the essential substance of the covenant relationship: God's covenant is precisely a matter of these personal pronouns, used in this way, as a basis for a life with God of friendship, peace and communicated love.

Thus, when God tells Abraham, 'I will establish *my* covenant as an everlasting covenant between *me* and *you* and *your* descendants after you . . . to be *your* God . . . I will be *their* God' (Gen. 17:6–8), the personal pronouns are the key words: God is committing himself to Abraham and Abraham's seed in a way in which he does not commit himself to others. God's covenant commitment expresses eternal election; his covenant love to individual sinners flows from his choice of them to be his for ever in the peace of justification and the joy of glorification. The verbal commit - ment in which electing sovereignty thus shows itself has the nature of a promise, the fulfilment of which is guaranteed by God's absolute fidelity and trustworthiness – the quality that David Livingstone the explorer celebrated by describing God as 'an honourable gentleman who never breaks his word.'

The covenant promise itself, 'I will be your God,' is an unconditional undertaking on God's part to be 'for us' (Rom. 8:31), 'on our side' (Ps. 124:15), using all his resources for the furthering of the ultimate good of those ('us') to whom he thus pledges himself. 'I will take you as my own people, and I will be your God' (Ex. 6:7), the covenant promise constantly repeated throughout both testaments (Gen. 17:6–8, Ex. 20:2, 29:45f.; Lev. 11:45; Jer. 32:38; Ezek. 11:20, 34:30f., 36:28; 2 Cor. 6:16–18; Rev. 21:2f.; etc.), may fairly be called the pantechnicon promise, inasmuch as every particular promise that God makes is packed into it – fellowship and communion first ('I will be with you,' 'I will dwell among them,' 'I will live among you,' etc.), and then the supply of every real need, here and hereafter. Sovereignty and salvation, love and largesse, election and enjoyment, affirmation and assurance, fidelity and fullness thus appear as the spectrum of themes (the second of each pair being the fruit of the first as its root) that combine to form the white light, glowing and glorious, of the gracious self-giving of God to sinners that covenant theology proclaims.

The God-given covenant carries, of course, obligations. The life of faith and repentance, and the obedience to which faith leads, constitute the covenant-keeping through which God's people receive the fullness of God's covenant blessing. 'I carried you on eagles' wings and brought you to myself. Now *if you obey me fully and keep my covenant*, then out of all nations you will be my treasured possession' (Ex. 19:4f.). Covenant faithfulness is the condition and means of receiving covenant benefits, and there is nothing arbitrary in that; for the blessings flow from the relation - ship, and human rebelliousness and unfaithfulness stop the flow by disrupting the relationship. Israel's infidelity was constantly doing this throughout the Old Testament story, and the New Testament makes it plain that churches and Christians will lose blessings that would otherwise be theirs, should covenant fidelity be lacking in their lives.

III

From what has been said so far, three things become apparent. First, *the gospel of God is not properly understood till it is viewed within a covenantal frame* .

Jesus Christ, whose saving ministry is the sum and substance of the gospel, is announced in Hebrews as the mediator and guarantor of the covenant relationship (Heb. 7:22, 8:6). The gospel promises, offering Christ and his benefits to sinner, are therefore invitations to enter and enjoy a covenant relationship with God. Faith in Jesus Christ is accord - ingly the embracing of the covenant, and the Christian life of glorifying God by one's words and works for the greatness of his goodness and grace has at its heart covenant communion between the Saviour and the sinner. The church, the fellowship of believers that the gospel creates, is the community of the covenant, and the preaching of the Word, the practice of pastoral care and discipline, the manifold exercises of worship together, and the administration of baptism and the Lord's supper (corresponding to circumcision and passover in former days) are all signs, tokens, expressions, and instruments of the covenant, through which covenantal enrichments from God constantly flow to those who believe. The hope of glory, as promised in the gospel, is the goal of the covenant relationship (Rev. 21:2f.), and Christian assurance is the knowledge of the content and stability of that relationship as it applies to oneself (Rom. 5:1–11,

8:1–39). The whole Bible is, as it were, presented by Jesus Christ to the whole church and to each Christian as the book of the covenant, and the whole record of the wars of the Word with the church as well as the world in the post-biblical Christian centuries, the record that is ordinarily called church history, is precisely the story of the covenant going on in space and time. As artists and decorators know, the frame is important for setting off the picture, and you do in fact see the picture better when it is appropriately framed. So with the riches of the gospel; the covenant is their proper frame, and you only see them in their full glory when this frame surrounds them, as in Scripture it actually does, and as in our theology it always should.

Second, *the Word of God is not properly understood till it is viewed within a covenantal frame.*

Covenant theology, as was said above, is a biblical hermeneutic as well as a formulation of biblical teaching. Not only does it spring from reading the Scriptures as a unity, it includes in itself specific claims as to how this should be done. Covenant theology offers a total view, which it is ready to validate from Scripture itself if challenged, as to how the various parts of the Bible stand related to each other. The essence of the view is as follows. The biblical revelation, which is the written Word of God, centres upon a God-given narrative of how successive and cumulative revelations of God's covenant purpose and provision were given and responded to at key points in history. The backbone of the Bible, to which all the expository, homiletical, moral, liturgical, and devotional material relates, is the unfolding in space and time of God's unchanging intention of having a people on earth to whom he would relate covenantally for his and their joy. The contents of Scripture cohere into a single consistent body of truth about God and mankind, by which every Christian – indeed, every human being – in every generation is called to live. The Bible in one sense, like Jesus Christ in another, is God's word to the world.

The story that forms this backbone of the Bible has to do with man's covenant relationship with God first ruined and then restored. The original covenantal arrangement, usually called the Covenant of Works, was one whereby God undertook to prolong and augment for all subsequent humanity the happy state in which he had made the first human pair – provided that the man observed, as part of the humble obedience that was then natural to him, one prohibition, specified in the narrative as not eating a forbidden fruit. The devil, presented as a serpent, seduced Adam and Eve into disobeying, so that they fell under the penal sanctions of the Covenant of Works (loss of good, and corruption of nature). But God at once revealed to them in embryo a redemptive economy that had in it both the covering of sin, and a prospective victory for the woman's seed (a human Saviour) over the serpent and his malice. The redemptive purpose of this new arrangement became clearer as God called Abraham, made a nation from his descendants, saved them from slavery, named himself not only their God but also their King and Father, taught them his law (the family code), drilled them in sacrificial liturgies, disciplined their disobedience, and sent messengers to hold up before them his holiness and his promise of a Saviour–King and a saving kingdom; which in due course became reality. The Westminster Confession summarizes what was going on in and through all this.

> Man, by his fall, having made himself incapable of life by (the first) covenant, the Lord was pleased to make a second, commonly called the covenant of grace: wherein he freely offereth unto sinners life and salvation by Jesus Christ, requiring of them faith in him, that they may be saved, and promising to give unto all those that are ordained unto eternal life his Holy Spirit, to make them willing and able to believe . . .
>
> This covenant was differently administered in the time of the law, and in the time of the gospel; under the law it was administered by promises, prophecies, sacrifices, circumcision, the paschal lamb, and other types and ordinances delivered to the people of the Jews, all foresignifying Christ to come, which were, for that time, sufficient and efficacious, through the operation of the Spirit, to instruct and build up the elect in faith in the promised Messiah, by whom they had full remission of sins, and eternal salvation; and is called the Old Testament.
>
> Under the gospel, when Christ, the substance, was exhibited, the ordinances in which this covenant is dispensed are the preaching of the Word, and the administration of the sacraments of Baptism and the Lord's Supper . . . in them: it is held forth in more fullness, evidence and spiritual efficacy, to all nations, both Jews and Gentiles; and is called the New Testament. There are not therefore two covenants of grace, differing in substance, but one and the same, under various dispensations (VII. iii, v, vi).

So the unifying strands that bind together the books of the Bible are, *first*, the one covenant promise, sloganized as 'I will be your God, and you shall be my people,' which God was fulfilling to his elect all through his successive orderings of covenant faith and life; *second*, the one messenger and mediator of the covenant, Jesus Christ the God–man, prophet and king, priest and sacrifice, the Messiah of Old Testament prophecy and New Testament proclamation; *third*, the one people of God, the covenant community, the company of the elect, whom God brings to faith and keeps in faith, from Abel, Noah and Abraham through the remnant of Israel to the world-wide New Testament church of believing Jews and Gentiles; and *fourth*, the one pattern of covenant piety, consisting of faith, repentance, love, joy, praise, hope, hatred of sin, desire for sanctity, a spirit of prayer, and readiness to battle the world, the flesh, and the devil in order to glorify God – a pattern displayed most fully, perhaps, in Luther's 'little Bible,' the Psalter, but seen also in the lives of God's servants in both Testaments and reflected more or less fully in each one of the Old and New Testament books. Covenant theologians insist that every book of the Bible in effect asks to be read in terms of these unities, and as contributing to the exposition of them, and is actually misunderstood if it is not so read.

Third, *the reality of God is not properly understood till it is viewed within a covenantal frame*.

Who is God? God is the triune Creator, who purposes to have a covenant people whom in love he will exalt for his glory. ('Glory' there means both God's demonstration of his praiseworthiness and the actual praising that results.) Why does God so purpose? – why, that is, does he desire covenantal fellowship with rational beings? The most we can say (for the question is not one to which God has given us a direct answer) is that the nature of such fellowship observably corresponds to the relationships of mutual honour and love between Father, Son and Holy Spirit within the unity of the divine being, so that the divine purpose appears to be, so to speak, an enlarging of this circle of eternal love and joy. In highlighting the thought that covenantal communion is the inner life of God, covenant theology makes the truth of the Trinity more meaningful than it can otherwise be.

Nor is this all. Scripture is explicit on the fact that from eternity, in light of human sin foreseen, a specific agreement existed between the Father and the Son that they would exalt each other in the following way: the Father would honour the Son by sending him to save lost sinners through a penal self-sacrifice leading to a cosmic reign in which the central activity would be the imparting to sinners through the Holy Spirit of the redemption he won for them; and the Son would honour the Father by becoming the Father's love-gift to sinners and by leading them through the Spirit to trust, love and glorify the Father on the model of his own obedience to the Father's will. This Covenant of Redemption, as it is commonly called, which underlies the Covenant of Grace, clarifies these three truths at least:

(1) The love of the Father and the Son, with the Holy Spirit, to lost sinners is shared, unanimous love. The tritheistic fantasy of a loving Son placating an unloving Father and commandeering an apathetic Holy Spirit in order to save us is a distressing nonsense.

(2) As our salvation derives from God's free and gracious initiative and is carried through, first to last, according to God's eternal plan by God's own sovereign power, so its ultimate purpose is to exalt and glorify the Father and the Son together. The man-centred distortion that pictures God as saving us more for our sake than for his is also a distressing nonsense.

(3) Jesus Christ is the focal figure, the proper centre of our faith-full attention, throughout the redemptive economy. He, as Mediator of the Covenant of Grace and of the grace of that covenant, is as truly an object of divine predestination as are we whom he saves. With him as our sponsor

and representative, the last Adam, the second 'public person' through whom the Father deals with our race, the Covenant of Grace is archetypally and fundamentally made, in order that it may now be established and ratified with us in him. ('With whom was the covenant of grace made?' asks question 31 of the Westminster Larger Catechism, and the prescribed answer is: 'The covenant of grace was made with Christ as the second Adam, and in him with all the elect as his seed.') From the vital union that we have with Christ through the Holy Spirit's action flows all the aliveness to God, all the faith, hope and love Godward, all the desire for him and urges to worship him and willingness to work for him, of which we ever were, are, or will be conscious; apart from Christ we should still be spiritually dead (objectively, lifeless; subjectively, unresponsive) in our trespasses and sins. Christ is therefore to be acknowledged, now and for ever, as our all in all, our Alpha and Omega, so far as our salvation is concerned – and that goes for salvation subjectively brought home to us, no less than for salvation objectively obtained for us. The legalistic, sub-spiritual Roman Catholic theology of Mass and merit, whereby Christians are required by the Father, and enabled by the Son, to take part in the achieving of their own salvation, is a further distressing nonsense.

These three truths together shape the authentic biblical and Reformed mentality, whereby God the Father through Christ, and Christ himself in his saving ministry, are given all the glory and all the praise for having quickened us the dead, helped us the helpless, and saved us the lost. Writes Geerhardus Vos:

> Only when the believer understands how he has to receive and has received everything from the Mediator and how God in no way whatever deals with him except through Christ, only then does a picture of the glorious work that God wrought through Christ emerge in his consciousness and the magnificent idea of grace begin to dominate and form in his life. For the Reformed, therefore, the entire *ordo salutis* [order of salvation], beginning with regeneration as its first stage, is bound to the mystical union with Christ. There is no gift that has not been earned by him. Neither is there a gift that is not bestowed by him and that does not elevate God's glory through his bestowal. *Now the basis for this order lies in none other than in the covenant of salvation with Christ* . In this covenant those chosen by the Father are given to Christ. In it he became the guarantor so that they would be planted into his body in the thought-world of grace through faith. As the application of salvation by Christ and by Christ's initiative is a fundamental principle of Reformed theology, this theology has correctly viewed this application as a covenantal requirement which fell to the Mediator and for the fulfilling of which he became the guarantor.[1]

---

[1] *Redemptive History and Biblical Interpretation* , ed. Richard B. Gaffin (Philadelphia: Presbyterian and Reformed, 1980), p. 248.

The full reality of God and God's work are not adequately grasped till the Covenant of Redemption — the specific covenantal agreement between Father and Son on which the Covenant of Grace rests — occupies its proper place in our minds.

Thus it appears that, confessionally and doxologically, covenant the - ology brings needed enrichment of insight to our hearts; and devotionally the same is true. Older evangelicals wrote hymns celebrating the covenant of grace in which they voiced fortissimos of triumphant assurance of a kind that we rarely hear today — so it will be worth our while to quote some of them. They merit memorizing, and meditating on, and making one's own; ceaseless strength flows to those saints who allow these sentiments to take root in their souls. Here, first, is the eighteenth-century leader, Philip Doddridge:

> 'Tis mine, *the covenant of his grace*,
>   And every promise mine;
> All sprung from everlasting love,
>   And sealed by blood divine.
> On my unworthy favoured head
>   Its blessings all unite;
> Blessings more numerous than the stars,
>   More lasting, and more bright.

And again:

> My God! *the covenant of thy love*
>   Abides for ever sure;
> And in its matchless grace I feel
>   My happiness secure.
> Since thou, the everlasting God.
>   My Father art become;
> Jesus, my Guardian and my Friend,
>   And heaven my final home;
> I welcome all thy sovereign will,
>   For all that will is love;
> And, when I know not what thou dost,
>   I wait the light above.

Also in the eighteenth century, Augustus Toplady wrote this:

> A debtor to mercy alone,
>   Of *covenant mercy* I sing;
> Nor fear, with thy righteousness on,
>   My person and offering to bring.

The terrors of law, and of God,
    With me can have nothing to do:
My Saviour's obedience and blood
    Hide all my transgressions from view.

The work which his goodness began
    The arm of his strength will complete;
His promise is Yea and Amen,
    And never was forfeited yet.
Things future, nor things that are now,
    Not all things below or above,
Can make him his purpose forego,
    Or sever my soul from his love.

Then, a hundred years later, Frances Ridley Havergal gave us the following:

Jehovah's covenant shall endure,
All ordered, everlasting, sure!
O child of God, rejoice to trace
Thy portion in its glorious grace.

'Tis thine, for Christ is given to be
The covenant of God to thee;
In him, God's golden scroll of light,
The darkest truths are clear and bright.

O sorrowing sinner, well he knew,
Ere time began, what he would do!
Then rest thy hope within the veil;
His covenant mercies shall not fail.

O doubting one, Eternal Three
Are pledged in faithfulness for thee;
Claim every promise sweet and sure,
By covenant oath of God secure.

O feeble one, look up and see
Strong consolation sworn for thee:
Jehovah's glorious arm is shown
His *covenant strength* is all thine own.

O mourning one, each stroke of love
A *covenant blessing* yet shall prove;
His *covenant love* shall be thy stay;
His *covenant grace* be as thy day.

O Love that chose, O Love that died,
O Love that sealed and sanctified,
All glory, glory, glory be,
O covenant Triune God, to thee!

One way of judging the quality of theologies is to see what sort of devotion they produce. The devotional perspective that covenant theology generates is accurately reflected in these lyrics. Readers will make up their own minds as to whether such devotion could significantly enrich the church today, and form their judgement on covenant theology accordingly.

IV

Earlier it was said that the Bible 'forces' covenant theology on all who receive it as what, in effect, it claims to be – God's witness to God's work of saving sinners for God's glory. 'Forces' is a strong work; how does Scripture 'force' covenant theology upon us? By the following four features, at least.

First, by *the story that it tells*. The books of the Bible, from Genesis to Revelation, are, as was said earlier, God's own record of the progressive unfolding of his purpose to have a people in covenant with himself here on earth. The covenantal character of God's relationships with human beings, first to last, has already been underlined, and is in fact reflected one way and another on just about every page of the Bible. The transition in Eden from the covenant of works to the covenant of grace, and the further transition from all that was involved in the preliminary (old) form of that covenant to its final (new) form, brought in through the death of Jesus Christ and now administered by him from his throne, are the key events in the covenant story. The significance of the fact that God caused his book of instruction to mankind to be put together with the history of his covenant as its backbone can hardly be overestimated. Covenant relationships between God and men, established by God's initiative, bringing temporal and eternal blessings to individuals and creating community among them, so that they have a corporate identity as God's people, are in fact the pervasive themes of the whole Bible; and it compels thoughtful readers to take note of the covenant as being central to God's concern.

Second, Scripture forces covenant theology upon us by the *place it gives to Jesus Christ* in the covenant story. That all Scripture, one way and another, is pointing its readers to Christ, teaching us truths and showing us patterns of divine action that help us understand him properly, is a principle that no reverent and enlightened Bible student will doubt. This being so, it is momentously significant that when Jesus explained the memorial rite for himself that he instituted as his people's regular form of worship, he spoke of the wine that they were to drink as symbolizing his blood, shed to ratify the new covenant – a clear announcement of the fulfilling of the pattern of Exodus 24 (Jesus echoes directly the words of verse 8) and the promise of Jeremiah 31:31–34. It is also momentously significant that when the writer to the Hebrews explains the uniqueness and finality of Jesus Christ as the only source of salvation for sinners he does so by focusing on Jesus as the mediator of the new covenant and depicts him as establishing this prophesied relationship between God and his people by superseding (transcending and thereby cancelling) the inadequate old covenant institutions for dealing with sins and giving access to God. It is also momentously significant that when in Galatians Paul tells Gentiles that their faith in Christ, as such, has already made them inheritors of all that was promised to Abraham, he makes the point by declaring that in union with Christ, as those who by baptism have 'put on' the Christ in whom they have trusted so as to become his own people, they are now the seed of Abraham with whom God has made his covenant for all time (Gal. 3) – the covenant that brings liberty from law as a supposed system of salvation and full fellowship for ever with God above (Gal. 4:24–31). Such Scriptures require us to interpret Christ in terms of God's covenant, just as they require us to interpret God's covenant in terms of Christ, and this fact also alerts thoughtful readers to the centrality of the covenant theme.

The third way in which Scripture directs us to covenantal thinking is by *the specific parallel between Christ and Adam* that Paul draws (Rom. 5:12–18; 1 Cor. 15:21f., 45–49). The solidarity of one person standing for a group, involving the whole group in the consequences of his action and receiving promises that apply to the whole group as well as to himself, is a familiar facet of biblical covenant thought, usually instanced in the case of family and national groups (Noah, Gen. 6:18, 9:9; Abraham, Gen. 17:7; the Israelites, Ex. 20:4–6, 8–12; 31:12–17 (16); Aaron, Lev. 24:8f.; Phinehas, Num. 25:13; David, 2 Chr. 13:5, 21:7; Jer. 33:19–22). In Rom. 5:12–18 Paul proclaims a solidarity between Christ and his people (believers, Rom. 3:22–5:2; the elect, God's chosen ones, 8:33) whereby the law-keeping, sin-bearing obedience of 'the one man' brings right - eousness with God, justification, and life to 'the many,' 'all;' and he sets this within the frame of a prior solidarity, namely that between Adam and his descendants, whereby our entire race was involved in the penal consequences of Adam's transgression. The 1 Corinthians passages con - firm that these are indeed covenantal solidarities; God deals with mankind through two representative men, Adam and Christ; all that are in Adam die; all that are in Christ are made alive. This far-reaching parallel is clearly foundational to Paul's understanding of God's ways with our race, and it is a covenantal way of thinking, showing from a third angle that covenant theology is indeed biblically basic.

The fourth way in which Scripture forces covenant theology upon us is by *the explicit declaring of the covenant of redemption*, most notably (though by no means exclusively) in the words of Jesus recorded in the Gospel of John. All Jesus' references to his purpose in the world as the doing of his Father's will, and to his actual words and works as obedience to his Father's command (John 4:32–34; 5:30; 6:38–40; 7:16–18; 8:28f.; 12:49f.; 14:31; 15:10; 17:4; 19:30); all his further references to his being sent by the Father into the world to perform a specific task (3:17, 34; 5:23, 30, 36, 38; 6:29, 57; 7:28, 29, 33; 8:16, 18, 26; 9:4; 10:36; 11:42; 12:44; 13:20; 14:24; 15:21; 16:5; 17:3, 8, 18, 21, 23, 25; 20:21; cf. 18:37); and all his references to the Father 'giving' him particular persons to save, and to his acceptance of the task of rescuing them from perishing both by dying for them and by calling and shepherding them to glory (6:37–44; 10:14–16, 27–30; 17:2, 6, 9, 19, 22, 24); are so many testimonies to the reality of the covenant of redemption. The emphasis is pervasive, arrest - ing, and inescapable: Jesus' own words force on thoughtful readers recognition of the covenant economy as foundational to all thought about the reality of God's saving grace.

V

Historically, covenant theology is a Reformed development: Huldreich Zwingli, Henry Bullinger, John Calvin, Zacharias Ursinus, Caspar Olevi - anus, Robert Rollock, John Preston, and John Ball, were among the contributors to its growth, and the Westminster Confession and Catechisms gave it confessional status. Johann Koch (Cocceius) was a Dutch stormy petrel who in a Latin work, *The Doctrine of the Covenant and Testament of God (Summa doctrinae de foedere et testamento dei*, 1648) not only worked out in detail what we would call a biblical–theological, redemptive–historical perspective for presenting covenant theology (three periods – the covenant of works, made with Adam; the covenant of grace, made with and through Moses; the new covenant, made through Christ), but muddied his exegesis by allegorical fancies and marginalized himself by needless attacks on the analytical doctrine-by-doctrine approach to theological exposition that was practised by his leading contemporaries in Holland, Maccovius, Maresius, and Voetius. It seems clear with hindsight that his method and theirs were complementary to each other, and that both were necessary then, as they are now. (Today we name the Cocceian procedure 'biblical theology' and that which he opposed 'systematic theology,' and in well-ordered teaching institutions students are required to study both.) But for more than half a century following the appearance of Cocceius' book clouds of controversy hung over Holland as Cocceians and Voetians grappled with each other, each side trying to prove the illegitimacy and wrong-headedness of what the other was attempting.

Within this embattled situation, Witsius tries to have the best of both worlds – and largely succeeds. His full title (*The Economy of the Covenants between God and Man: comprehending a complete Body of Divinity*) might seem to claim too much; but it is clearly a friendly wave to the Cocceians, who were insisting that the only way to organize theology and set out Christian truths was in terms of the historical unfolding of God's covenant dealings. His four books, the first on the Covenant of Works, the second on the Covenant of Redemption, the third on the Covenant of Grace, and the fourth on covenant ordinances at different times, and on the knowledge and experience of God's grace that these conveyed, are a journey over Cocceian ground, in the course of which Witsius, excellent exegete that he is, manages to correct some inadequacies and errors that poor exegesis in the Cocceian camp had fathered. But he treats each topic analytically, and draws with evident happiness on the expository resources produced by systematicians during the previous 150 years including, be it said, much deep wisdom from the Puritan–Pietist tradition, which is particularly evident in Book Three. This is a head-clearing, mind-forming, heart-warming treatise of very great value; we possess nothing like it today, and to have it available once more is a real boon. I thank the publishers most warmly for taking a risk on it, and I commend it enthusiastically to God's people everywhere.

Chapter 3

Jesus Christ the Lord

What think ye of Christ? That's the test
To try both your state and your scheme.
You cannot be right in the rest
Unless you think rightly of him.

So, two centuries ago, wrote John Newton, 'the old converted slave-trader.' Was he right?

By biblical standards he most certainly was. 'State' means 'spiritual condition'; 'scheme' means 'theological system'; claims to hold a 'scheme' of truth and to be in a 'state' of grace become vulnerable where one's Christology – that is, one's thoughts about the person and place of Jesus of Nazareth, whom Christians since Pentecost have called Christ (cf. Acts 2:36) – is suspect. John showed this when he condemned both the 'scheme' and the 'state' of Gnostic separatists on the grounds that 'every spirit which does not confess Jesus [sc. as Son of God come in the flesh] . . . is the spirit of antichrist' (1 John 4:2f; cf. 2 John 7), and that 'any one who goes ahead and does not abide in the [sc. apostolic] doctrine of Christ does not have God' (2 John 9).

Historically, it has not been seriously doubted till modern times that belief in the incarnation – that is, the taking of full humanity by the Son of God or, putting it the other way round, the full personal deity of the man Jesus – is essential to Christianity. Two sets of reasons have been held to show that this is so.

Christology and Christian Belief

Set one has to do with *theology*, that is, our understanding of God and his relation to everything everywhere that is distinct from himself. The Christian consensus has been that, as Scripture is the proper source from

JESUS CHRIST THE LORD was originally published in *Obeying Christ in a Changing World*, vol. 1; *The Lord Christ*, ed. John R. W. Stott (London: Harper Collins, 1977), pp. 32–60. Reprinted by permission.

which theology should flow, so Christology is the true hub round which the wheel of theology revolves, and to which its separate spokes must each be correctly anchored if the wheel is not to get bent. That all historic Christianity's most distinctive convictions have been decisively shaped by belief in the incarnation is not hard to see. Let me illustrate.

Take *God*. Why do Christians hold that the one God is plural (triple, to be exact), and that he is at once intolerably severe, terrifyingly perceptive, and infinitely good? Ultimately, it is because they hold that Jesus, who prayed to his Father and promised the Spirit, and whose character was as described, was personally divine.

Or take *humanity*. Why do Christians hold that personal relationships matter more than anything in this world, and that the truly human way to live – in the last analysis, the only non-bestial way – is lovingly, constantly, unreservedly to give yourself away to God and to others, and that anything less offends God? Ultimately, it is because they hold that Jesus was as fully human as he was divine, and that as he taught these things so he lived them, and that at the deepest level of personhood his was the one perfect human life that the world has seen.

Or take *God's Word*. Why are Christians sure, despite all the difficulties, that the Bible is God's own inspired and authoritative instruction? Ultimately, it is because Jesus, the Son of God, showed constantly that the Old Testament Scriptures were to him his Father's word, teaching him his Father's way.[1]

Or take *God's Church*. Why do Christians view their thousands of congregations as not just a chain of clubs or interest groups, but as outcrops of a single organic entity, the one 'body' of ransomed, healed, restored and forgiven sinners, brothers and sisters in one family sharing a new supernatural life through common links with Christ their 'head'? Ultimately, it is because Jesus taught his disciples to see his Father as their Father, his death as their ransom sacrifice, and himself as their way to the Father, their bread of life, and the vine in which, as branches, they must abide.

Or take *human destiny*. Why do Christians hold, despite the felt limitations which aging bodies impose, and despite endless speculations and superstitions about the larger life of departed spirits, that full humanness requires re-embodiment, and hence anticipate physical resurrection? Ultimately, it is because they are sure that Jesus rose physically from death, and that his rising is the model for ours.

---

[1] Scholars vary in their understanding of Jesus' attitude to the Old Testament, but Rudolf Bultmann's statement seems to hit the nail on the head: 'Its authority stands just as fast for him (Jesus) as for the Scribes, and he feels himself in opposition to them only in the way he understands and applies the Old Testament.' *Theology of the New Testament* (London: SCM Press, 1952), I.16. For extended discussion, see John W. Wenham, *Christ and the Bible* (Leicester: Tyndale Press, 1972).

Or, lastly, take *world history*, Why do Christians, facing the chaos of an overcrowded world in which technological titans are spiritual pyg -mies and mass starvation seems the only alternative to nuclear holocaust, cling to the hope of a cosmic triumph of divine justice and power? Ultimately, it is because they believe that God's risen Son reigns, really if hiddenly, over all things, and is pledged to return in glory to judge and renew that world which he, with the Father and the Holy Spirit, first created.

So we see that all the main distinctives of the Christian creed spring from Christian Christology. What *follows?* This: that if you alter the Christology, you should alter the derived beliefs as well, since there is now no good reason for maintaining them in their original form.

Thus, if we think that Jesus, though a fine, God-filled man, was not personally divine, we should follow Unitarians in treating Trinitarianism as a mistake, and give it up.

Again, if we think that Jesus did not rise, but 'lives' and 'reigns' only in his followers' memories and imaginations, and is not actively and objectively 'there' in the place of power, irrespective of whether he is acknowledged or not, we should give up hope of our own rising, and of Jesus' public return, and admit that the idea of churches and Christians being sustained by the Spirit-given energy of a living Lord was never more than a pleasing illusion.

And in that case we ought frankly to affirm that, though the New Testament is an amazing witness to the religious creativity of the human spirit, its actual message is more wrong than right, more misleading than helpful, and we must reconstruct our gospel accordingly. Only a weak, muddled or cowardly mind will hesitate to do this. [2] But then it will be a misuse of language to call our theology Christian; for, as we have seen, the forms of faith and thought to which that name has been given over the best part of two millennia all depend on belief in the incarnation. [3]

Christology and Christian Experience

Set two of reasons for regarding belief in Jesus' deity as central to Christianity must now be noted. This has to do with *religion* – that is, our actual response to God. The relevant facts here are that it is

---

[2] In this connection it is worth recalling C. S. Lewis' trenchant words to theological students in *Fern-seed and Elephants* (London: Fontana, 1975), pp. 105f.
[3] Maurice Wiles urges that 'any theology that emerges out of a serious attention to the Christian tradition has a prima facie claim to being considered a Christian theology' (*Working Papers in Doctrine*, London: SCM Press, 1976, p. 192). But to be Christian, a theology must do more than engage with Christian themes; it must make recognisably Christian affirmations.

characteristic of Christians to *approach* Jesus Christ in prayer and worship, and to *commune* with him in a relationship of faith and hope, loyalty and love, openness and dependence; and both activities implicitly assert his deity.

Take the latter first. The Christian claim from New Testament time has been that God confronts men not only in those intimations of creaturely dependence and obligation which come to all persons alive in God's world,[4] but also in the person of the risen Christ, the divine Saviour whose portrait is in the gospels and whose place in God's purpose is the theme of the whole New Testament. Christianity (so Christians love to say) is Christ – not just theological notions plus a code of practice, but fellowship with the Father and Jesus Christ his Son (cf. 1 John 1:3). More particularly, Christianity (so it is affirmed) is a prolonging and universalizing for all disciples of that one-to-one rela - tionship with Jesus which his first followers enjoyed in Palestine in his earthly ministry.

There are, indeed, two differences. First, we know more of who and what Jesus is than anyone knew before his passion. Secondly, once Jesus is now physically absent from us, our connection with him is not via our physical senses, but through his own inward application of biblical material to mind and heart in a way which is as familiar to believers as it is mysterious to others.[5] But the actual sense of being confronted, claimed, taught, restored, upheld and empowered by the Jesus of the gospels has been the essence of Christian experience over nineteen centuries, just as it is demonstrably of the essence of what New Testament writers knew, promised and expected.[6] To assume, however, that Jesus is alive, univer - sally available, and able to give full attention simultaneously to every disciple everywhere (and this is the biblical and Christian assumption) is, in effect, to declare his divinity.

Moreover, Christians have from the start addressed prayer and praise to the Son as well as to the Father.[7] It seems that Jesus taught the propriety of praying to him once he had returned to the Father,[8] and in any case if his disciples could rightly make requests of him while he was on earth it could hardly become wrong for them to do so when 'the days of his flesh' gave way to the days of his reign. In AD 112 the younger Pliny found

---

[4] cf. Rom. 1:18–21, 28, 32; 2:12–15.

[5] 'The watershed of the Resurrection led to the discovery by the Church of the continuing impact of the risen Lord, different in idiom but identical in impact with his fellowship with the disciples during his earthly life'. (H. E. W. Turner, *Jesus the Christ*, London: A. R. Mowbray, 1976, p. 109).

[6] cf. 2 Tim. 4:17f.; 2:7, etc.

[7] cf. Acts 7:59f.; 22:7–21; 2 Cor. 12:8f.; Heb. 4:14–16.

[8] John 14:13f.

Christians meeting before dawn to 'recite a hymn of praise to Christ, as to a god,'[9] and much Christian liturgy and hymnody goes the same way. Typical is the *Te Deum*: 'Thou art the King of glory, O Christ . . . we therefore pray thee, help thy servants . . .' And also the Prayer Book Litany:

> By the mystery of thy holy Incarnation . . . by thy Cross and Passion . . . by the coming of the Holy Ghost, good Lord, deliver us . . . Graciously hear us, O Christ; graciously hear us, O Lord Christ.

All this, however, as Athanasius told the Arians long ago, would be the height of irreverence were Jesus not held to be divine.

What has been said so far highlights two facts about biblical and later Christianity: first, that belief in Jesus' deity is so essential to it that at no significant point could it have become what it is had this belief not operated; secondly, that Christian faith means not just acknowledging Jesus' deity, but also seeking and finding a personal relationship with him in which we receive of his fulness and respond to his love in the devotion of discipleship. Christians have not always achieved agreement on how this relationship is mediated (some stressing sacraments as an alternative to the gospel word), but they agree that the relationship is real, and that the deepest and saddest division in the Christian world, deeper than any gulf dividing denominations, is and always was the division within congregations between those who know Jesus Christ in experience and those who do not. It is the reality of this relationship for Christian people that explains the pain they feel when confronted with what seems to them Christological misbelief which insults and diminishes their Saviour; just as it is (so they fear) ignorance of this relationship which produces the misbelief in the first place and then creates an audience for it.

A generation ago, Dietrich Bonhoeffer posed for enquiry the theme 'Who Christ really is, for us today.'[10] Since his time, Christology has become a matter of new debate, and of fresh tension too. Teilhard de Chardin, in maximizing Christ's cosmic significance, has appeared to depersonalize him. And Protestant theologians, in stressing Jesus' human - ness and historicality, have appeared to dissolve away the substance of his godhead. Should such Christologies be taken as the last word, the faith-relationship with Jesus of which we spoke would not be 'on.' And merely by existing they make that relationship harder to hold on to, just as do the current 'secular' pictures of Jesus as a troubled hysteric (e.g.

---

[9] *Epistolae* X.xcvi.

[10] Dietrich Bonhoeffer, *Letters and Papers from Prison*, enlarged edition, ed. Eberhard Bethge (London: SCM Press, 1971), p. 279.

Dennis Potter, *Son of Man*) and as a pleasant song-and-dance man (e.g. *Godspell; Jesus Christ Superstar*). Fresh clarification is called for, urgently!

This essay seeks to show how the record may be put straight, and the way to true faith reopened. We shall start to work out an answer to the question which Bonhoeffer left us, not subjectively, in terms of what in this confused age men feel, fancy or (worse!) 'like to think,' but objectively, in terms of what is *there*, given and abiding, according to the nineteen-hundred-year-old principle that 'Jesus Christ is the same yesterday and today and for ever' (Heb. 13:8).

We shall in fact address ourselves to a question which underlies Bonhoeffer's, namely this: what must be said of our Lord Jesus Christ today in order first to secure for him that acknowledgement in praise, worship and obedient trust which apostolic witness and theology require, and secondly to prevent the nature and scope of his saving ministry being so misunderstood as to produce mistaken – indeed, by biblical standards unbelieving – proclamation and practice?

In order to answer this question, we shall (1) sketch out the main lines of New Testament Christology, (2) bring into focus some of the claims which it entails, (3) note some characteristic methods, assumptions, theses and problems of the 'humanitarian' Christology of our time, and (4) reaffirm an 'incarnational' account of Jesus. (The point of contrasting 'humanitarian' with 'incarnational,' be it said, is not that exponents of the former approach reject incarnation of set purpose, but that their way of explaining it is an abandoning of it in fact.) Thus, hopefully, our theologizing will pay true homage to Jesus Christ the Lord.

New Testament Christology

'I have come to the point,' wrote Francis Schaeffer in 1968, where, when I hear the word 'Jesus' – which means so much to me because of the Person of the historic Jesus and His work – I listen carefully because I have with sorrow become more afraid of the word 'Jesus' than almost any other word in the modern world. The word is used as a contentless banner . . . there is no rational scriptural content by which to test it . . . Increasingly over the past few years the word 'Jesus,' separated from the content of the Scriptures, has been the enemy of the Jesus of history, the Jesus who died and rose and is coming again and who is the eternal Son of God.[11]

Dr. Schaeffer's protest against allowing the name 'Jesus' to become a 'non-defined symbol,' a 'connotation word' in a world of 'semantic mysticism,' is timely. That the only real Jesus is the Christ of New Testament history and theology, and that by parting company with the

---

[11] Francis Schaeffer, *Escape from Reason* (Leicester: IVP, 1968), pp. 78f.

New Testament we do not find him, but only lose him, is a truth that cannot be too often emphasized today.

But do we find the real Jesus in the New Testament? Can we trust the records and interpretations which we find there? Do not the New Testament presentations of Jesus differ so widely as to cancel each other out, and create uncertainty at every point? Skepticism abounds, we know, but we shall be forearmed against it if we will learn to weigh the following three points.

First, the current fashion of treating the varieties of vocabulary, emphasis and development of themes within the New Testament as indicating a plurality of inconsistent theological outlooks is merely a revival of an elderly mistake which has already been many times corrected. A century and a half of scientific New Testament study has seen abundant hypotheses of this kind, setting Paul against the synoptic evangelists, or the synoptists against John, or James against Paul, or the Pastorals against the rest of Paul's letters, and so forth. None of them can be said to have stood the test of sustained scholarly examination. On the contrary, investigation has again and again underlined the real unity of the New Testament witness to Christ.[12]

Secondly, the current habit of disbelieving gospel narratives, and treating Jesus' real history as mostly unrecoverable – a last-century habit, which owes most of its recent vogue to one outstanding but idiosyncratic teacher, the late Rudolf Bultmann, who died in 1976 at the age of 91 – comes to look silly once one realizes that the bulk of the New Testament dates from the lifetime of persons who knew Jesus (all from before AD 70, claims John A. T. Robinson[13]), and moreover that the culture of Palestinian Judaism was based on memory to a far greater extent than ours is. Nobody alive in 1977 who remembers the Second World War should think it possible that key facts of Jesus' life and teaching were forgotten, or misremembered, among his disciples before the gospels were written; particularly in view of the importance ascribed to these facts, and Luke's

---

[12] Current interest in the development of traditions within the Bible, and the pluriformity of Scripture as we have it tends to obscure the solid achievement of the 'biblical theology' movement in exhibiting the inner unity of the scriptural message. Among books embodying this achievement are E. C. Hoskyns and F. N. Davey, *The Riddle of the New Testament* (London: Faber, 1931); A. M. Hunter, *The Unity of the New Testament* (London: SCM Press, 1943); H. H. Rowley, *The Rediscovery of the Bible* (London: James Clarke, 1945); *The Unity of the Bible* (London: Carey Kingsgate, 1953); A. G. Hebert, *The Bible from Within* (Oxford: Oxford University Press, 1950); O. Cullmann, *Christ and Time* (London: SCM Press, 1950); Alan Richardson, *Introduction to the Theology of the New Testament* (London: SCM Press, 1958).

[13] John A. T. Robinson, *Redating the New Testament*, (London: SCM Press, 1976).

emphatic claim to be well informed (Luke 1:1–4), and the attestation given to John's witness in the fourth gospel (John 19:25; 21:24). [14]

Thirdly, the current readiness to think that the Jesus of the gospels could have been made up is nonsensically naive. In 1904 Bishop Handley Moule wrote of 'that supreme miracle, the Lord,' declaring that 'there is no miracle more properly miraculous than the Jesus of the Evangelists, in the profound contrasts and sublime harmony of his character.' [15] 'If anything whatever is common to all believers, and even to many unbelievers,' wrote C. S. Lewis,

> it is the sense that in the Gospels they have met a personality . . . So strong is the flavour of that personality that, even while he says things which, on any other assumption than that of divine Incarnation in the fullest sense, would be appallingly arrogant, yet we – and many unbelievers too – accept him at his own valuation when he says 'I am meek and lowly of heart.' [16]

Surely it is clear that to suppose that the sayings and doings which communicate the unique flavour of Jesus' personality are products of pious imagination, while the real Jesus was in undiscoverable ways different, is embracing the incredible. To take just one point: the Jesus of the gospels is free from any sense of sin or dissatisfaction with himself (traits that are ordinarily psychopathic, and the negation of virtue), yet he impresses us as a supreme moral realist, and a person of supreme goodness. The *remembering* of so mind-blowing a personality is no problem, suppos-ing he really existed, but the idea that he might have been *invented* by imagination alone is as wild as the idea that pigs may some day fly. No biblical miracle takes so much believing as that!

So we approach the New Testament with confidence, which the discovery in it of a substantial unity of witness to Christ bears out. This

---

[14] On John, the following extract from C. S. Lewis is worth pondering: 'Turn to *John*. Read the dialogues: that with the Samaritan woman at the well, or that which follows the healing of the man born blind . . . I have been reading poems, romances, vision-literature, legends, myths, all my life. I know what they are like. Of this text there are only two possible views. Either this is reportage . . . pretty close up to the facts . . . Or else, some unknown writer in the second century, without known predecessors or successors, suddenly anticipated the whole technique of modern, novelistic, realistic narrative. If it is untrue, it must be narrative of that kind. The reader who doesn't see this has simply not learned to read.' *Fern-seed and Elephants*, p. 108.

[15] Cited from J. B. Harford and F. C. Macdonald, *Handley Carr Glyn Moule* (London: Hodder & Stoughton, n.d. [1922?]), p. 294.

[16] C. S. Lewis, *Fern-seed and Elephants*, pp. 110f.

witness, about which there is no dispute save on details, [17] may be summed up in four propositions, thus:

1. Jesus of Nazareth is God's promised Christ

'Christ' is, of course, not a surname(!) but an 'office-title,' meaning literally 'anointed one' (which is what 'Messiah' also means), and desig-nating God's promised Saviour-King. That the Galilean rabbi who rose from death is the Christ was always the basic Christian conviction, [18] and all strands of the New Testament express it. The Messiah's fulfilment of his earthly ministry in face of incomprehension and hostility, right up to his dying and rising, is the 'plot' of all four gospels. That 'Son of man,' Jesus' own mysterious title for himself, and 'Lord,' the title given him from Pentecost on, point first to the reality of his Messianic rule is nowadays generally agreed. [19]

Not that Jesus' concept of Messiahship corresponded to Jewish expec-tation. His notion reflected his view of God's eschatological kingdom, which he preached as a reality brought into being by his own ministry. He saw the kingdom as a new relationship between penitent sinners and God as their heavenly Father, a relationship achieved through commit-ment to himself as their sovereign Saviour; and he saw his lordship as based on his call to be God's suffering servant, the innocent one who, having died for others' sin, is then vindicated by being restored to life, according to Isaiah 53. Calvin well summarized Jesus' notion of

---

[17] Among the best surveys of the material are B. B. Warfield, *The Lord of Glory* (Grand Rapids: Baker, 1974 [1907]); A. E. J. Rawlinson, *The New Testament Doctrine of the Christ* (London: Longmans, 1926); Vincent Taylor, *The Person of Christ in New Testament Teaching* (London: Macmillan, 1958); O. Cullman, *The Christology of the New Testament* (London: SCM, 1959); Leon Morris, *The Lord from Heaven* (London: IVF, 1958).

[18] cf. Acts 2:36; 9:22; Matt. 16:13–17.

[19] G. W. H. Lampe writes of 'the two-way assertion implied by the credal confession, "Jesus Christ is LORD": that Jesus is the Messiah and the Messiah is none other than the man Jesus . . . the same Jesus who was known before his death . . . the title "LORD" signified the exaltation of Jesus to God's throne (Ps. 110:1). Against the background of its application to the patron and saviour deities of Hellenistic personal religion, on the one hand, and its reference in the Hebraic tradition to the Lord God, on the other, "LORD" expresses the conviction that Jesus uniquely mediated God's authority, that he transcended the category of ordinary humanity, and that he stood, as it were, on the side of God over against all other men, as one who exercised God's sovereignty over them.' (*Christ, Faith and History*, ed. S. W. Sykes and J. P. Clayton (Cambridge: Cambridge University Press, 1972), pp. 111f.

Messiahship, and the overall New Testament view of his role, when he spoke of Jesus as fulfilling a threefold office, as prophet (bringer of messages from God), priest (offerer of sacrifice to God) and king (ruler of the people of God).

2. *Jesus of Nazareth is the unique Son of God*

There are places in the first three gospels and Acts where 'Son of God' may be an honorific title for the Messiah, modelled on Ps. 2:6ff.; [20] but it is certain that in the epistles and in John's gospel it signifies a unique relation of solidarity with the Father, a relation entailing both a revelatory function [21] and also a share in the Father's work of creating, sustaining, reconciling, ruling and renewing his world; [22] and whatever 'Son of God' means in the first three gospels, their direct witness to Jesus' knowledge of his unique filial identity is very clear. [23] Personal distinctions within the unity of God constitute perhaps the hardest notion round which the human mind has ever been asked to wrap itself, and the thought was never adequately conceptualized till the fourth century. But faith that Jesus was in a true sense the Son of God made flesh, and an emphatic rejection of docetism (the view of Jesus as a theophany, an appearance of God, not a real or complete man at all) marked Christians from the first.

3. *Jesus of Nazareth is the only way to the Father*

The New Testament views knowing your Maker as your Father, and yourself as his child and heir, as the highest privilege and richest relation – ship of which any human being is capable. Not to know God in this way is, by contrast, to be in a state of fallenness and guilt, cut off from God's life, exposed to his judgement, and under demonic control, whence flows only misery. But this is every man's natural condition.

Can it be changed? Jesus said: 'I am the way, and the truth, and the life; no one comes to the Father, but by me' (John 14:6). It is as if he said: Yes, a filial relationship to God is possible through relating to me and my mediatorial ministry – though not otherwise. For sonship of God, in the sense that guarantees mercy and glory, is not a fact of natural life, but a gift of supernatural grace. 'To all who received him, who believed in his name he gave power' [or the right, the prerogative] 'to become children of God' (John 1:12). The doctrine of the bestowal of sonship is part of the proper exposition of 1 Peter 3:18: 'Christ . . . died for sins once for

---

[20] cf. Matt. 26:63; Acts 9:20–22.
[21] cf. John 1:18; 14:9; Heb. 1:1–2:4.
[22] cf. John 1:1–18; Eph. 1:9f.; Col. 1:15–20; Heb. 1:2f.
[23] cf. Mark 1:9ff.; 9:7; 12:6; 13:32; Matt. 11:27; Luke 2:49.

all, the righteous for the unrighteous, that he might bring us to God.' The only-begotten Son, who died for us, presents us to his Father as his brothers and sisters; thus we are adopted. But to this privilege unbelievers remain strangers, to their own infinite loss.

As contractors-out gain no benefit from a pension scheme, so one who shrugs off the gospel gains nothing from the mediation of Jesus Christ. 'You refuse to come to me that you may have life,' says Jesus (John 5:40). As unadopted roads are just pebbles and puddles, lacking a surface, so the spiritually unadopted lack a God they can call Father, and their living, however hectic, is drab in consequence. However vivid their sense of God may be, and however ardent their quest to know more of him, there is only one way they can find him as Father, and that is by coming to terms with – that is, accepting terms already announced by – God's Son, Jesus Christ, the living Lord. As no other relation to God save sonship brings salvation, so apart from Jesus, who effects our adoption, 'there is no other name under heaven given among men by which we must be saved.'[24]

4. Jesus of Nazareth is the only hope for any person

Hopelessness is hell – literally. As God made us to fulfil a function and attain an end (for 'man's chief end is to glorify God, and to enjoy him for ever'), so he made us creatures for whom hope is life, and whose lives become living deaths when we have nothing good to look forward to. As the deep hopelessness of post-Christian western culture tightens its chilly grip on us, we are made to feel this increasingly, and so can better appreciate the infinite value for life today of that exuberant, unstoppable, intoxicating, energizing hope of joy with Jesus in the Father's presence for ever which is so pervasive a mark of New Testament Christianity.

Whereas those without Christ are without God and without hope, living already in a dusk of the spirit that is destined to grow darker and colder, Christians are in the sunshine, endlessly rejoicing in 'Christ Jesus our hope.'[25] The inescapable alternatives are *false* hope (Marxism? spiritism? happiness through having things? endless good health? – false hopes, every one), or else *no* hope (total pessimism, inviting suicide), or else *Christian* hope, the electrifying knowledge of 'Christ in you, the hope of

---

[24] Acts 4:12. So John A. T. Robinson writes that the Christian 'judges that empirically it is true that no one comes – or has come – to the *Father*, that is, to God conceived in the intimacy of "*abba*," but by Jesus Christ. Jeremias is justified in calling this one of the distinctive marks of Christianity. Certainly it is not true of Moses or Mohammed, Buddha or Vishnu, Confucius or Lao Tzu.' *The Human Face of God* (Cambridge: Cambridge University Press, 1973), p. 222.

[25] 1 Tim. 1:1; cf. Eph. 2:11–13.

glory.'[26] It is a pity that so little is heard these days about what has been called 'the unknown world with its well-known inhabitant' to which the New Testament teaches Christians to look forward; for, as the hymn says: 'The lamb is all the glory of Emmanuel's land,' and declaring that glory is part of what it means to relate the New Testament witness to the person and place of Jesus Christ.

Five Crucial Claims

Let us now be analytical, and spell out to ourselves five particular claims which this witness involves. Each relates to both Jesus and ourselves, and each has vital importance for present-day discussion of both. Then we shall better see the significance of what has just been written.

The first claim relates to *history*, and the meaning of our own place in it. Concerning Jesus, the claim is that his incarnation, death, rising and present reign are events that give saving significance to present and future occurrences. A divine plan for history is in operation, and a new community, indeed a race of new persons – is being created. The power that made the world from nothing is now active to renovate it from the chaos and disorder that sin has brought. This power of new creation first transformed Jesus' humanity when he rose. Now, through the Spirit whom Jesus sends, it touches our own personal being in the great change which Jesus, John, James and Peter referred to as *new birth* and which Paul described as *co-resurrection with Christ*.[27] One day, when Jesus reappears, it will transform our physicality as completely as it trans-formed his, and in that transformation the whole external universe will in some unimaginable way be involved.[28] Meanwhile, Jesus Christ is in control, world history is 'his story,' and we may live in the certain knowledge that the predestined reintegration of all things in him[29] is on its way.

Concerning *ourselves*, the claim is that as God's rational creatures and our Lord's redeemed subjects we find the true purpose and fulfilment of our lives by embracing God's announced goals and working for them – for the spread of the gospel, the good of others, the enriching of human life, and the eliminating of what is morally evil and practically harmful. The alternative would be to turn one's back on world history as an area of meaninglessness and seek to realize God, Hindu-style, in the privacies of the psyche: a drop-out philosophy which through disillusionment with

---

[26] Col. 1:27.

[27] For 'new birth' see John 3:3–8; Jas. 1:18; 1 Pet. 1:3,23, and for 'co-resurrection with Christ' Eph. 2:4–6; Col. 2:11–13; 3:1; cf. Rom. 6:5–13.

[28] Rom. 8:18–23.

[29] cf. Eph. 1:9f.

the rat-race of the 'great society' has recently had a new vogue. But Christians must set their faces against it.

The second claim relates to *humanity*, and the meaning of our humanness. Concerning *Jesus*, it is claimed, that he is the yardstick at the level of motivation and attitudes of what it means to be fully human. Concerning *ourselves*, the claim is that only as we set ourselves to imitate Christ at this level are we fulfilling and developing (as distinct from violating and diminishing) our own human nature, which is already much diminished through sin; and only in this way can we find true joy, which is always integrally bound up with a sense of fulfilment. When Jesus said: 'My *food is* to do the will of him who sent me, and to accomplish his work,'[30] he was testifying to the joy which he found in his Father's service – service which, in his humanity no less than before he took flesh, was the fulfilling of his nature as the Son. But it was also, and equally, the fulfilling of his nature as man.

For us then, as for him, full realization of all that potential which is distinctively human (a realization which is both the heart of freedom and the height of joy) is found, not in self-will, but in service – service of God (which for us means service of the Son with the Father), and of others for the Lord's sake. Other paths may bring temporary pleasure, but lead neither to fulfilment, nor to freedom, nor to joy; and enlargement of one's experience will be little enough compensation for the shrinkage of one's real humanity.

The third claim relates to *encounter*, and the meaning of our person-hood. Concerning Jesus, it is claimed that he, the risen and enthroned Lord, is, though physically withdrawn from us, none the less 'there,' indeed 'here,' by his Spirit, in terms of personal presence for personal encounter. From such encounter (so the claim runs) trust in him, and love and loyalty to him, derive. The experience of Paul on the Damascus road, and that of Zacchaeus up and down the sycamore tree,[31] classically illustrate this. Fellowship with Jesus is not a metaphor or parable or myth of something else, but is a basic ingredient of distinctively Christian experience.

Concerning *ourselves*, the claim is that we were made for relationships, first with God and then with created persons; that this, indeed, is part of God's image in us, inasmuch as God himself is triune, each divine person existing in constant conscious relationship to the other two; and that through the re-creative effect of God's saving relationship to us through Jesus Christ, our capacity for relationships at the deepest level with other human beings, a capacity which sin has in large measure impaired, is progressively restored to us, so that we find ourselves free in Christ for genuinely human relationships in a way that was never true before.

---

[30] John 4:34.

[31] Acts 9:1–22; Luke 19:1–10.

The fourth claim relates to *dominion*, and the meaning of our circum-stances. Concerning *Jesus*, the claim is that at every point and in every space-time event the cosmos is under the authoritative control [32] of Jesus the risen Lord, who is both the Jesus of history whom we meet in the gospel story and Jesus our saviour and friend. Concerning *ourselves*, the claim is that whatever happens to us, however bewildering or harrowing, has positive meaning because it was planned in love for us, and willed for our good, and others' good through us, in one way or another. Not that this good meaning is always apparent (except in the sense that we see some appropriate exercise of faith, patience and continuing obedience being called for); but what a difference it makes to living to know that a meaning is there!

The fifth claim relates to *destiny*, and the meaning of present choices. Concerning Jesus, the claim is that at the end of the road of each man's life Jesus the judge stands inescapable, and that each man will at that time know that this final encounter with Jesus has had final significance for determining his own final state. This is the reality of the judgement-seat of Christ, which is central in biblical thinking about both death and the *parousia* (royal visit) of the returning Son. [33]

Concerning *ourselves*, the claim is that present decisions determine ultimate destiny, for they have, in von Hügel's phrase, 'abiding conse-quences.' Christ as judge will from one standpoint simply ratify the choice to have God, or not to have him, which we have already made in this life.

Surely it is in terms of these claims that our answer to Bonhoeffer's question: 'Who is Jesus Christ for us today?,' must be given. Whatever should be added to the above analysis, this is where thinking must start.

Humanitarian Christology

The richest theological statement of the incarnation in Scripture is, beyond question, the prologue of John's gospel (John 1:1–18), the climactic sentence of which is verse 14: 'So the Word became flesh; he came to dwell among us, and we saw his glory, such glory as befits the Father's only Son, full of grace and truth' (NEB). 'The Word' (*logos*) here is the mysterious being who was God with God at the beginning, agent of creation, source of life and light (i.e. knowledge of the Creator), rejected visitor to his world, and yet donor of sonship to God by adoption through a new divine birth (1–13). 'Flesh' signifies those qualities of weakness, vulnerability, and limitedness in space, time and knowledge in this world which are the marks of created humanity. 'Became' implies

---

[32] *exousia*: Matt. 28:18.

[33] See John 5:26–29; Acts 17:31; Rom. 2:5–16; 2 Cor. 5:6–10 and Heb. 9:27.

the unimaginable reality of God assuming these qualities as modes of his own life.

The verse says that witnesses ('we') discerned in the Word thus made flesh the divine glory of God's only Son. John is clearly asserting two things: first, that the personal Son who is also God's expressive and executive Word existed and was active prior to the incarnation;[34] secondly, that he is the personal subject whose human name is Jesus, and whose humanness is as apparent, as his deity in the story John goes on to tell.

Naturally, mainstream Christian thinking about Jesus has stayed within these limits, and it is right to see the terms of theological art which the Fathers used at the Council of Chalcedon (451) when they confessed one person (*hypostasis*; better, 'entity') in two natures (*physeis*) as intended not to explain, but simply to surround and safeguard this area of mystery – namely, that a man named Jesus, a real human being, was truly and fully God, God the creator, God the Son. The general Christian consensus has been that the incarnation, no less than the divine triunity, cannot in any ordinary sense of the word be explained at all; it is a transcendent reality that confounds our finite minds; all we can do (and all we are asked to do) is acknowledge and adore.

In modern times, however, an approach to Christology quite different from John's has been tried. Its theme, of which there have been many variants over a century and a half, is this: Jesus of Nazareth was a prophetic man in whom God was manifest and through whom God acted, exerting an influence that produced a community with distinctive goals, experi - ences, views of itself and modes of God-consciousness, of all of which the New Testament is a record. The man from Galilee was not God personally, nor did he in any sense exist before conception and birth, nor (probably) did he rise bodily from death, nor (certainly) can he be expected to 'come to be our judge.' But his life was a supreme revelation of godliness, and facing it mediates the touch of God to us with unique effectiveness.

This justifies worship of him. The fact that John and other New Testament writers speak differently is dealt with by urging that their authority lies in their witness to Christian origins and experience in a general way rather than in the particular way they put it into words. That was conditioned by their culture; so that once we have taken the measure of their experience and sense of things, we are free to express it in different words and concepts if we think they fit it better. In this case, what they are telling us, and what we need to be carefully picking up from them, is the impact of Jesus; but we are not obliged to endorse their first-century notions of who he was.

Space prohibits full and fair dealing with any one exponent of this 'humanitarian' Christology, so it is best that we should name none of the

---

[34] cf. Col. 1:15–17; Heb. 1:2, 6.

current ones, notorious though some of them have become. Instead, we shall make some general comments on this approach, as it has been developed from Friedrich Schleiermacher, the 'father of liberalism,' who died in 1834, up to the present day.

First, what has given rise to it? Three factors operating together. The first is a habit of not treating the teaching of biblical writers as divinely revealed truth. Secondly, an interest in feelings and experiences which is a spin-off from the Romantic movement in European culture, and which has prompted folk to try to imagine what it felt like to be Jesus. This is a psychological question, reflecting concerns which New Testament writ - ers do not manifest or help us much to pursue, and one wonders how far they are worth pursuing; but certainly, for many today one test of the adequacy of an account of Jesus is that it makes him psychologically comprehensible. This obviously favours 'humanitarian' Christology; to envisage a godly man's state of mind is practicable in a way that mapping the consciousness of God incarnate could hardly be.

The third factor, following from the second, is a recoil from Chalce - donian Christology; not just because it uses elusive philosophical terms ('nature,' 'substance,' 'entity'), but chiefly because (so it is argued) it cannot properly recognize Jesus' humanness, and so is in effect docetic. Now it is true that some Fathers who went the Chalcedonian way talked with maximum awkwardness about Jesus 'suffering impassibly,' and divided out his experiences between his divine and human natures in a way that is quite impossible (hereby deferring to Greek rather than to biblical ideas of God). It is also true that some latter day Chalcedonians, deprecating the smell of docetism, have felt it needful to adopt the 'kenosis' theory, which speculates – that is, guesses – that for the Son to experience human limitations properly he had to abandon some divine powers when becoming man.

But the conviction now being discussed goes further: its burden is, quite simply, that only human persons have human experiences, and the idea of God having them is impossible. (Which begs the whole question of the incarnation! – although to many professed Christians it has none the less seemed a self-evident truth.)

Other modern dogmas have favoured humanitarian Christology: the anti-supernatural 'scientific world-view,' for which incarnation was in - admissible; the evolutionary outlook, for which incarnation was an intrusion; and the scepticism of biblical historians who severed the Christ of apostolic faith from the Jesus of history and then reconstructed the latter by eliminating the miraculous from the gospel story.

But insuperable difficulties dog this Christology in all its forms. Not only does it involve in general terms a painfully low view of biblical authority, apostolic intelligence and two millennia of Christian devotion; it also invites particular objection along at least the following lines.

First, in relation to *Jesus himself*, humanitarian Christology calls in question not only his godhead but also his goodness. We must insist, in face of the common inability of 'humanitarians' to see it, that no view of Jesus as a uniquely God-filled, God-possessed man can ever amount to faith in his deity, nor can it function as an explanation of that faith. It is not an explanation of it, but an alternative to it. And we must also insist, in face once again of the inability of 'humanitarians' to see it, that the old dilemma, either he was God or he was not good (*aut Deus aut non bonus*), still applies. All the records (and it takes prodigies of special pleading to doubt them all) show Jesus conscious of divine sonship, claiming divine prerogatives as men's saviour and judge, and matter-of-factly demanding, expecting and accepting the unqualified trust and loyalty which by common consent are God's due alone. If he was not divine, we cannot avoid saying that he was deluded and (unwittingly, we assume) deluded others. This is compatible, no doubt, with perfect sincerity, but hardly with perfect goodness.

Secondly, in relation to *the doctrine of God*, the failure of the humanitarian view to distinguish the incarnation of the Son from the Spirit's indwelling a saint, and its reduction of the former to the latter, makes trinitarian faith impossible. The humanitarian view can be understood in either unitarian or binitarian terms, according to whether the Spirit's distinct personality is affirmed or denied, but it cannot be understood in trinitarian terms because, though it affirms that God was in Christ, it denies that Christ was personally divine. So the whole biblical picture of God in three persons fulfilling a saving purpose in which the incarnate Son has the key role as mediator – God for humanity and human for God, bringing God and humanity out of estrangement into fellowship – will have to be redrawn. The loss is surely as intolerable as it is inescapable.

Thirdly, in relation to *the doctrine of grace*, non-acknowledgement of Jesus as God incarnate requires a re-defining of the gospel. The best we can now say is that by his example of faith and faithfulness, his moral and spiritual trail-blazing, and the impact of his teaching and character, Jesus (the figure in the gospels) moves us to imitate him. (Which, as it stands, is moralism, luring us back into the world of justification by works.) What we can never now say is that Jesus' death is God propitiating his own wrath against our sins, and that Jesus' resurrection is God arising to bring us pardon and peace, and to raise us from spiritual death to new life in fellowship with himself.

So salvation is not of the Lord, nor is Jesus the object of faith, in the sense that we once thought; and prayer to Jesus as distinct from the Father seems improper, while talk of Jesus as our present help and hope must be hyperbolical. But that is a terrible impoverishing of the gospel, indeed a destruction of it, for there is no gospel left. Here again, the loss which is inescapable is also intolerable.

Fourthly, in relation to *Christian experience*, and also to the God-given Scriptures which shape that experience, the witness of the Holy Spirit

leads away from humanitarian Christology to something higher. G. W.
H. Lampe asks 'what Christians mean when they claim to "encounter
Jesus Christ," ' and puts alternatives. Would they say

> that they encounter, here and now, or are encountered by God, the Spirit
> who was in Jesus, meeting them with the identical judgement, mercy,
> forgiveness and love which were at work in Jesus, inspiring and recreating
> them according to the pattern of Jesus; and that they worship God, the Spirit
> who was in Jesus . . . ? Or would they, rather, assert that in their experience
> Jesus of Nazareth, the man fully possessed by the Spirit and thus united with
> God, meets them from the other side of death? Or must Spirit Christology
> after all give way at this point to the concept of the incarnation of the
> pre-existent divine being, the Logos/Son?[35]

Surely the Christian consensus, today as yesterday, is that the first analysis
is incomplete, because it is Jesus personally, the Jesus of the gospels, whom
we meet; that the second analysis is uncouth, because it is precisely of
Jesus as divine saviour, calling for our faith and worship, that we are made
aware; and that nothing less than acknowledging Jesus as God's pre-
existent Son will express the sense of reality in the Spirit-taught heart.
But when the speculations of theologians contradict the Spirit's witness
to worshippers, it is time to call a halt.

Christ Unchanging

It is not the case that by contrast with humanitarian Christology the
incarnationalism of the New Testament and of Chalcedon is problem-
free; though whereas humanitarianism ran into trouble through its deep
disharmony with Scripture, the problems of incarnationalism concern
only the 'how' of the biblically-declared reality.

Here are three sample problems: how does the Son uphold the universe
(Heb. 1:3; Col. 1:17) while living within the limits of his humanity? – for
that humanity, though glorified, remains human and therefore limited still.
Again, how could temptation and moral conflict have been real for Jesus
when the Son, being God, cannot sin? And how could Jesus truly not have
known the time of his return (Mark 13:32), when as the divine Son he was
omniscient? Our life of faith does not necessitate our knowing the answer
to these or any similar questions, and the full answers are likely to exceed
our mind's reach anyway. None the less, the questions are real and not
improper, and a quick comment on each may be ventured.

On the first: are we entitled (God being God) to assume that because
the fullness of a divine-human personal life appears in Jesus, therefore the

---

[35] Lampe in *Christ, Faith and History*, pp. 129f.

Son now does all his work through his humanity? Surely not. We simply do not know. And if it worries us that we cannot imagine how the Son has upheld the universe since the incarnation, we should remind ourselves that we cannot imagine how he did it before the incarnation either. The whole matter is too high for us.

On the second: is it not a matter of experience that often the person least likely to yield to temptation is most sensitive to it, and has what feels like the hardest and most sustained battle with it?

On the third: kenoticists (those who, as we saw, understand the Son's self-emptying at the incarnation as involving loss of powers as well as of glory) suggest that omniscience was given up at the time of the incarna - tion; but surely omniscience should be defined as power to know all that one wills to know, and the Son's ignorance be explained in terms of the fact that he never willed to know by supernatural means more than he knew that his Father willed him to know. If he knew that his Father did not wish him to have in his mind the date of his return, that settled it; the knowledge was not there. The Son, being Son, knows, just as he acts, in dependence on the Father, never on his independent initiative. [36]

To say these things, however, is to point up a further question. If the personal subject whom we know as Jesus is in his true identity Son of God, co-creator and upholder of all things, is it possible, in the nature of the case, for him to be a man in the full sense? The Chalcedonian tradition proclaims him as one person, and that must mean one personality, and that must mean one centre of consciousness, one subject-self, one psychological ego.

So Chalcedonian incarnationalism must imply that Jesus' knowledge of himself as 'I,' a distinct personal subject, involved knowing himself as divine. But is it not essential to true humanness to know that one is not God, however vividly aware of God one may be? How then can Jesus be genuinely human?

In reply, note first that this is not a new question. Older exponents of Chalcedon have faced it. Their line was to define the Son's humanity as precisely a set of qualities and capabilities for experience, both passive and active, the acquiring of which conditioned his entire personal life. The Son's humanity, once acquired, never was and never will be 'switched off,' or laid aside in the way kenoticists think divine powers were laid aside when the Son took flesh; yet this humanity was and is, so to speak, adjectival to the person whose it is, and who lives for ever in the consciousness of his identity as God's Son.

The thought is that the self-awareness – that is, the being-present-to-oneself that comes with awareness of other realities – which began to crystallize in the mind of Jesus as baby and toddler, and which developed, as it does in us all through adolescence into adulthood, had in it from the start awareness of a unique relationship, not just potential but actual,

---

[36] cf. John 5:19.

between himself and the ultimate Person, a relation of dependence within co-eternity, of subordination within co-equality, and of filial obedience within total mutual love.

No doubt Jesus stood in need of that knowledge of objective facts which comes through temporal and bodily existence in the world with other selves and things, and grew and developed in that knowledge, as indeed Luke 2:52 affirms. No doubt he gained his mature understanding of the kingdom and service of God, and of his own mission as Son of Man and servant-Messiah from commerce with the Scriptures (everything in the records suggests that), and so may rightly be said to have lived by faith (rather than vision, or immediate revelation, as older thinkers tended to say) so far as his vocation was concerned. (Is it wrong to see Jesus' going to a foreseen death in Jerusalem as an act of faith that the Father would then raise him, by willing him to raise himself, from the dead? Surely not.) No doubt too, although supernatural modes of knowledge at a distance, knowledge of men's secret thoughts, and knowledge of the future and of the past, were available to him,[37] no more came into his mind by these means at any time, as we said earlier, than his Father wished him to be aware of, so that while on earth he never knew all that he could have known, had the Father so willed, and was sometimes ignorant of matters of a kind which at other times he knew supernaturally.[38] But for all that, the sense of being God's Son related to his Father in an abiding fellowship of love in which each glorifies the other[39] was always in his mind, as it was expressed in all that he did.

Therefore Chalcedonians have usually said that Jesus, the Word-made-flesh, was man generically and qualitatively, but not 'a man' in the sense of an individual human being with a creaturely identity, and they have wed the technical terms *hypostatic* union and *enhypostasia* to express the thought that Jesus' manhood exists only as the manhood – that is, the sum of human characteristics – of the divine person who is God's eternal Son. And in voicing this thought they certainly have the backing of the apostle John! Any alternative position would be open to the criticism of not taking the fourth gospel seriously enough. (That some distrust John's gospel these days is true, but not in our view good, for their scepticism is not adequately justified nor, we think, adequately justifiable, by argument.)

Of course, if in calling Jesus 'a man' we mean only to say that no constituent human quality was lacking to him, without raising the question whether his demonstrable dependence on and submission to the

---

[37] cf. For knowledge at a distance, Matt. 17:24–27; Mark 11:2; 14:13f.; John 1:48f.; for knowledge of men's secret thoughts, Mark 2:6–8; Luke 9:46f.; John 2:24; for knowledge of the past, John 4:17f.; for knowledge of the future, Mark 13:6–83; John 13:19; 14:29; 21:18f.

[38] cf. Mark 5:30 with John 1:47f.

[39] cf. John 17:1, 4f.

Father reflected a consciousness of creaturehood or not, there is no reason why we should not do it; the usage described in the previous paragraph was developed to make a different point.

Does this line of thought really impair the full humanity of our divine Lord? Not if we understand personhood and personality in the modern and, surely, correct way – that is, in terms of relatedness to other realities. If Jesus was related to the Father in terms of co-eternity, co-equality and co-creatorship, then he was a divine person. If his experience of relatedness to things and people – experience, that is, of thinking, feeling, choosing, giving, receiving; of being hungry, hurt, excited, tired, disappointed; of being aware of the opposite sex, and so on – corresponded in a fundamental and comprehensive way, not indeed to ours as it is, under sin's taint, but to what ours and Adam's would have been had the Fall not happened, then he was a human person. Both things are true so we speak of him as a divine-human person. Is there really a problem here? I think not.

Bonhoeffer's question 'Who is Christ for us today?' could be taken as a plea for Christological novelty, as if only a novel account of Jesus Christ could catch men's ears today. Certainly, in our time much Christological novelty has been provided – in the reduced Jesus of humanitarianism, the revolutionary 'political Christ' drawn by some, and the concept of Christ as a principle of evolution which we find in Teilhard de Chardin, to look no further. But this essay has sought to commend the conviction that the Christ of whom the modern West, with its vast problems and growing alienation from its Christian roots, most needs to hear is precisely the Christ of the New Testament and of historic Christian teaching – the incarnate Son of God who lives, reigns, judges and saves; the Christ who prompts the confession, 'My Lord and my God' (cf. John 20:28).

For what, after all, are the world's deepest problems? They are what they always have been, the individual's problems – the meaning of life and death, the mastery of self, the quest for value and worth-whileness and freedom within, the transcending of loneliness, the longing for love and a sense of significance, and for peace.

Society's problems are deep, but the individual's problems go deeper; Solzhenitsyn, Dostoevsky or Shakespeare will show us that, if we hesitate to take it from the Bible. And Jesus Christ the God-man, who is the same yesterday, today and for ever, still ministers to these problems in the only way that finally resolves them. 'Him we proclaim,' said Paul long ago, 'warning every man and teaching every man in all wisdom, that we may present every man mature in Christ.'[40] It is for us, his late-twentieth-century servants, to proclaim him still, for the same end.

'The old converted slave-trader' opened this essay for us with words of theological warning. Now let him close it, leading us this time into doxology and devotion.

---

[40] Col. 1:28.

Jesus ! my Shepherd, Husband, Friend,
  My Prophet, Priest, and King;
My Lord, my Life, my Way, my End,
  Accept the praise I bring.

Weak is the effort of my heart,
  And cold my warmest thought;
But when I see thee as thou art,
  I'll praise thee as I ought.

Till then I would thy love proclaim
  With every fleeting breath;
And may the music of thy name
  Refresh my soul in death.

Chapter 4

Jesus Christ, the Only Saviour

'Praise, My Soul, the King of Heaven' and 'Abide with Me' are the only
hymns by Henry Francis Lyte that are sung much today. But he wrote
other good ones, and one of them, using the same metre as 'Praise, My
Soul,' starts like this:

> O how blest the congregation
> Who the gospel know and prize;
> Joyful tidings of salvation
> Brought by Jesus from the skies!
> He is near them,
> Knows their wants and hears their cries.
>
> In his name rejoicing ever,
> Walking in his light and love,
> And foretasting, in his favour,
> Something here of bliss above;
> Happy people!
> Who shall harm them? what shall move?
>
> In his righteousness exalted,
> On from strength to strength they go;
> By ten thousand ills assaulted,
> Yet preserved from every foe,
> On to glory
> Safe they speed through all below.

Lyte's formula of blessing for your congregation and mine is that we
should know and prize the gospel of salvation, which was Jesus' central
message, and with it know and prize Jesus and his love-gift of new life,

JESUS CHRIST, THE ONLY SAVIOUR, was originally presented to Essentials '94, the Anglican conference held June 16–21, 1994 in Montreal, Quebec,
and subsequently published in *Anglican Essentials*, George Egerton, ed. (Toronto:
Anglican Book Centre, 1995), pp. 98–110. Reprinted by permission.

new joy, new strength, and new security. Lyte is right! Whatever cultural shifts take place around us, whatever socio-political concerns claim our attention, whatever anxieties we may feel about the church as an institution, Jesus Christ crucified, risen, reigning, and now in the power of his atonement, calling, drawing, welcoming, pardoning, renewing, strengthening, preserving, and bringing joy, remains the heart of the Christian message, the focus of Christian worship, and the fountain of Christian life. Other things may change; this does not.

Thus it was from the beginning, as the New Testament shows. 'Jesus is Lord' (Rom. 10:9) was, by scholarly consensus, the first Christian confession of faith. Invoking and worshipping 'our Lord and Saviour Jesus Christ' (2 Pet. 1:11; 2:20; 3:18) alongside the Father (his and ours) was the primary form of Christian devotion. Celebrating Jesus as 'our God and Saviour' (Titus 2:13; 2 Pet. 1:1) was a basic focus of early Christian doctrinal teaching. 'Believe in the Lord Jesus, and you will be saved' (Acts 16:31) was the original Christian message to the world. Reconciliation with God and pardon of sin through Christ's atoning death, adoption and new birth into God's family through regeneration in Christ and co-resurrection with Christ, life in the power of the Spirit of Christ, and hope of everlasting glory in the presence of Christ were the staple themes of the apostolic explanation of what salvation means. 'Christianity is Christ,' the slogan beloved of so many preachers, sums it up most perfectly. When Lyte wrote, 'O how blest the congregation / Who the gospel know and prize,' it was of the gospel of salvation from sin and death through Jesus Christ that he was thinking – the gospel that finds us lost and broken and leaves us 'ransomed, healed, restored, forgiven.' Thus he anchored himself in the centre of the Christian mainstream, glorying in 'the old, old story / Of Jesus and his love.' That is the place where today's Christians, with you and me among them, should be anchored also.

Christology and Theology

From the New Testament mindset that sees Christ at the centre of things grew mainstream Christian theology – that is, our understanding of God and his relation to everything everywhere that is not himself. The Christian consensus has always been that, as Scripture is the proper source from which theology should be derived, so Christology – that is, our knowledge of the person, place, and work of Christ – is the true hub around which the wheel of theology must revolve, and to which each of its spokes must be correctly fastened if the wheel is not to get bent out of shape. Take some examples.

Why do Christians hold that the one God is plural (tri-personal, to be exact), and that he is at once intolerably severe, terrifyingly perceptive, and infinitely gracious and good? Ultimately it is because they hold that Jesus, who prayed to the Father and promised the Spirit, and whose character was as described, was himself God.

Why are Christians sure, despite all the difficulties, that Scripture is God's own inspired and authoritative instruction? Ultimately it is because Jesus, the divine Son, always treated the Old Testament Scriptures as his Father's word, given to show him and his disciples his Father's way.

Why do Christians hold that personal relationships matter more than anything in this world, and that the truly human way to live is lovingly, constantly, unreservedly to give yourself away to God and others, and that anything less than this offends God? Ultimately it is because they hold that Jesus was as fully human as he was divine, and that as he taught these things, so he lived them, and that at the deepest level of personhood, his was the one perfect human life that the world has seen.

Why do Christians insist that God's forgiveness of sins is only ever possible on the basis of an atoning sacrifice? Ultimately it is because Jesus saw the making of atonement as the main purpose of his coming, and after three years as a preacher, went up to Jerusalem, deliberately courting death, in order that the Father's will in this matter might be done.

Why do Christians view their thousands of gatherings – congregations, as we call them – as not just a chain of clubs or interest groups, but as outcrops of a single organic entity called the church, within which they are brothers and sisters in one family of redeemed sinners, one 'body' sharing a new supernatural life through common links with Christ their 'head'? Ultimately it is because Jesus taught his disciples to see his Father as their Father, his death as their ransom-price, and himself as their way to the Father, and now as their bread of life and the vine in which, as branches, they must abide.

Why do Christians counter the world's endless speculations about the larger life of disembodied spirits by maintaining that full humanness requires embodiment, and hence look forward to physical resurrection? Ultimately it is because they are sure that Jesus rose bodily from the state of death and that his risen life is the model for ours.

And why do Christians cling to the hope of a cosmic triumph of divine justice and power when the world around them seems to be slipping, despite humanity's best efforts, into chaos at every level? Ultimately it is because they believe that God's risen Son reigns, really, if hiddenly, over all things, and is pledged to return in glory to judge and renew this world which he, with the Father and the Holy Spirit, first created.

These examples illustrate how historic Christianity conceives, defines, and explains itself in the Trinitarian, Christological, and Christocentric terms that are native to it. Christianity is what it is because Jesus of Nazareth was what he was, and every suggestion as to what Christianity should be today and tomorrow must be measured by Christ himself as its criterion. The fact that some versions of Christianity lose sight of this principle is a modern tragedy and a source of enormous confusion. We ourselves must try to avoid any such lapse.

Universality and Universalism

A further principle of original Christianity was the universality of Jesus' claim on the human race, and of every person's need to know about, and respond to, the claim he makes and so to receive the gift of salvation that he gives. 'All authority in heaven and on earth has been given to me,' said the risen Jesus to his apostles, announcing his appointment as this world's proper king. 'Therefore go and make disciples of all nations' (Matt. 28:18–19). Paul defined his ministry in terms of this universality: 'We proclaim him [Jesus], admonishing and teaching everyone with all wisdom, so that we may present everyone perfect in Christ' (Col. 1:28). The great missionary movements of the early Christian centuries and the past two hundred years sought to implement the insights of Christ's universal claim and humankind's universal need. We should rejoice that in Asia, Africa. and Latin America, evangelism goes on apace today, with great fidelity to the New Testament and great fruitfulness among the common people, whatever may be happening in the modern and post – modern West. Soul-winning, church-planting outreach must always have pride of place in Christian strategy. For of all the tasks to which love of God and neighbour should lead us, disciple-making comes first.

Here, however, we find that something of an intellectual landslide has occurred in certain sections of the church. In place of a clear declaration of the universality of Christ's claim as Saviour, with salvation requiring faithful response, we find ourselves confronted with understandings of God's purpose for humanity, and of Christ's achievement on the cross, which produce either the dogmatic assertion that all human beings will finally attain eternal life or at least a confidence that sincere adherents of non-Christian faiths, and maybe others too, will be saved alongside Christian believers. Two identifiable new positions have emerged. *Pluralism*, championed by the universalist John Hick, is a restyled version of the old idea that all religions are climbing the same mountain and will meet at the top – in other words, that all religious persons are actually converging on the same goal, and all the key teachings of all the world's major religions actually direct their adherents on this convergent course. [1]

[1] See John Hick, *God and the Universe of Faiths* (New York: St. Martin's Press, 1973); *God has Many Names* (Philadelphia: Westminster Press, 1982); *An Interpretation of Religion: Human Responses to the Transcendent* (New Haven: Yale University Press, 1989); J. Hick, ed., *The Myth of God Incarnate* (London: SCM Press, 1977); J. Hick and P. Knitter, eds., *The Myth of Christian Uniqueness* (Maryknoll, N.Y.: Orbis, 1987). See also Harold A. Netland, *Dissonant Voices: Religious Pluralism and the Question of Truth* (Grand Rapids: Eerdmans, 1991).

Inclusivism is the idea, which takes many forms, that Christ does actually save persons who knew nothing of him but were serious and sincere in practising whatever their religion was. Each position makes the momen - tous claim that it does justice to the reality of God's love to humankind in a way that other positions do not. In a multi-ethnic, multi-religious society like today's Canada, these views generate no small bewilderment as to what we should hope, pray, and work for in evangelism, both at home and abroad.

Our present agenda is to try to dispel this bewilderment by offering some clarifications, and our first step to that end will be to analyse from Scripture the salvation that Jesus Christ the Saviour has wrought.

The Saviour and the Salvation

It is hardly possible to overstress the magnitude of the intellectual achieve - ment embodied in the New Testament. The New Testament, as we know, is a consensus collection of apostolic writings that were brought together after each had been separately produced as particular needs required. None of these twenty-seven books was written to be part of any such collection, or to back up any other items that are part of it, and all of them were produced within seventy years – indeed most, if not all, within forty years – of Jesus' resurrection when Christian theology might have been expected to be still in a rudimentary stage. But in fact they have within them a coherent body of thought that is fully homogenous in its substance and thrust, despite the independent individuality of each writer and the way in which all their thinking cuts across the dogmas of the Judaism out of which it came. The central place of Jesus Christ in creation, providence, the divine plan of salvation, the history of our race, and the coming universal judgement and new creation of the cosmos is the theme throughout, and amazingly there are no internal contradictions or loose ends.

This revolutionary consensus, involving as it does trinitarian and incarnational beliefs within a monotheistic frame – perhaps the hardest bit of thinking that the human mind has ever been asked to do – is so stunning that it is hard to doubt its supernatural origin. As from one standpoint the person, power, and performance of the Lord Jesus is its main focus, so from another standpoint all the books dilate in their different ways on the need and glory of the saving grace that he gives, thus furnishing a wealth of material to guide us in our enquiry.

Here, now, in a nutshell, are the basic lines of thought about Jesus Christ the Saviour to which the New Testament materials boil down.

1. Jesus Christ is the divine Word made flesh, the unique Son of God.

By being virginally conceived and born of Mary, with Joseph as his official father, the Son of God became a Jew of David's line while remaining as fully divine as he was in his pre-incarnate life. All that was involved in being fully human he acquired, though without ever becoming a sinner. His words, works, and personal life on earth displayed his divinity to those with eyes to see and ears to hear, and in so doing revealed the true nature and character of 'God the Father Almighty.' Through incarnation he added to his cosmic role as creator, upholder, and future renovator of all things, the further role of saving lost humankind. The church is currently emerging from two centuries of vacillation with regard to Jesus' personal deity; it is worth highlighting the fact that the first Christians had no doubt about it, and no reluctance to affirm it.[2]

2. Jesus Christ is our prophet, priest, and king, the one mediator between humankind and God.

The themes of Jesus as messenger from heaven, bringing news of God's saving mercy, as fulfiller of the priestly role of offering to God an atoning sacrifice for his people's sins, and as king now enthroned in the kingdom of God over all things and all people, pervade the entire New Testament. Mediation, which means bringing together alienated parties and estab - lishing a firm basis for their future relationship, is the biblical term for the saving ministry that Christ in his triple office fulfils. 'God our Saviour . . . desires everyone to be saved and to come to the knowledge of the truth. For there is one God; there is also one mediator between God and humankind, Christ Jesus, himself human. who gave himself a ransom for all' (1 Tim. 2:34, NRSV).

The writer to the Hebrews develops the thought that as high priest, the incarnate Son is the mediator who deals with humans on behalf of God, and with God on behalf of humans, and so brings and keeps them together. Before his passion the Son learned by experience to empathize with people under temptation, so that now he can minister to us in times of moral and spiritual need (Heb. 2:18; 4:15–5:3; 5:7–10). Following his passion, in which he 'offered' to the Father 'for all time one sacrifice for sins,' and having 'sat down at the right hand of God,' 'he is able to save

---

[2] On the incarnation as a fact, see John's Gospel, especially the prologue, 1:1–18; also the many references to Jesus' unique divine Sonship in the other Gospels (Matt. 3:17; 4:3, 5,11–27; 14:33; 16:16; 17:5; 21:37; 27:54; 28:19; and parallels); also Paul's words in Rom. 1:4; 9:5, KJV, NASB, NIV, and NRSV; Col. 1:15–20; 2:9; also Heb. 1–2; 1 John 1; Rev. 1. On the virgin birth and Davidic identity, see the independent narratives and genealogies of Matt. 1; Luke 1–2, and 3:23–37; Rom. 1:3; Rev. 22:16. On the sinlessness of Jesus, see John 8:46; 2 Cor. 5:21; Heb. 4:15, and 7:26; 1 Pet. 2:22–23; 1 John 3:5. On Jesus as revealer of God, see John 1:18 and 14:9–11; 2 Cor. 4:4; Col. 1:15; Heb. 1:3–5. On the conjunction of the Son's cosmic and saving roles, see John 1:3–5; Col. 1:16–20; Heb. 1:31.

completely those who come to God through him, because he ever lives to intercede for them' (Heb. 10:12; 7:25; cf. Rom. 8:34). Through his two-sided ministry of intercession for us – based on his cross, and succour to us, based on his own temptation experience – he now communicates God's pardon and peace of conscience to believers, leads them in their worship, and shepherds them through life's vicissitudes to their heavenly home. This is the ongoing reality of his mediatorial ministry.

3. Jesus Christ is lover and lord of his people, and head of the body that is the church of God.

The New Testament views Jesus as having come to found a new community, and apostolic teaching is consistently church-centred. Chris - tian 'Lone Rangerism' is really a contradiction in terms. Corporateness is fundamental to New Testament Christianity, which everywhere appears as a practice of personal devotion within a communal life that all are to share. Having been made 'one new man' out of their distinct individu - alities (Eph. 2:15), 'all one in Christ Jesus' (Gal. 3:28), believers must now relate to one another within the solidarity of their new identity. And where this communion of hearts is realized, wonderful things are found to happen. The church in Christ is supernaturalized by Christ; loving it, he animates and invigorates it, pouring out the Holy Spirit on it and leading those who make it up into a unique mode of interactive life in fellowship with his Father and himself on the one hand, and with fellow-believers, viewed as spiritual siblings, on the other. The power of united praise is experienced, and love and care overflow.

In Romans 12, 1 Corinthians 12, and Ephesians 4, Paul expresses this by using the organic image of the church as the body of Christ and each Christian, under Christ the head, as a unit within it – a distinct and individual unit, corresponding to the great variety of separate units (particular limbs, joints, muscles, nerves, and so on) in the human body. This image yields the particular implications that the church is one in its diversity, and diverse in its unity; that all the church's authentic worship, witness, and work is directed by Christ himself; that all service within the community is the ministry of Christ the head to his body through his body; that every-member ministry, with each believer contributing at Christ's behest to the health of the whole complex, is meant to be the rule within the body of Christ; and that some ability to contribute in this way (that is, some spiritual gift) is supplied by Christ the head to every Christian.

The headship of Christ is central to the thought that the body-image expresses in Ephesians 4:15 (see also 1:22; 5:23; Col. 1:18; 2:19). There has been debate as to whether, in the places cited, headship signifies Christ as the source of the body's life or as the authority over its functioning, which is what headship evidently signifies in 1 Corinthians 11:3. Perhaps the answer is both/and, rather than either/or; for certainly the church's existence and spiritual energies do come from Christ, and submission to the lordship of the heavenly lover is set forth repeatedly in the New Testament as basic to the church's life.

Such, then, is Jesus the Saviour, according to the consistent witness of the New Testament and the sustained faith of the universal church across a wide range of contrasting milieux and cultures over nearly two thousand years. The self-sustaining and life-transforming power that these beliefs about Jesus have displayed from the first century to the present day needs to be explained, and the most rational explanation is that they are true, and have been proving themselves true through the Holy Spirit's application of them to human minds and hearts all the time. Of the confusions and diminutions of belief about Christ that have abounded in theological academia for more than a century, and are still being actively generated in some quarters, it need only be said that their a priori has always been some skepticism about the supernatural, and that without this prejudice to sustain them their arbitrariness and lack of inner cogency become apparent at once. Belief in the incarnation and the Trinity (the two belong together, for the doctrine of the Trinity is in the first instance just a clear spelling out of the divinity of Jesus Christ) is fully coherent and reasonable in a way that scaled-down revisionist Christologies simply are not. So we take it as a fixed point, and move on to further explore the salvation which, according to the New Testament, the Saviour bestows.

Salvation Analyzed

Salvation means, in broadest terms, deliverance from evil: rescue, that is, from a state of jeopardy and misery into one of safety and therefore of joy. God is revealed in the Old Testament as one who brings salvation from various evils, and in the New Testament, the gift of salvation is the focal centre of the gospel.

New Testament salvation is the divine gift, to persons who know themselves to be godless and guilty, of a new relationship of reconciliation with God the Creator through the mediatorial ministry of Jesus Christ the Saviour. In this relationship sinful human beings are no longer exposed to the prospect of God's wrath (judicial rejection and retribution) on judgement day, but are justified – that is, pardoned for the past, accepted in the present for the future, and guaranteed the eternal reward of the righteous, although in themselves they are sinners still. Justification by grace, on the basis of what Jesus did and suffered for us, is truly the last judgement so far as we are concerned; it is God the judge pronouncing here and now the verdict that determines how we shall spend eternity. Paul treats justification, 'the gift of righteousness' as he calls it (Rom. 5:17), as the fundamental blessing that the gospel brings, and on which every other blessing rests (see Rom. 3:21–5:21; Gal. 2:15–3:29; Phil. 3:7–14). Linked specifically with justification is the gift of *adoption*, whereby the judge takes us into his family as his sons and heirs – 'heirs of God and co-heirs with Christ' (Rom. 8:17). The gift is free, to sinners only; it cannot be earned on a basis of merit, only received on a basis of mercy. The receiving is by *faith*, which means the empty hands of the heart outstretched to embrace Jesus Christ as Saviour and Lord in the knowledge that he brings this salvation with him to make it ours. Faith involves *repentance*, a saying no to sin and self-centredness in order to say yes to the Christ who tells us to follow him, to take his yoke upon us and learn of him, and to sense him henceforth and forever. Such is salvation relationally, in its underlying dimensions.

And there is more to it than that. Those whose lives become a matter of faith and repentance in sustained exercise thereby show themselves to have been *regenerated*, or 'born of the Spirit' (John 3:8; cf. 3–7); that is, they have been united by the Holy Spirit with Jesus Christ in his death and resurrection. The effect of this is that without losing their own personal identity they have become, in the most fundamental sense, new creatures in Christ, living with him a new life (2 Cor. 5:17; Gal. 6:15; see Rom. 6:1–14). The newness of the new life springs from the fact that the Son of God now reproduces and sustains in us at the motivational core of our being the same thrusting and controlling desire to love, honour, and glorify the Father that drove him throughout his life on earth (as it had driven him from all eternity, and drives him still, and will go on driving him in heaven for ever). With this desire, the Holy Spirit – Christ's emissary and deputy in this world – maintains residence within us to transform our character from being Adamic and Satanic to being Christlike, and to empower us for the obedience and usefulness that will please God. To have renounced deliberate sinning, and in steady purpose to have 'crucified the sinful nature with its passions and desires' (Gal. 5:24), is what it means to be dead with Christ (Rom. 6:24, 6; Gal. 2:20). To be driven by Christ's implanted desires while being changed by Christ's Spirit into Christ's moral image is what it means to be risen with Christ (Rom. 7:4, 6). Thus the regenerate person is no longer ruled by the world, the flesh, and the devil, but is led by the Spirit through the biblical word into paths of enterprising and zealous obedience, and this constitutes *sanctification*, that is, heaven's glorification in the bud.

Salvation is a blessing of the kingdom of God, and like everything else in that kingdom it is both 'now' and 'not yet': *now* in beginnings and foretaste, *not yet* in completion and fullness. Hope of more grace and future glory, springing from faith that rejoices in present salvation and life in Christ, is therefore central to the Christ mind-set (see Heb. 10:38–12:3). One day Jesus will have returned to consummate all God's purposes for this world; then the believers' character-change will be complete; they will have bodies to match that change, bodies through which they can perfectly express their Christlike longings; they will be part of a new world order in which sin and pain have no place; and they will endlessly enjoy the celestial vision of the Father and the Son, whom they love. This is a hope of glory indeed! The church is the fellowship of those who, having been saved from sin's penalty by justification, are now being saved from its power by sanctification and who look ahead to the day when they will be saved from sin's presence and perfected in holiness and joy through glorification. As Lyte's hymn put it: 'On to glory / Safe' – saved! – 'they speed through all below.' Such, according to Scripture, is the full reality of the salvation that is mediated through Jesus Christ, our Saviour and our Lord.

A Church Year Salvation

A convenient way to analyse salvation further is provided by the church's liturgical year.

It is an Advent salvation

God painstakingly prepared the way over many centuries for the coming of Christ the Saviour to this world. He did this by means of promises, prophecies, and types that one way or another patterned out the rescue from sin and hell that Christ would achieve for his people when he appeared. Advent reminds us that we should understand salvation as the New Testament writers do, as the fulfilment of these foreshadowings. Also, as Advent looks ahead to Christ's return, it teaches us to hope for the completing of our salvation that his return will bring (Heb. 9:28).

It is a Christmas salvation

The incarnation of the Son of God, so Paul tells us, should be viewed as a step towards the cross (Phil. 2:5–8); but it has two further meanings in its own right. One is *identification*. The Son of God, by becoming human, came to know the human condition from the inside, as it were; his empathetic insight into our state and needs, gained through his experience of human living, is now as full as it could possibly be. The second meaning is *revelation*. As John says, 'truth came through Jesus Christ. No one has ever seen God. It is God the only Son, who is close to the Father's heart, who has made him known' (John 1:17–18, NRSV; 'made him known' carries the idea of 'explained' or 'expounded' him). Jesus himself said: 'Anyone who has seen me has seen the Father' (John 14:9). Since God is Jesus-like, hearing and watching Jesus gives full knowledge of the divine character. Integral to salvation is the assurance that God knows us as we really are, and that we know God as he really is. The incarnation is foundational for that assurance.

It is a Good Friday salvation

Central to the New Testament, in the Gospels, Acts, Epistles, and Revelation alike, is the cross of Jesus, viewed as the atoning event through which our salvation was achieved. Paul is the great theologian of atonement, and his many-sided thought about the cross seems to be structured as follows. How does the cross save? By being a *blood sacrifice* (its sacrificial status is affirmed in Eph. 5:2; and 'blood' in Rom. 3:25, 5:9, and Eph. 1:7 certainly means 'life laid down in sacrificial death'). How did Christ's sacrifice save us? By *redeeming* us from the jeopardy of guilt and exposure to God's vindicatory wrath that we were in before (Gal. 3:13; 4:5; Eph. 1:7). How did Christ's sacrifice redeem us? By *reconciling* God to us and us to God, cancelling our sins (2 Cor. 5:18–21) and ending our mutual hostility (Rom. 5:10). How did Christ's sacrifice end God's enmity to us? By being a *propitiation* – that is, as the NIV margin on Romans 3:25 puts it, 'one who would turn aside his wrath, taking away sin' (see also the margin on 1 John 2:2; 4:10). How did Christ's sacrifice have this propitiatory effect? By being a *substitution* – that is, a vicarious enduring of the retributive judgement declared against us (the curse of the law, Gal. 3:13; the tally of our sins nailed to the cross to account for Christ's execution, Col. 2:14; cf. Matt. 27:37). Our justification 'by [Christ's] blood' (Rom. 5:9), which, as we saw, is the foundational blessing in God's salvation package, is based not on judgement waived or suspended, but on justice actually done: it is *just* and *justified* justification, grounded on payment of the penalty by Christ in our place. He died for us, and now we go free. Salvation by substitution is the heart of the gospel message.

It is an Easter salvation

The bodily rising of Jesus into imperishable life, which showed forth his divinity (Rom. 1:4) and defeat of death (Acts 2:24), also guaranteed our forgiveness and justification by showing that our sins really had been dealt with (1 Cor. 15:17; cf. Rom. 4:25) and made certain our own resurrection into transformed bodily life when Christ returns (1 Cor. 15:18–21, 51–57; cf. Phil. 3:20–21). That will be our salvation completed.

It is an Ascension Day salvation

Jesus' journey from the tomb to the throne at the Father's right hand – that is, the place of executive rule – was like a two-flight air trip, with the forty days of the post-resurrection appearances as an extended stopover, and the ascension as the second flight, intended from the start (see John 20:17). Jesus' ascension is significant, not only because of the personal ascendancy and powerful intercession it betokened, but also because God the Father, in quickening us out of spiritual death (that is, separation from and unresponsiveness to himself), 'raised us up with Christ and seated us with him in the heavenly realms in Christ Jesus' (Eph. 2:4–6). Christians may thus remain 'on top,' as we say, in relation to everything that happens, living as conquerors in the confidence that Lyte expressed in the final verse of the hymn with which we began:

> God will keep his own anointed,
> Nought shall harm them, none condemn;
> All their trials are appointed,
> All must work for good to them;
> All shall help them
> To their heavenly diadem.

This confidence is part of the reality of Christian salvation.

It is a Pentecost salvation

Since other chapters in this volume deal with life in the Spirit, all we shall say about it here is that every Christian shares in the Pentecostal coming of the Paraclete to display Christ to us continually (see John 16:14) and to change us into his likeness as we gaze at his glory. 'All of us, with unveiled faces, seeing the glory of the Lord as though reflected in a mirror, are being transformed into the same image from one degree of glory to another; for this comes from the Lord, the Spirit' (2 Cor. 3:18, NRSV). Here is the essence of present salvation – deliverance, that is, from the blinding and enslaving power of sin.

It is a Trinity salvation

Trinity Sunday points to the climactic New Testament truth that our salvation is, if I may so phrase it, a team job in which the Father, the Son, and the Holy Spirit work together. It is in this shared task that the divine tri-personhood is revealed; should the truth of the Trinity be denied, the apostolic gospel could not be stated. What God in grace does to save us sinners shows that *he* is *they*, essentially and eternally a society of mutual love engaged in enlarging the fellowship of that love by bringing us into it. Salvation means, in the final analysis, our unending personal fulfilment in adoring and pleasing the Father, the Son, and the Holy Spirit, as the divine Three lead the church ever deeper into the eternal enrichment that has been prepared for saved sinners to enjoy together. The triune God is love in the relational reality of the divine being, and is love to penitent believers in the further relational reality of the work of saving grace. Living in the life-transforming experience of God's sovereign salvation – trusting Christ, honouring the Father, and relying on the Holy Spirit – is this world's supreme good now, and the best is yet to be.

Jesus Christ is the only Saviour because it is through him alone that we find forgiveness and come to the Father and are re-created in love by the Holy Spirit, and are finally brought to the everlasting enrichment of the next world. 'Thanks be to God for his indescribable gift!' (2 Cor. 9:15).

Implications

From what has been said it follows that any watering down, distorting, or obscuring of this gospel of salvation through Jesus Christ, any dismissal of it as untrustworthy fantasy, any distraction from contemplating and celebrating it as the centrepiece of worship, any suggestion that other faiths are adequate alternatives to it, and any attempt to fit it into a theological frame that is not incarnational or trinitarian or structured around the three 'R's' of Christianity – namely, ruin, redemption, and regeneration – will weaken the church by corrupting its liturgy, its ministry, its message, and its mission. The sincerity with which non-Christian faiths are promoted in the world, and revisionist theologies are put forward in the church, is undoubted, but sincerity does not guarantee either truth or realism, and where the revelation of Christ the Redeemer, set forth in Scripture and embraced in the Creeds, the Articles, and the Solemn Declaration of 1893 (to look no further), is denied or imperfectly grasped, both truth and realism, and therefore both life and power, will be lacking. Experience in the present century has surely proved this up to the hilt.

What then should we say of *pluralism*, the relativistic notion that all theological clashes between religions can be transcended and that an ultimate oneness of worldwide religious outlooks can be demonstrated? Space forbids any extensive discussion of this idea, attractive in many ways as it is; but, speaking in general terms, three points seem to stand insuperably against it. First, the accounts of the religious ultimate (God), the human predicament (sin), and the nature and path of true life (salvation) that the world's religions offer are neither compatible nor convergent, but diverge radically. Second, all attempts to achieve an umbrella account of what they say on these three issues (the highest-common-factor quest in multifaith theology) have so far failed to produce anything substantial for which the exponents of the various world religions can settle, and the most careful analysis yields no likelihood of any greater success in the future. Third, New Testament theology is explicitly exclusivist. 'I am the way and the truth and the life,' said Jesus. 'No one comes to the Father' – that is, no one comes to know God as Father, however strong they are on God's reality – 'except through me' (John 14:6). 'There is no other name under heaven given to men,' preached Peter, 'by which we' – who? Clearly in context, anybody and everybody – 'must be saved' (Acts 4:12). 'Must' implies that people both need to be saved and may be saved through Jesus: this is the universality of the Christian claim, of which we spoke at the outset, breaking surface once more. Pluralism, however, is categorically ruled out by such statements as these.

What should we say of *inclusivism*, the hopeful idea long embraced by Roman Catholicism and more recently by various Protestants also, that some, perhaps many, who did not encounter the Christian message in this world are nonetheless saved by Christ through a divinely induced disposition that is the equivalent of repentance and faith? Here again, full discussion is not possible in this chapter, but all who recognize the authority of the biblical revelation and the hazardous status of guesswork that goes beyond it will plead for reverent agnosticism at this point. We are not forbidden to hope for what Clark Pinnock calls 'a wideness in God's mercy'[3] to at least some of those who do not hear the gospel, but the attempts that he and others have made to find in Scripture a doctrine of wideness in this sense cannot be regarded as a success, and this means that we are obligated in practice to evangelize on the basis that there is no salvation for anyone whom we encounter apart from faith in Christ. If we cannot be confident that there would have been any hope for us had we not learned of Christ and been brought to personal faith in him, we have no basis for holding out such hope in the case of anyone else, however strongly charity prompts us to want to do so. Inclusivist speculation about salvation for the unevangelized is thus necessarily unfruitful, and is likely to distract us from our present witnessing task.

What, finally, should we say of the Anglican Church of Canada? Why, simply what Lyte says, in a statement whose force we can now perhaps better appreciate than when we first took note of it:

> O how blest the congregation
> Who the gospel know and prize;
> Joyful tidings of salvation
> Brought by Jesus from the skies!
> He is near them,
> Knows their wants and hears their cries.

---

[3] See Clark Pinnock, *A Wideness in God's Mercy* (Grand Rapids: Zondervan, 1992). See also John Sanders, *No Other Name: An Investigation into the Destiny of the Unevangelized* (Grand Rapids: Eerdmans, 1992).

It is as such congregations multiply in the Anglican Church that there is hope for us, and not otherwise. Our future depends on how faithfully we maintain faith in, and fidelity to, Jesus Christ the only Saviour. The way is clear; the only question is whether we will walk in it. Lyte has indicated what is essential, and no more need now be said.

Chapter 5

The Lamb Upon His Throne

The proclamation of Christ today tends to move straight from vindicating the Resurrection to present encounter with the risen Lord. This sequence of themes is meant partly to challenge sceptics who deny miracles and partly to engage liberals, formalists, moralists, Jews, New Agers, and adherents of ethnic religions for whom the Jesus of history is a great teacher a wonderful example and a potent memory, but not a living Saviour. Let us by all means maintain this focus; let us go on telling people that Jesus' resurrection is one of the best attested facts of history, for indeed it is. But let us not lose sight of the fact that the Resurrection was the prelude to the Ascension. We should never forget that from the moment Jesus left the tomb, he was heading for the heavenly throne.

Resurrection and Ascension

The Creed ties Christ's resurrection directly to his ascension and heavenly session. 'The third day he rose again from the dead; He ascended into heaven; and sitteth on the right hand of God the Father Almighty.' The Resurrection began – and his ascension completed – the return to glory he knew before.

Jesus' first conversation after being raised from death showed this clearly. Mary of Magdala, meeting him alive again, wanted to embrace him. Matthew 28:9 says that she and the other Mary did what one did in those days to show affection to a superior: they got down and grasped His feet. But Jesus prevented her: 'Stop clinging to Me; for I have not yet ascended to the Father, but go to My brethren, and say to them, "I ascend to My Father and your Father, and My God and your God." ' [1] 'I ascend' meant 'I am about to ascend.' Jesus' words were not a cold-hearted brush-off but a compassionate re-education. The Marys, and the rest of

THE LAMB UPON HIS THRONE was originally published in *Tabletalk* Ligonier Ministries, Orlando, Florida, December, 1992, pp. 13–15. Reprinted by permission.

[1] John 20:17, NASB.

his disciples with them, had to get used to practising fellowship with a Saviour whom they could not touch or even see, for he would shortly ascend to heaven and so withdraw from human sight till his second coming.

Incarnation and Mystery

The Resurrection and Ascension involve *mystery* – basically, the mystery of incarnation itself.

What immediate changes in the human body of the Son of God did his resurrection bring? Continuity was evident: the risen Lord looked and sounded as before; he was solid flesh and bone, and ate food, [2] and could be touched and held. [3] But change was evident too: he could vanish, and appear as it were from nowhere, even passing through locked doors. [4] Some guess that Jesus' body became immaterial and invisible at the moment of resurrection but rematerialized in some way for each of his post-resurrection encounters. That certainly goes beyond the biblical evidence, and arguably raises more problems for the mind than it removes.

What exactly happened to Jesus in the Ascension? The disciples' perception of this was that after he commissioned and blessed them, [5] a cloud came down, [6] and Jesus was drawn, not downward, not sideways, but up – up into the cloud, leaving them goggling skyward. [7] That upward movement signified not only that the Father was withdrawing the Son from this world-order and taking him home but also that he was advancing the Son to new dignity (as when we speak of someone 'going up in the world'). So Christ's ascension implies Christ's ascendancy, it is as if, having travelled successfully in the firm's interest, the Son was now recalled to headquarters to become managing director.

Thus, the risen Lamb returned to glory to be enthroned at the Father's right hand, in the Grand Vizier position at the ancient Persian court, the place of executive government in the monarch's name; and there he reigns today, as Lord of the entire universe.

As Jesus said himself, the Father has committed all authority in heaven and on earth into His hand. [8] And 'He must reign until He has put all His

---

[2] Luke 24:39–43.

[3] Matthew 28:9; John 20:27.

[4] Luke 24:31, 36; John 20:19, 26.

[5] Acts 1:8; Luke 24:50.

[6] A sign of the Father being present to act, as at the Transfiguration: Luke 9:34–36.

[7] Acts 1:9f.

[8] Matthew 28:18; John 5:20–23, 26f.

enemies under His feet.'[9] But what should we make of Jesus' bodily exit in the cloud? It was certainly miraculous, involving a unique exercise of divine creative power just as his entry into the world by virgin birth had done, but what sort of miracle was it? We should not think of Jesus as the first space traveller, zooming instantaneously through light-years of dis - tance away from us. We should find our clue, rather, in the realization that after his resurrection, as we have seen, the three dimensions of space that confine us confined him no more. C. S. Lewis spoke somewhere of the Son being withdrawn through a 'fold' in space, like an actor who having taken his bow appears to vanish into a fold in the stage curtain (actually stepping into the gap between the two curtains), and this image gives us perhaps the best idea we can form of the mystery involved here.

The fact to be grasped is that though Jesus' *personal* presence is now available through the Holy Spirit to all who call on him everywhere, his *bodily* presence is gone. Physically, Jesus has returned to heaven, there to serve as his Father's right-hand man (how apt that phrase is!) until he reappears for judgement.

No doubt Jesus' body in heaven is now 'glorious,'[10] shining as it did at the Transfiguration, though not, it seems, in any of the post-resurrec - tion appearances that are recorded for us. Something more has happened to it through the Ascension, though we shall have to wait till we ourselves get to heaven to find out just what.

Session and Intercession

The key to understanding Jesus' present life in heaven, and with it his previous life on earth, is to grasp that he is there, as once he was here, *for us*. 'Us' in this phrase, as always in the New Testament, means not the human race as such but past, present, and future believers, all whom God has chosen to save. 'Intercede' means 'intervene in our interest,' in a way that guarantees our welfare by ensuring that what he died to secure for us actually becomes ours. The Son does not supplicate the Father on our behalf in uncertainty as to whether his requests will be granted; he speaks to the Father from the throne on which the Father has set him, fully aware that his will for our good is the Father's will also. Jesus' ongoing intercession for his people is therefore sovereignly efficacious.

What benefits does his intercession bring us? Quite simply, every one that relates to our relationship with our triune God, from every stand - point, at every level. On the one hand, Jesus' intercession maintains our justified status.[11] On the other hand, Jesus' intercession ensures that when

---

[9] 1 Corinthians 15:25.

[10] Philippians 3:21.

[11] Romans 8:34.

we approach his throne in our weakness and inadequacy, we find it to be a 'throne of grace' where we 'receive mercy and find grace to help us in our time of need.'[12] No spiritual benefit of any kind comes to any child of God apart from the mediatorial intercession of Jesus the Lord.

War and Peace

Spiritually, there is a war on, and the Lamb on his throne is a war commander, directing a global campaign. It has been so from the start. This fallen world lies under Satan's power.[13] He will not let go of any part of it without a struggle, and wherever he is dispossessed, he will try to regain control, or if he cannot do that, at least spoil God's work and thwart his purposes. Yet Satan is a defeated foe; Christ overcame him decisively while on earth, and now from heaven he pours out his Spirit to enable his servants to ram home his victory by freeing lost souls from Satan's sway and bringing them new life.

The warfare, intellectual, moral, and ideological, if not actually physi-cal, between the Lord's people and the forces of spiritual lawlessness is constant and bitter, and in the short term, it is not always clear who is on top.

One day Jesus Christ will reappear to close the book of this world's history, and then all spiritual rebellion will end, for power to oppose him will then be abolished everywhere for ever. But until that day the war goes on, and the battles for truth, wisdom, and righteousness in the church, the world, and each Christian's personal life are not to be evaded; they are to be fought and won, in the strength that flows from heeding the directive: 'Let us fix our eyes on Jesus, the author and perfector of our faith, who for the joy set before Him endured the cross, scorning the shame, and sat down at the right hand of the throne of God.'[14]

Such is the real Christian life, under the really reigning Lord: a life of war and peace, war without and peace within. Is it ours? Christian realists will not settle for anything less: nor should they. So don't you.

---

[12] Hebrews 4:16.
[13] 1 John 5:19; cf. 2 Corinthians 4:4.
[14] Hebrews 12:2.

Chapter 6

A Modern View of Jesus

The late W. H. Griffith Thomas entitled one of his books *Christianity is Christ*. He was right; so it is. To describe Christianity as a creed plus a code would be more usual, but would not go so deep. That Christianity involves both a creed and a code is a truth that none should query. Where basic beliefs about Jesus are denied and Christian behavior is not practised, Christianity does not exist, whatever may be claimed to the contrary.

But Thomas' point was that you can know the creed and embrace the code and still be a stranger to Christianity. Martin Luther, George Whitefield and John Wesley, to name but three, had to learn that through humbling experience; so did I; and so many more.

For the essence of Christianity is neither beliefs nor behaviour patterns; it is the communion here and now with Christianity's living founder, the Mediator, Jesus Christ.

Stages of Decline

Christianity proclaims that Jesus of Nazareth, the Galilean preacher, was a divine person, the incarnate Son of God. Christianity calls him 'Christ' because that is his official title: it identifies him as the long-awaited, God-appointed Saviour-King of mankind.

Christianity interprets the criminal's death that he suffered as fulfilling a divine purpose, the salvation of sinners. And Christianity affirms that after his death Jesus came alive again, in human flesh, mysteriously transformed, and has from that time been exercising full supremacy over the entire cosmic order.

Invisibly present to uphold us as we trust, love, honor and obey him, he supernaturalizes our natural existence, re-making our characters on the model of his own, constantly energizing us to serve and succor others for his sake. When life ends, whether through the coming of our own heartstop day or through his public reappearance to end history

A MODERN VIEW OF JESUS first appeared in *Faith Today*, January/February, 1987, pp. 28, 30, 32–33. Reprinted by permission.

with judgment, he will take us to be with him. Then we shall see his face, share his life, do his will, and praise his name, with a joy that will exceed any ecstasy of which we are now capable and that will go on literally forever.

That is the gospel. It is indeed good news.

Being a Christian, therefore, is a matter of constantly reaching out to the invisibly present Saviour by words and actions that express three things: faith in him as the one who secured, and now bestows, forgiveness of our sins, so setting us right with the God who is his Father by essence and becomes ours by adoption; love for him as the one who loved us enough to endure an unimaginably dreadful death in order to save us; and hope in him as the sovereign Lord through whose grace our life here, with all its pains, is experienced as infinitely rich and our life hereafter will be experienced as infinitely richer.

It thus appears that Christianity is Christ *relationally*. Being a Christian is knowing Christ, which is more than just knowing about him. Real faith involves real fellowship. 'Our fellowship,' explained the apostle John, 'is with the Father and with his Son, Jesus Christ.'[1] Credence without this communion is only half-way to Christianity. Personal homage, trust and obedience Christ-ward is what finally counts.

The Christian centuries have seen a vast company of believers who have shown that they understood this well, even when their official teachers were not stating it well. This knowledge of Christ sustained Christians in the catacombs and in the arena during 250 years of persecution before Constantine. This same knowledge upheld Protestant martyrs in Britain and Western Europe in the 16th century and the persecuted Puritans, Covenanters and Huguenots of the 17th. This knowledge has supported missionaries, who have been laying down their lives for Christ since the days of the Jesuit pioneers, and countless thousands who have suffered for Christ in our time in Africa and behind the Iron Curtain.

What should we make, and what should we ask the world to make, of these heroic believers who remained so peaceful, patient and sweet through all they endured? Their secret was an open one; it is really no secret at all. They embraced Paul's certainty that nothing can separate us from the love of God that is in Christ Jesus our Lord (Romans 8:38f.).

They took to themselves Christ's words to the church at Smyrna: 'Be faithful, even to the point of death, and I will give you the crown of life' (Rev. 2:10). By these assurances they died, as they had lived, in joy and triumph. Their faith in, and love for, their divine Saviour and their readiness to exchange the present life for a better one at his call are the authentic marks of Bible Christianity. This is the real thing.

---

[1] 1 John 1:3.

Christ Changing Lives

Against the background of this supernatural, faithful heroism which demonstrates so fully the credibility of Christianity as stated, if you were told that many in the churches have come to minimize and even deny the deity, dominion and sole saviourhood of Jesus Christ, you would conclude that they were in a state of spiritual delirium of some kind.

But such is true; sleeping sickness of the spirit, with talking in the sleep, is in fact my own diagnosis of this state of affairs. Let me describe more exactly what I see.

For a century now, not just among outsiders but within Protestant bodies too, there has been a massive drift into a lowered view of Jesus as a good and godly man who is simply an inspiring example rather than an almighty Saviour. This trend has produced great confusion and weakness. Folk nowadays do not know what the truth is about Jesus. And if they were in a church (which most of them are not), they do not know what they would be expected to believe about him; for they see the clergy as confused on the subject, and many church people holding views about Jesus that are quite different from what their church professes.

What seems to be assumed by all is that to say anything more about Jesus than that he was a fine man is to enter the realm of speculation, where no norms for thought exist and no-one has any right to impose his or her views on anyone else.

A sad scene? Yes, very. How did it come to be? By stages, thus: Three centuries ago, Protestant intellectual culture – philosophical, scientific, literary and aesthetic – tugged loose from its historic moorings in Christian faith. Brilliant men shrank the thought of God smaller and smaller, distorting it in the process, and distorting belief about Jesus with it. That is why today's man-in-the-street has only out of shape notions about the Father and the Son, seen, as it were, through the wrong end of a telescope.

Specifically, the Reformers had proclaimed the sovereign Lord of scriptural faith, the God who says what the Bible says and who saves sinners through Christ by grace. But 17th century Deists ruled out miracles and set a fashion of denying that God is Lord over his world. In the 18th century the philosopher Immanuel Kant set a fashion of denying verbal revelation, and 19th century thinkers domesticated God as the power behind the universal evolutionary processes that they posited. Our own 20th century has settled for a finite, kind-hearted, ineffective, suffering God, a kind of heavenly uncle whose goodwill makes no real difference to anything, a being who it is nice to think exists but who, ultimately, is not worth bothering about. You have met this rather pathetic figure: he is the God in whom the average North American today believes.

Thoughts about Jesus shrank similarly. Seventeenth-century scepti-cism about miracles made the incarnation an embarrassment, and 18th-century scepticism about revelation reduced the words of Jesus from divine disclosures to something far less. Since the 19th century, Jesus has been viewed as a supreme instance of human religious development, who probably did not rise from the dead and certainly does not rule the world at present, but whose memory still has influence, as does that of Socrates or Winston Churchill. This, however, does not affirm Jesus' continuing personal ministry, but denies it. It says he was not God incarnate but was a man whom God indwelt, and that he is important to us as a sample of sainthood rather than as a supernatural Saviour from the guilt and power of sin.

This was bad enough, but four further factors in world Protestantism have made it worse.

First, the theological colleges and seminaries and, in Germany particu - larly, the theological faculties of universities, which prepare each genera - tion of clergy for their life's work, have largely surrendered to this scepticism about Christ. They teach it to their students, who naturally swallow it neat and spread it in the churches where they serve.

Second, the so-called 'higher' biblical criticism (which is no more than the necessary attempt to find out when, where, how, by whom and why each book was written) has for more than a century been controlled by the anti-miraculous assumptions about God of which we spoke above. As a result, it has come to be thought, quite wrongly, that scientific scholarship has shown the untrustworthiness of much of the Bible, including its delineation of Jesus as the supernatural Saviour, and that any attitude of belief in the Bible and its Christ must hence be judged unscholarly.

Third, the practice of making children memorize catechisms stating Christian doctrine has fallen out of use. Modern Sunday schools mostly limit themselves to teaching Bible stories. Children thus grow up in the church without being drilled in its creed. They learn of Jesus as friend and helper without ever hearing that he is the second person of the Trinity, and so become adults to whom this fact is altogether strange.

Fourth, as the West's sense of human sinfulness has diminished and its awareness of other religions has intensified, the idea has taken root that Christianity is a mind-set and behavior pattern that is seen in all good men, whatever faith or lack of faith they may profess; and that it is acquired by instinct and osmosis rather than instruction.

Since no one knows about Jesus without instruction, this view would seem to imply that Jesus himself is not essential to Christianity. That, I suspect, is what many believe deep down, though few are bold enough to say it aloud.

With all these factors as part of the scene, it is small wonder that great companies of churchgoers today should think of God in a unitarian rather than Trinitarian way, of Christ in terms of God-indwelt humanity rather than of incarnate deity, and of salvation in terms of being accepted through

God's forbearance for trying to do right rather than of being forgiven through Christ's atonement for actually doing wrong. But it is tragic that we who inherit so rich a legacy of true faith, past and present, should have gone so far astray on matters so fundamental. It shows of course that, as has often been said, God has no grandchildren; grace and wisdom do not run in the blood. No doubt the devil laughs at our lapses, but I hope no one else does. They are too serious for that.

Rebuilding Belief in Christ

What this all amounts to is that in today's church historic Christian belief in Jesus Christ is like Humpty Dumpty: it has had a great fall, and now lies before us broken in pieces. Everyone picks up some of these, but few have them all or know what to do with those they have.

There is much genuine perplexity. Persons of good will who want to be Christians look to clergy and theologians for help, find them in disarray regarding the person and place of Jesus and, with some impatience and disgust, turn away from them to settle for their own private thoughts about the man from Galilee. Yet they know that these are no more than amateurish fancies and guesses, and they would be very glad if they could be given something surer and more definite.

So for their sake as well as that of others, we ask with some urgency, Can Christian certainty about Jesus Christ be reconstructed? Can Humpty Dumpty be put together again? I think the answer is yes, and I move on now to offer guidelines for doing this.

1. Link the person of Jesus with his work

All accounts of Jesus Christ really answer two questions together: not just the question about his person (who he was, and is), but also that which concerns his work (what he did and does). The first question is ontologi - cal, the second functional and they are distinct; nonetheless, one's answer to the second is likely to affect one's answer to the first.

If, under the influence of scepticism about the Bible, one should limit Jesus' work to instruction (teaching God's will) and demonstration (of God's love and of godliness) and play down as unreal all thoughts of his present heavenly reign and future return to judge mankind, and reduce communion with him to being moved by his example, then one will lose nothing by reducing him to the status of a uniquely enlightened human being, a man who reflected God in a specially clear way. Such a non-supernatural view of Jesus will seem simple, sufficient and appealing.

But for sober Christians who heed the apostles' understanding of Jesus, and his own recorded understanding of himself, as sole mediator between God and men, our substitutionary sin-bearer on the cross, our risen

Redeemer here and now and the one in whom and through whom we have eternal life, it is a very different story.

Such Christians give full weight to the New Testament depiction of Christ's salvation as a matter of literal union and communion with him here and hereafter. They note that the New Testament sees prayer and praise to Jesus as no less proper than praise and prayer to the Father; that the New Testament actually hails him as the living Lord who, alongside the Father, is personally divine; and that in the New Testament, as in the Christian community since, personal fellowship with the risen Lord is a reality of experience.

Their conclusion is that to categorize Jesus as a God-indwelt man, now dead, is to fall grievously short, for such a Christ could not bring us the salvation that the New Testament proclaims.

Where the dimensions of salvation are diminished or obscured, there the New Testament account of Jesus' role as redeemer is likely to be scaled down to match. What else would you expect? This is the explanation for most of the poor Christology that the world has seen in our time.

2. Understand Jesus' identity in Trinitarian terms

The one God is a complex unity, to whose personal life oneness and threeness are equally basic. For this unique and unparalleled fact the New Testament has no technical terminology, and it took Christians 300 years of debate before they learned to express and safeguard it by confessing one God in three persons, the Son and Spirit being one in essence with the Father.

But Trinitarian thinking about God is found constantly throughout the New Testament, most strikingly so when Jesus explains that after his going to the Father 'another counselor,' the Holy Spirit, will come to replace him, and that through the Spirit's coming he himself will come to the disciples in personal presence. They will then know that they live in him. [2]

The New Testament writers see salvation as the joint work of Father, Son and Holy Spirit, the Father arranging it, the Son accomplishing and administering it, and the Holy Spirit applying it. Therefore if one denies the Trinity, the truth about salvation will inevitably be lost also. It is basic to Christianity, as distinct from all other world religions, always to think about God in Trinitarian terms.

So rather than loosely referring to Jesus as ' *God* incarnate,' as if unitarianism is true and 'Jesus' is a second role that the eternal Father has played, we should always describe him as ' *the Son of God* incarnate.' For it was only the second person of the eternal three who took humanity to himself.

Among New Testament scholars today it is fashionable to maintain that passages like John 1:1–14, Phil. 2:5–7, Col. 1:15–17 and Hebrews

---

[2] John 14:12–23; 16:5–28.

1–2 affirm that the Son pre-existed before the Incarnation only as a thought in the Father's mind, not as an eternal person distinct from the Father. Whether they see that this view denies the Trinity I do not know, but it does. It is so unnatural and forced as an interpretation, however, that we need not spend time discussing it here.

3. Do not soft-pedal Jesus' humanness

John's statement that the Word became flesh[3] means more than that he encased himself in a physical body. It means that he took to himself, and entered right into, everything that contributes to a fully human experi - ence. From the moment he became a fetus in Mary's womb up to the present, human experience has been one dimension of the life of the son of God, and will continue so forever.

By virtue of what he experienced as a healthy first-century Jewish male before his death at thirty-three, he can now enter sympathetically into all human experiences, those of girls and women, sick folk, the aged, and addicts (for instance) no less than those of young males like himself.[4] Thus he is able to give to all the help towards right living that we all need.

The church has always known this. That is why such ideas as that Jesus really was not human (though he appeared to be), or that the incarnate Son had no human mind or will, have always been condemned as heresy. And that is why Christians have been constantly asking Jesus to help them in their struggles ever since the days of the apostles, and constantly declaring that he does.

For more than a hundred years it has been argued that those who believe that Jesus' humanness is adjectival, so to speak, to his deity cannot take his humanness seriously. Such people certainly do believe that the deepest secret of his identity is that he is 'God plus,' a divine person ontologically and experientially enlarged by his manhood rather than being 'man plus,' a human person uniquely indwelt and enriched by his God. That does not however leave him less human than you or me.

It is certainly true that believers in the incarnation have often trailed their coat at this point by talking as if there were some experience – the suffering of Calvary, for one – that Jesus went through 'in his humanity' but not 'in his deity.' But that idea should be replaced by the thought that the Jesus of the New Testament experienced everything in the unity of his divine-human person, and that his experiencing of life was more vivid than ours because his sensitivity had not been dulled at any point.

The true Christian claim here is that incarnation made direct entry into human frustration and pain possible for the Son of God, who then out of love actually entered in person into the agony of crucifixion and

---

[3] John 1:14.
[4] See Heb. 2:18; 4:15–16.

the greater agony of God-forsakeness[5] in order to bear our sins and so redeem us. Never let this claim be played down.

4. *Do not diminish Jesus' divinity*

An unhappy speculation that has mesmerized many during the past century is the so-called 'kenosis theory,' which suggests that in order to enter into a fully human experience of limitation, the Son of God at his incarnation forfeited his natural powers of omnipotence and omniscience; as a result, there were things that he wanted to do that he could not do, and mistakes due to ignorance could enter into his teaching. Four comments seem to be called for by way of reaction.

First, there is no hint of any such forfeiture in Scripture.

Second, the suggestion seems to undermine Jesus' authority as a teacher and thus dishonor him.

Third, it raises a problem about Jesus' present heavenly life. If Jesus' exercise of the two abilities mentioned (the Son's natural power to do and know whatever he willed to do and know) is incompatible with a fully human experience, it would seem to follow that *either* – having in heaven affirmed these powers – his experience is not now fully human, or, since his heavenly experience remains fully human, he has not regained these powers, and never will. I leave it to the proponents of the kenosis theory to struggle with this dilemma; it is not my problem, nor I hope yours.

Fourth, the natural explanation of the one bit of evidence from the gospels cited in support of the theory – Jesus' acknowledged ignorance of the time of his return[6] – is that since the Son's nature is not to take initiatives[7] but to follow his Father's prompting, his reason for not doing certain things, or bringing to conscious knowledge certain facts was simply that he knew that his Father did not wish this done.

In other words, Jesus' human limitations should be explained in terms, not of the special conditions of the incarnation, but of the eternal life of the Trinity.

To follow these paths of thought is, I believe, to avoid the pit-falls that in our day threaten incarnational thinking.

Then we will be led back out of confusion to regain a truly biblical faith in Jesus Christ. How we in our churches today need to do this! Surely there will be no renewal of life and power from God among us until we learn again to see the glory of Jesus Christ, our incarnate Lord. May God teach us all this – soon!

---

[5] See Mark 15:34.

[6] Mark 13:32.

[7] See John 5:19.

Chapter 7

The Uniqueness of Jesus Christ

Some Evangelical Reflections on Historic Evangelicalism

Our conference theme is evangelical identity today. We are asking ourselves what makes one an evangelical, as distinct from a Christian of some other brand, and how one's evangelical identity can be preserved (if indeed it can be) when one parts company with long-standing evangelical conventions: as one does (for instance) by taking westward position instead of north side at the communion table, or by admitting ritual gestures and aesthetic ornament in worship instead of going for plainness at all costs, or by using modern services as alternatives to 1662, or by not observing customary abstinences in areas of Christian liberty, or by pointing out what seems good in Anglo-Catholicism and Roman Catholicism and Eastern Orthodoxy and talking constructively with their spokesmen, or by saying with F. D. Maurice and many since that the gospel yields among other things a theology of social institutions which summons us to social action. I count it a privilege, and a congenial one, to be sharing in this important and timely enquiry; but I must ask leave to spend a moment at the outset defining the nature of my interest in it, for here I often feel myself out of step with others and, indeed, somewhat over a barrel. So please allow me three ground-clearing remarks.

First, as one who is much less ready than some to leave behind the historic externals – the symbols, if you like – of Anglican evangelical churchmanship as I learned it thirty years ago, and who remains convinced that the main services of the Prayer Book, though pastorally limited nowadays as the alternatives of Series I, II and III are not, are of far higher quality than any of them, and who still recommends the Thirty-nine Articles as a teaching tool, may I say that my interest in evangelical identity is conscientiously not shaped by sectarian or atavistic or escapist motives, and I hope the same is true of yours. None of us, I hope, has any interest in belonging to a party, in the sense of an inner ring of folk who are always

THE UNIQUENESS OF JESUS CHRIST was presented at the Islington Conference, 23 January, 1978, and originally published in *Churchman*, XCII, 1978, 2, pp. 101–111. Reprinted by permission.

'us' as opposed to 'them.' None of us, I hope, would allow his concern to be a thorough evangelical to get mixed up with our secular English love of the quaint and traditional for its own sake, or with middle-aged nostalgia for the 'good old days' (whenever we take them to have been), or with neurotic urges to take mental flight from the jarring confusions of the present to the comfortable clarities of the past.

I think that on occasion I have seen these false motives surface in church discussions to destroy the credibility of wise conservationist policies and to spark off reactions of practical Athenianism – 'anything, provided it be different' (I might have said Gadarene-swine reactions: 'anywhere, provided it be forward!') – and I have been most unhappy to see it, for it is not thus that the best decisions get made: rarely will the reaction of man work the righteousness of God. So I hope I carry you with me in my first remark: that there is no place in anyone's evangelical identity for sectarian, regressive or escapist impulses, and we should consciously declare war on all three.

Second: as one who remains committed to the Church of England, for all its free-wheeling goofiness, because of the value and hope which I find in its heritage of truth, wisdom, worship, devotion and pastoral concern, and as one who fully identifies with the 1967 Keele stance (while wondering if Nottingham '77 was not a mistake), may I say that my interest in evangelical identity, and my resolve to hold on to it, reflects a belief about history. The word 'evangelical' has, after all, in the first instance an historical definition: it signifies the Christianity, both convic - tional and behavioural, which we inherit from the New Testament via the Reformers, the Puritans, and the revival and missionary leaders of the eighteenth and nineteenth centuries. This Christian tradition, as expressed in the lives and writings of its past and present exponents, constantly functions as our hermeneutical aid in understanding the Bible – sometimes in more far-reaching ways than we are aware. Most of us are much more children of the evangelical past than we realize.

Now, the reason why I call myself an evangelical, and mean to go on doing so, is my belief that as this historic evangelicalism has never sought to be anything other than New Testament Christianity, so in essentials it has succeeded in its aim. Its preaching, devotional writing and pastoral practice show, even more clearly than its formal theology, that it has known the real essence of the gospel (Jesus Christ as Saviour from sin), that it has practised the real essence of church life (worship and fellowship in the Spirit), and that it has fulfilled the real essence of the Christian mission (church-centred, church-planting, church-strengthening evangelism, to which all other works of love are ancil - lary). Whatever its defects in other respects, this is its record regarding the central things, the things that matter most. It is a very honourable record indeed.

So I speak to you as one who is frankly proud in the Lord of his evangelical heritage, both from within and outside the Church of England: the heritage, I mean, which includes Athanasius and Augustine, Martin Luther and John Calvin, Richard Hooker (demonstrably an evangelical) and John Owen, Jonathan Edwards, George Whitefield and John Wesley, Charles Spurgeon and John Charles Ryle, Robert Aitken and William Booth, the great Presbyterian theologians of Scotland and North America, the spirituality of the English Puritans and the East African revival, and much, much more. To me, historic evangelicalism is an ecumenical reality constituting the nearest approach to New Testa - ment Christianity that the world has yet seen, and as such represents the mainstream of Christian development into which all the wealth found in other traditions is meant to flow; and my interest in defining and maintaining evangelical identity springs from my desire that we should all enter into this heritage to the fullest extent.

I see evangelicalism as something which evangelicals hold in trust for the world, and I want to see all men everywhere sharing that faith which the men and movements aforementioned unite to mediate to us. 'Faith,' by the way, in that last sentence means not only creed and theology but also what my Welsh friends, following St. John, call 'the life': that is, God-given experiential communion with the Father and the Son in the fellowship of Christian people. Creed and theology are vital, for it is only through truth that God gives life; but to hold the truth outwardly without experiencing the life inwardly is pathetically hollow.

Here, then, is my second remark: that the ingredients in evangelical identity, and the special glories of that identity, are found in history, both remote and recent, so that we must be in touch with our history and with God's legacy to today through that history if we are to be worthy heirs of those who were evangelicals before us. Though you and I are children of an age which, because of its own rapid and kaleidoscopic cultural shifts, is notoriously insensitive to history, and are therefore strongly tempted to impoverish ourselves by disregarding our evangelical history (thus yielding to worldliness in one of its present-day forms), I hope I carry you with me in this remark also.

My third remark is a quickie. It follows from what has been said, that what makes an evangelical will be that which in the eyes of the New Testament writers makes a Christian. What is that? In a phrase, it is true faith in the real Jesus Christ. One who does not display this will not only not be an evangelical; the question will arise whether they are a Christian at all, and evangelicals will judge that they cannot be unless they are better and sounder at heart than appearances would suggest.

From these three remarks you see where I am coming from, as the Americans say, in my approach to the question of the uniqueness of Jesus Christ.

The Vital Question

Christology is in dispute today, and the differences under discussion are crucial. The question is whether the man Christ Jesus was and remains God in person or not: whether God incarnate is, as one recent book maintains, an item of factual truth [1] or, as another book has urged, a notion with the status of a non-factual myth. [2] We may excuse ourselves from trying to state in positive terms just what a myth is, for those who use this category of explanation do not seem to be fully agreed among themselves on that; suffice it for our purposes to say that myth is in one way or another an imaginative declaration of personal significance or communal vision which does not correspond to, or rest on, public, objective, cosmic, space-time fact. So the issue is whether, as a matter of public, objective, space-time fact, Jesus Christ was a divine person – the Word made flesh without ceasing to be God's Son, which is what John affirms explicitly in the famous fourteenth verse of the first chapter of his gospel – or whether, despite what John and other New Testament writers, notably Paul and the writer to the Hebrews, thought and taught, Jesus was not God become man and ought to be accounted for in other terms.

This is as far-reaching an issue as can well be imagined. On it hangs your view both of God and of salvation. Take the matter of God first. We need to realize that, as the doctrine of the Trinity is not an idle fancy or speculation about God in the abstract but a specific claim about our Lord Jesus Christ, so the doctrine of the Incarnation is not an idle fancy or speculation about Jesus in isolation but a specific claim about God. For what the doctrine of the Trinity says is that the relationship of Jesus the Son to the Father and the Spirit, which the gospels depict and the epistles affirm, is a revelation of that endless fellowship of mutual love and honour which is the final, definitive description of God's eternal reality. And what the doctrine of the Incarnation says is that the Triune God loves sinners, and therefore in unity with God the Father and God the Spirit, God the Son has come to us where we are and identified wholly with the human condition in order to save us.

All the works of the Trinity external to the Godhead are undivided, says the old tag (*omnia opera Trinitatis ad extra indivisa sunt*): so it needs to be understood that, as indeed the gospel records make very plain, the Son became human at the command of the Father, by the power of the Holy Spirit and in the joy of loving union with both; and that when in his cry of dereliction on the cross Jesus testified to god-forsakenness at conscious level, at a deeper level the togetherness of the Godhead remained intact. That Jesus knew this, even if for those three dark hours he could not feel

---

[1] *The Truth of God Incarnate*, ed. Michael Green (London: Hodder & Stoughton, 1977).
[2] *The Myth of God Incarnate*, ed. John Hick (London: SCM, 1977).

it, is surely clear from his first and last words on the cross: 'Father, forgive them,' and 'Father, into thy hands I commit my spirit' (Luke 23:34, 46).

Denial that the Incarnation is fact, however, undercuts the whole of this. On the one hand, it takes away at a stroke all grounds for supposing the Trinity to be fact (as clear-headed myth-men like Professor Maurice Wiles cheerfully admit). On the other hand, it constitutes a denial that, when mankind was perishing in sin and had forfeited God's favour and provoked his wrath, the Father loved the world enough to give his only Son to become poor so that we might be made rich, and to bear unimaginable agony in enduring the sinner's death so that we might know righteousness and life. There is no escaping this point: what non-incarnational Christologies say is that, contrary to what Christians always thought and what their liturgies and hymns have hitherto expressed, God did not come in person to save the world after all; for whoever Jesus was, and whatever he did, he was not God.

Putting this point biblically, Paul's great statement that the Father 'did not spare his own Son' (the verb speaks of the cost to the Father) 'but gave him up for us all' (that verb speaks of the cost to the Son), is being denied; and the effect of this denial is to rob us of all warrant for embracing Paul's glorious inference – 'will he (the Father) not also give us all things with him?' (Rom. 8:32). In other words: deny the Incarnation, and Jesus' death, just because it is not now the death of God's Son and not therefore the most costly gift God could bestow, loses its significance as the guarantee of every other gift that God can devise. This is a heavy loss which, one feels, should make advocates of the new Christology pause and reconsider.

What, now, of the link between the Incarnation and salvation? Here the basic point is that if we are going to deny that Jesus was God incarnate, we cannot ascribe to him any mediatorial ministry involving anything which it takes God to do. How much then, do we stand to lose of the Saviour's ministry as we have hitherto understood it? The answer of the New Testament from its own standpoint, and equally of the protagonists of 'humanitarian' Christologies from theirs, seems to be: practically all of it. For both objective reconciliation through Christ, and personal renewal in Christ as its consequence, will have to go.

Take reconciliation first. Paul tells us, if I read him right, that God's reconciling work in Christ took the form of a substitutionary sacrifice in which 'for our sake he (the Father) made him (the Son) to be sin who knew no sin' (2 Cor. 5:19, 21): that is to say, our sins were imputed to Christ as the personally innocent and sinless sacrificial victim, according to the typical Old Testament pattern, and he died under God's curse in our place. 'Christ redeemed us from the curse of the law, having become' – the natural rendering would be, '*by becoming*' – 'a curse for us' (Gal. 3:13). The curse is, of course, the sentence of spiritual death, the appropriate judicial retribution.

But if Jesus Christ had not been God incarnate, he would have been simply a man in Adam; and in that case, however Spirit-filled and godly he was, he would not have been personally sinless, for no child of Adam is. How then could he have been our substitutionary sacrifice?

Again, if the substitutionary sacrifice goes, the free gift of justification that is based upon it goes also. When, in the verse (2 Cor. 5:21) which we started to quote above, Paul said that for our sake the Father made the Son 'to be sin who knew no sin, so that in him we might become the righteousness of God,' he linked reconciliation and justification together as two aspects of what Luther called the 'wonderful exchange' whereby our penal liability has passed to Christ and been dealt with on the cross; while his righteousness, that is his acceptance by the Father, which was maintained by his perfect obedience, is now extended to us for the taking. If we do not see our justification as based on 'the redemption that is in Christ Jesus, whom God put forward as a propitia - tion by his blood' (Rom. 3:24f.), it is not justification according to Paul that we are talking about: we have lost his frame of reference. A non-incarnational Christology, however, seems to make this inevitable.

Again, the New Testament sees our subjective renewal – that is, according to Paul, our co-resurrection with Christ – as taking place 'in Christ,' through life-giving union and communion with the risen Lord. But those who insist that Jesus was no more than a godly man are naturally sceptical as to whether his resurrection, if indeed it happened, could in reality be the vitalizing archetype of ours. It is really impossible on a non-incarnational basis to make anything of that present rising with Christ which baptism proclaims, or of waiting for 'a Saviour, the Lord Jesus Christ, who will change our lowly body to be like his glorious body, by the power which enables him even to subject all things to himself' (Phil. 3:20f.). So on this basis renewal in Christ, as the New Testament presents it, must also be given up, as must that fellowship with the living Lord, in the power of the Spirit whom he sends, which is the distinctive and essential feature of New Testament devotion; and now very little of New Testament salvation remains, as you can see.

Both pro- and anti-incarnationists (not all the latter, but most) affirm the uniqueness of Christ. They do it, however, in contrasting ways, and it is instructive to compare the two kinds of accounts.

1) All mainstream Christian traditions since the patristic period (the evangelical included) have followed the lead of the New Testament writers, whose presentations of Jesus – though seemingly independent, apart from the Synoptic evangelists, and at verbal and conceptual level quite distinct – harmoniously converge upon the 'two-nature' Christol - ogy, and the account of mediation built on it, which is set out in the fourth gospel and the letters to the Colossians and Hebrews. On this view, Jesus' uniqueness, that is his one-and-only, once-for-all quality, appears at two points: first in his divine human person, and second in his

mediatorial work as, in Barth's phrase, God for man and man for God. Take the two separately.

In the constitution of his person, Jesus is 'God plus': the second person of the Godhead who through being born of Mary became the subject of all the physical and psychological awarenesses that make up distinctively human experience. This does not, of course, mean that he experienced everything that actually happens to each one of us (he did not, for instance, experience marriage or old age); nor does it mean that it was into fallen human experience, of which disordered desire is a constant element, that he entered. All we can say is that his human experience was of such a comprehensive kind as to enable him to understand and feel with us in all situations, as Hebrews 2:18 and 4:15 tell us he does.

A question arises about his knowledge while on earth: though some - times he knew facts at a distance, and seems always to have been utterly and immediately clear on spiritual issues, there were times when he showed ignorance, and it has been suggested that rather than put this down to play-acting (as the Fathers sometimes did) we should posit some pre-incarnate self-emptying of divine powers – in this case, of the capacity to know whatever he willed to know, the capacity which we call omniscience. This *kenosis*-theory is not, however, easy to make fit the facts (because Jesus knew, not only so little, but also so much); nor is it easy to make sense of in its own terms (because it sounds like a di- or tri-theistic fairy story rather than Trinitarian theology).

It seems better to explain Jesus' ignorances in terms not of an induced inability to know but rather of dependence on his Father's will and unwillingness to call to mind facts which he knew that his Father did not direct him to have in his mind at that time. The paradigm for this view is Jesus' own statement that 'the Son can do nothing of his own accord' (John 5:19).

I wish I could go on here to speak at length of Jesus' mediatorial ministry as our prophet, priest and king; of the solitariness, permanence and power of that ministry; and of his solidarity with both his Father and us, a solidarity which he indicated in deceptively simple terms by saying, according to John's gospel, that he and his Father are 'in' each other, and that his people live 'in' him and he 'in' them (John 14:11; 15:4; 17:23, etc.). But time does not allow that.

2) The non-incarnational account of Jesus' uniqueness places it entirely in his *impact*: that is, in the instrumentality of his example to bring about effective identification with, and experience of, the 'Jesus way' of life – whether this is analysed at the level of feeling (Schleier - macher) or of ethics (Ritschl, Harnack, Albert Schweitzer), or of openness to God and self-understanding (Bultmann, Bornkamm and their successors), or however. Jesus on this view is 'man-plus': plus, that is, a unique sense of God and unique, God-given, insight. But his significance for us is wholly as a revelation of godliness rather than of

God. Teacher and brother-man and example to us he may be, but Son of God and Saviour he is not: and one cannot think it surprising that myth-men like Dennis Nineham and Don Cupitt are prepared to wonder aloud whether, even as teacher and example, Jesus has very much real importance for us today.

Whence does such thinking – such painful thinking, to many of us – derive? From three obvious sources. Source one is hermeneutical arbi - trariness (interpretive individualism, if you like) whereby, with Bultmann, scholars treat apostolic witness to Christ as myth despite the apostles' own constant insistence that they are declaring historical fact and revealed truth. Source two is historical scepticism whereby, following Deism ancient and modern, scholars assume that God never does anything genuinely new, despite sustained biblical proclamation to the contrary; so that they discount miracles, and particularly what C. S. Lewis calls 'the grand miracle,' namely the Incarnation, as necessarily non-factual.

Source three is philosophical dogmatism whereby they affirm *a priori* that God the Creator cannot take to himself the nature of created man, despite New Testament declarations that he has actually done so. One can understand non-incarnationists wishing to affirm this hazardous *a priori* (for hazardous it is: how could anyone possibly prove it? How can one show it to be even plausible?).

Certainly, any denial that God came in person to save will sound less shocking and impoverishing when based on a confident assurance that incarnation could not have happened anyway, in the nature of things. But surely setting limits to God in this way is really the acme of crass and even suicidal irreverence. Ecclesiastes pronounced woe on the land whose king is a child (Eccles. 10:16), a child presumably in matters of statecraft and government. It is hard to refrain from pronouncing similar woe on the church whose theologians and teachers, however technically accom - plished and sophisticated in speech, are children in understanding; and that is the point we seem to have reached. I am sorry to have to speak like this, but lest my words should be thought intemperate and unwar - rantable I would like to refer you to E. L. Mascall's magisterial essay *Theology and the Gospel of Christ*, which makes this precise point by sustained argument and with devastating conclusiveness.

Realism and Solidarity

What shall we say to these developments? I have three things to say concerning them as I close.

First, I fear that we must interpret the situation in which university theologians go into print with the effect – however unintended – of denying the Lord who bought them, as a tragedy of judgement on us all for long-standing Laodiceanism and unconcern about revealed truth.

On the personal level, we echo Stephen Neill's charitable comment that irrational factors touch the minds of the best and most well-meaning of men, causing us all sometimes to take up with theories and ideas which are objectively crazy and disastrous. Living in glass houses as we all do, we had better be careful with our stones. We note that a number of those who now challenge the Incarnation came out of university Christian Unions, where hurtful forms of obscurantism, insensitiveness and group pressure have sometimes been known to operate; and we lay our hands on our mouths. But behind all that lies the fact, for fact it surely is, that we are living through an era which spiritually is like that of Jeremiah: a time in which consciences are calloused, sin – the 'gay' life-style, for instance – can pass as virtue, shame for shortcomings is scarcely felt, and minds, even the ablest, over and over again are unable to distinguish things that differ.

That this frightening time is one of judgement, bringing loss of strength, expense of spirit and waste of good throughout the church's life, seems too plain to be denied. Statistically, financially, spiritually, theo - logically, the Protestant churches in our country appear to be dying on their feet. Please do not tell me that the charismatic movement and the increased and increasing numbers of evangelical clergy and laity, as compared with twenty years ago, have changed all that: for they have not. These things are merely new ripples on the surface of a pond whose waters continue to drain away. Whether they will ever amount to more than that we do not yet know.

At present, our complacent way of talking to each other about the future comes through as a spiritual death rattle, just as at another point on the spiritual and theological front non-incarnational Christology also does. Realism compels us to recognize that judgement, theological, moral and spiritual, has overtaken English Protestantism; and to see the humani - tarian scaling-down of Jesus Christ to someone who is no longer the divine Saviour whom we need, as a symptom no less than a cause of what is going on.

Second, I urge that in these bleak conditions we must consider carefully who our true allies are in the defence and confirmation of the gospel. Once it was felt that what chiefly endangered the gospel in the Church of England was a mechanical sacramentalism, and that those to whom we should look to help us oppose it were the Low and Broad Churchmen – those whom Newman would have called 'liberals.' But now that which chiefly endangers the gospel is the humanitarian Chris - tology which denies us a living divine Saviour; and our allies against it are chiefly our catholic brethren, whose views of Christ are in step with the Creeds.

The debates about the Godhead, and latterly the Incarnation, over the past fifteen years have shown that the things which unite evangelical and catholic Anglicans give them closer links with each other than either group has with the Broad Church constituency, especially its radical wing. Furthermore, the unity which derives from a common acceptance of Nicene and Chalcedonian convictions, together with a common love for the living Lord Jesus as our risen, reigning Saviour from sin, goes far deeper than do any specific differences of view about church, ministry and sacraments. Thus, whatever reservations I may have about the ecclesiology, Mariology and eucharistic teaching of such a man as my learned friend Dr. Eric Mascall, I am profoundly grateful to him for books like *Up and Down in Adria*, *The Secularization of Christianity* and *Theology and the Gospel of Christ*, and I hope you are too. Should the future see a catholic renewal in the Church of England, having the same non- triumphalist, non-partisan character as has marked the evangelical renewal of the past generation, I am bold to predict both that the church will benefit and that evangelical-catholic solidarity against views which erode the supernatural in the realm of redemption will become yet stronger. Such co-belligerence will not compromise either side, and will be tactically appropriate for furthering faith in those fundamentals concerning our incarnate Lord on which we are truly agreed.

Third, I urge that, as those who define evangelical identity in terms of a New Testament-based faith in Jesus Christ as God incarnate, our prophet, priest and king, our wisdom and our righteousness, our Lord, our life, our way and our end, we should watch like hawks against any fragmenting of the seamless robe of scriptural testimony to Jesus' person and place. One of the theological failings of our age is our habit of isolating individual doctrines for treatment and reconstruction without weighing the full consequences of that reconstruction for the rest of the body of divinity. But Christian theology, both in Scripture and in our own minds, is an organism, a unity of interrelated parts, a circle in which everything links up with everything else; and if we are clear-headed we shall keep in view the long-range implications of each position when evaluating it. We have already seen how humanitarian Christology demolishes the received doctrines both of the Trinity and of salvation, and the same is true of the doctrine of the church as the new humanity in the Lord.

The worship of Jesus Christ alongside the Father, to which the New Testament leads us, the Christian's saving relationship with him and the church's corporate solidarity with him in his risen life, all assume that he died as an effective sacrifice for our sins, rose again as proof that his atoning work was done, reigns here and now and will one day return to judge the living and the dead. None of this can be convincingly affirmed if his divine-human glory as God incarnate be denied. It really is not true that the less you set yourself to defend of New Testament Christology, the easier it will prove to defend it. On the contrary, if you take away any of its component bricks, and particularly the reality of the Incarnation, which is the keystone of the arch, the whole structure falls down. Clarity of thought requires us to acknowledge that only when the whole New

Testament story concerning Christ is told in all its parts will credibility attach to any of it.

If the Incarnation is denied, the whole New Testament account of Jesus the Christ should certainly be categorized as mythological fantasy (we may agree with the humanitarians on that). But then there is no reason why it should any longer claim our interest; the proper place for it then would be the dustbin. We need to realize the inter-locking and interde - pendent character of the truths concerning Jesus, to see that divided they fall, and to make it a matter of deliberate care to tell the whole story – man's creation and fall; Christ's incarnation, atonement, resurrection, reign, and future return – when bearing testimony to the Son of God in this clashing, confused and disordered age.

Chapter 8

What Did the Cross Achieve?

The Logic of Penal Substitution

The task which I have set myself in this lecture is to focus and explicate a belief which, by and large, is a distinguishing mark of the worldwide evangelical fraternity: namely, the belief that Christ's death on the cross had the character of *penal substitution*, and that it was in virtue of this fact that it brought salvation to humankind.

Two considerations prompt my attempt. First, the significance of penal substitution is not always stated as exactly as is desirable, so that the idea often gets misunderstood and caricatured by its critics; and I should like, if I can, to make such misunderstanding more difficult. Second, I am one of those who believe that this notion takes us to the very heart of the Christian gospel, and I welcome the opportunity of commending my conviction by analysis and argument.

My plan is this: first, to clear up some questions of method, so that there will be no doubt as to what I am doing; second, to explore what it means to call Christ's death *substitutionary*; third, to see what further meaning is added when Christ's substitutionary suffering is called *penal*; fourth, to note in closing that the analysis offered is not out of harmony with learned exegetical opinion. These are, I believe, needful preliminaries to any serious theological estimate of this view.

Mystery and Model

Every theological question has behind it a history of study, and narrow eccentricity in handling it is unavoidable unless the history is taken into

WHAT DID THE CROSS ACHIEVE?: THE LOGIC OF PENAL SUBSTI-TUTION was originally delivered as the Tyndale Biblical Theology Lecture at Tyndale House, Cambridge, on July 17th, 1973. Reprinted from the *Tyndale Bulletin*, 25 (1974), pp. 1–43, by permission.

account. Adverse comment on the concept of penal substitution often betrays narrow eccentricity of this kind.

The two main historical points relating to this idea are, first, that Luther, Calvin, Zwingli, Melanchthon and their reforming contempo - raries were the pioneers in stating it and, second, that the arguments brought against it in 1578 by the Unitarian Pelagian, Faustus Socinus, in his brilliant polemic *De Jesu Christo Servatore* (*Of Jesus Christ the Saviour*)[1] have been central in discussion of it ever since. What the Reformers did was to redefine *satisfactio* (satisfaction), the main mediaeval category for thought about the cross.

Anselm's *Cur Deus Homo?*, which largely determined the mediaeval development, saw Christ's *satisfactio* for our sins as the offering of compensation or damages for dishonour done, but the Reformers saw it as the undergoing of vicarious punishment (*poena*) to meet the claims on us of God's holy law and wrath (i.e. his punitive justice). What Socinus did was to arraign this idea as irrational, incoherent, immoral and impossible.

Giving pardon, he argued, does not square with taking satisfaction, nor does the transferring of punishment from the guilty to the innocent square with justice; nor is the temporary death of one a true substitute for the eternal death of many; and a perfect substitutionary satisfaction, could such a thing be, would necessarily confer on us unlimited permission to continue in sin. Socinus' alternative account of New Testament soteriol - ogy, based on the axiom that God forgives without requiring any satisfaction save the repentance which makes us forgivable, was evasive and unconvincing, and had little influence. But his classic critique proved momentous: it held the attention of all exponents of the Reformation view for more than a century, and created a tradition of rationalistic prejudice against that view which has effectively shaped debate about it right down to our own day.

The almost mesmeric effect of Socinus' critique on Reformed scho - lastics in particular was on the whole unhappy. It forced them to develop rational strength in stating and connecting up the various parts of their position, which was good, but it also led them to fight back on the challenger's own ground, using the Socinian technique of arguing a priori about God as if he were a man – to be precise, a sixteenth- or seventeenth-century monarch, head of both the legislature and the judiciary in his own realm but bound nonetheless to respect existing law and judicial practice at every point. So the God of Calvary came to be

---

[1] Socinus' arguments were incorporated in the *Racovian Catechism*, published at Racow (the modern Cracow) in 1605 which set forth the Unitarianism of the Polish Brethren. After several revisions of detail down to 1680, the text was finalized and in due course translated into English by Thomas Rees (London, 1818). It is a document of classical importance in Unitarian history.

presented in a whole series of expositions right down to that of Louis Berkhof (1938) as successfully avoiding all the moral and legal lapses which Socinus claimed to find in the Reformation view.[2]

But these demonstrations, however skilfully done (and demonstrators like Francis Turretin and A. A. Hodge, to name but two,[3] were very skilful indeed), had built-in weaknesses. Their stance was defensive rather than declaratory, analytical and apologetic rather than doxological and kerygmatic. They made the word of the cross sound more like a conundrum than a confession of faith – more like a puzzle, we might say, than a gospel.

What was happening? Just this: that in trying to beat Socinian rationalism at its own game, Reformed theologians were conceding the Socinian assumption that every aspect of God's work of reconciliation will be exhaustively explicable in terms of a natural theology of divine government, drawn from the world of contemporary legal and political thought. Thus, in their zeal to show themselves rational, they became rationalistic.[4] Here

---

[2] See L. Berkhof, *Systematic Theology* (Grand Rapids: Eerdmans, and London: Banner of Truth, 1949), pp. 373–383. Berkhof's zeal to show that God did nothing illegal or unjust makes a strange impression on the post-Watergate reader.

[3] See F. Turretin, *Institutio Theologiae Elencticae* (Geneva, 1682) II. xiv, 'De Officio Christi Mediatoris,' and A. A. Hodge, *The Atonement* (London: Nelson, 1868). Turretin's position is usefully summarized in L. W. Grensted, *A Short History of the Doctrine of the Atonement* (Manchester: Manchester University Press, 1920) pp. 241–252. Cf. J. F. Heidegger's parallel account in his *Corpus Theologiae Christianae* (Zurich, 1700), which R. S. Franks reviews in *The Work of Christ* (London: Nelson, 1962) pp. 426ff.

[4] In his influential book *Christus Victor*, tr. A. G. Herbert (London: SPCK, 1931), which advocated a 'dramatic', non-rational way of declaring God's conquest of evil through the cross, Gustaf Aulén describes the 'Latin' account of the atonement (i.e. that of Anselm and Protestant orthodoxy) as 'juridical in its inmost essence' (p. 106), and says: 'It concentrates its effort upon a rational attempt to explain how the Divine Love and the Divine Justice can be reconciled. The Love of God is regulated by His Justice, and is only free to act within the limits that Justice marks out. *Ratio* and *Lex*, rationality and justice, go hand in hand . . . The attempt is made by the scholastics to elaborate a theology which shall provide a comprehensive explanation of the Divine government of the world, which shall answer all questions and solve all riddles' (pp. 173f.). What Aulén fails to note is how much of this implicitly rationalistic cast of thought was a direct reaction to Socinus' rationalistic critique. In fact, Aulén does not mention Socinus at all; nor does he refer to Calvin, who asserts penal substitution as strongly as any, but follows an exegetical and Christocentric method which is not in the least scholastic or rationalistic. Calvin shows no interest in the reconciling of God's love and justice as a theoretical problem; his only interest is in the mysterious but blessed fact that at the cross God did act in both love and justice to save us from our sins. Cf. P. van Buren, *Christ in our Place: The Substitutionary Character of Calvin's Doctrine of Reconciliation* (Edinburgh: Oliver and Boyd, 1957).

as elsewhere, methodological rationalism became in the seventeenth cen -
tury a worm in the Reformed bud, leading in the next two centuries to a
large-scale withering of its theological flower.

Now I do not query the substantial rightness of the Reformed view
of the atonement; on the contrary, I hope to confirm it, as will appear;
but I think it is vital that we should unambiguously renounce any such
intellectual method as that which I have described, and look for a better
one. I shall now try to commend what seems to me a sounder method
by offering answers to two questions: (1) What sort of knowledge of
Christ's achievement on the cross is open to us? (2) From what source
and by what means do we gain it?

First: what sort of knowledge of God's action in Christ's death may
we have? That a man named Jesus was crucified under Pontius Pilate
about AD 30 is common historical knowledge, but Christian beliefs about
his divine identity and the significance of his dying cannot be deduced
from that fact alone. What further sort of knowledge about the cross,
then, may Christians enjoy?

The answer, we may say, is *faith-knowledge*: by faith we know that God
was in Christ reconciling the world to himself. Yes, indeed; but what sort
of knowledge is faith-knowledge? It is a kind of knowledge of which God
is both giver and content. It is a Spirit-given acquaintance with divine
realities, given through acquaintance with God's word. It is a kind of
knowledge which makes the knower say in one and the same breath both
'whereas I was blind, now I see' (John 9:25) and also 'now we see as in
a mirror, darkly . . . now I know in part' (1 Cor. 13:12). For it is a unique
kind of knowledge which, though real, is not full; it is knowledge of what
is discernible within a circle of light against the background of a larger
darkness; it is, in short, knowledge of a *mystery*, the mystery of the living
God at work.

'Mystery' is used here as it was by Charles Wesley when he wrote:

> 'Tis mystery all! The immortal dies!
> Who can explore his strange design?
> In vain the first-born seraph tries
> To sound the depths of love divine!

'Mystery' in this sense (traditional in theology) means a reality distinct
from us which in our very apprehending of it remains unfathomable to
us: a reality which we acknowledge as actual without knowing how it is
possible, and which we therefore describe as *incomprehensible*. Christian
metaphysicians, moved by wonder at the world, speak of the created order
as 'mystery,' meaning that there is more to it, and more of God in it, than
they can grasp; and similarly Christian theologians, taught by revelation,
apply the same word for parallel reasons to the self-revealed and self-
revealing God, and to his work of reconciliation and redemption through

Christ. It will be seen that this definition of mystery corresponds less to Paul's use of the word μυστήριον (which he applied to the open secret of God's saving purpose, set forth in the gospel) than to his prayer that the Ephesians might 'know the love of Christ *which passes knowledge*' (Eph. 3:19).

Knowing through divine enlightenment that which passes knowledge is precisely what it means to be acquainted with the mystery of God. The revealed 'mystery' (in Paul's sense) of Christ confronts us with the unfathomable 'mystery' (in the sense I defined) of the Creator who exceeds the comprehension of his creatures. Accordingly, Paul ends his full-dress, richest-ever exposition of the mystery of Christ by crying:

> O depth of wealth, wisdom, and knowledge in God! How unsearchable his judgements, how untraceable his ways! Who knows the mind of the Lord? . . . Source, Guide and Goal of all that is – to him be glory for ever! Amen.[5]

Here Paul shows, and shares, his awareness that the God of Jesus remains the God of Job, and that the highest wisdom of the theological theorist, even when working under divine inspiration as Paul did, is to recognize that he is, as it were, gazing into the sun, whose very brightness makes it impossible for him fully to see it; so that at the end of the day he has to admit that God has much more to him than theories can ever contain, and to humble himself in adoration before the one whom he can never fully analyse.

Now the atonement is a mystery in the defined sense, one aspect of the total mystery of God. But it does not stand alone in this. Every aspect of God's reality and work, without exception, is mystery. The eternal Trinity; God's sovereignty in creation, providence, and grace; the incar - nation, exaltation, present reign and approaching return of Jesus Christ; the inspiring of the Holy Scriptures; and the ministry of the Spirit in the Christian and the Church – each of these (to look no further) is a reality beyond our full fathoming, just as the cross is. And theories about any of these things which used human analogies to dispel the dimension of mystery would deserve our distrust, just as rationalistic theories about the cross do.

It must be stressed that the mystery is in each case the reality itself, as distinct from anything in our apprehension of it, and as distinct therefore from our theories, problems, affirmations and denials about it. What makes it a mystery is that creatures like ourselves can comprehend it only in part. To say this does not open the door to scepticism, for our knowledge of divine realities (like our knowledge of each other) is genuine knowledge expressed in notions which, so far as they go, are true. But it does close the door against rationalism, in the sense of

---

[5] Rom. 11:33ff., NEB.

theorizing that claims to explain with finality any aspect of God's way of existing and working. And with that, it alerts us to the fact that the presence in our theology of unsolved problems is not necessarily a reflection on the truth or adequacy of our thoughts.

Inadequate and untrue theories do of course exist: a theory (the word comes from θεωρειν, 'to look at') is a 'view' or 'sight' of something, and if one's way of looking at it is perverse one's view will be distorted, and distorted views are always full of problems. But the mere presence of problems is not enough to prove a view distorted; true views in theology also entail unsolved problems, while any view that was problem-free would certainly be rationalistic and reductionist. True theories in theol - ogy, whether about the atonement or anything else, will suspect them - selves of being inadequate to their object throughout. One thing that Christians know by faith is that they know only in part.

None of this, of course, is new or unfamiliar; it all belongs to the main historic stream of Christian thought. But I state it here, perhaps too laboriously, because it has not always been brought to bear rigor - ously enough on the doctrine of the atonement. Also, this position has linguistic implications which touch the doctrine of the atonement in ways which are not always fully grasped; and my next task is to show what these are.

Human knowledge and thoughts are expressed in words, and what we must note now is that all attempts to speak of the mystery of the unique and transcendent God involve many kinds of *stretching* of ordinary language. We say, for instance, that God is both plural and singular, being three in one; that he directs and determines our free acts; that he is wise, good and sovereign when he allows Christians to starve or die of cancer; that the divine Son has always upheld the universe, even when he was a human baby; and so forth. At first sight, such statements might appear nonsensical (either meaningless or false). But Christians say that, though they would be nonsensical if made about us, they are true as statements about God. If so, however, it is clear that the key words are not being used in an everyday way.

Whatever our views on the origins of human language and the inspiration of the Scriptures (both matters on which it seems that options are currently being broadened rather than reduced), there can be no dispute that the meaning of all the nouns, adjectives and verbs that we use for stating facts and giving descriptions is anchored, at least in the first instance, in our experience of knowing things and people (ourselves included) in this world. Ordinary language is thus being adapted for an extraordinary purpose when we use it to speak of God.

Christians have always made this adaptation easily in their prayers, praises and proclamations, as if it were a natural thing to do (as indeed I think it is), and the doubts articulated by skeptical and somewhat old-fashioned philosophers like A. J. Ayer and Antony Flew as to whether such utterances express knowledge and convey information about anything more than private attitudes seem curiously provincial as well as paradoxical.[6] Moreover, it is noticeable that the common Christian verbal forms for expressing divine mysteries have from the first shown remark - able consistency and steadiness in maintaining their built-in logical strangeness, as if the apprehended reality of God was itself sustaining them (as indeed I think it was).

Language about the cross illustrates this clearly: liturgies, hymns and literature, homiletical, catechetical and apologetic, all show that Christians have from the start lived by faith in Christ's death as a sacrifice made to God in reparation for their sins, however uncouth and mythological such talk sounds (and must always have sounded), however varied the presen - tations of atonement which teachers tried out, and however little actual theologizing about the cross went on in particular periods, especially the early centuries.[7]

Christian language, with its peculiarities, has been much studied during the past twenty years, and two things about it have become clear. First, all its odd, 'stretched,' contradictory and incoherent-sounding features derive directly from the unique Christian notion of the tran - scendent, tripersonal Creator-God. Christians regard God as free from the limits that bind creatures like ourselves, who bear God's image while not existing on his level, and Christian language, following biblical precedent, shakes free from ordinary limits in a way that reflects this fact.

---

[6] Ayer voiced his doubts in *Language, Truth and Logic* (London: Gollancz, 1936, 2nd ed. 1946), Flew his in 'Theology and Falsification,' *New Essays in Philosophical Theology*, ed. A. G. N. Flew and Alasdair MacIntyre (London: SCM, 1955) pp. 96–130. There are replies in, among other books, E. L. Mascall, *Words and Images* (London: Longmans, 1957); *Faith and Logic*, ed. Basil Mitchell (London: George Allen and Unwin, 1957), Frederick Ferré, *Language, Logic and God* (London: Eyre and Spottiswood, 1962; Fontana ed. 1970); W. Hordern, *Speaking of God* (New York: Macmillan, 1964).

[7] Of the church in the patristic period H. E. W. Turner writes: 'Its experience of Redemption through Christ was far richer than its attempted formulations of this experience' (*The Patristic Doctrine of Redemption*, [London: Mowbray, 1952], p. 13; cf. chapter V, 'Christ our Victim'). On T. F. Torrance's sharp-edged thesis in *The Doctrine of Grace in the Apostolic Fathers* (Edinburgh: Oliver and Boyd, 1948) that the Apostolic Fathers lapsed from New Testament faith in the cross to a legalism of self-salvation, Robert S. Paul's comment in *The Atonement and The Sacraments* (London: Hodder & Stoughton, 1961) p. 37, note 2, is just: 'To me he has made his case almost too well, for at the end I am left asking the question "In what sense, then, could the Church change this much and still be the Church?" ' In fact, Torrance's thesis needs the qualification of Turner's statement quoted above.

So, for instance, faced with John's declaration in 1 John 4:8–10, 'God is love. . . . Herein is love, not that we loved God, but that he loved us, and sent his Son to be the propitiation for our sins,' Calvin can write without hesitation: 'The word *propitiation* (*placatio*; Greek, ἱλασμός) has great weight: for God, in a way that cannot be put into words (*ineffabili quodam modo*), at the very time when he loved us, was hostile (*infensus*) to us till he was reconciled in Christ.' [8] Calvin's phrase 'in a way that cannot be put into words' is his acknowledgement that the mystery of God is beyond our grasp. To Calvin, this duality of attitude, love and hostility, which in human psychological terms is inconceivable, is part of God's moral glory; a sentiment which might make rationalistic theologians shake their heads, but at which John certainly would have nodded his.

Second, Christian speech verbalizes the apprehended mystery of God by using a distinctive non-representational 'picture language.' This con - sists of parables, analogies, metaphors and images piled up in balance with each other, as in the Bible itself (from which this language is first learned), and all pointing to the reality of God's presence and action in order to evoke awareness of it and response to it. Analysis of the functioning of this language is currently in full swing, [9] and no doubt much remains to be said. Already, however, the discussion has produced one firm result of major importance – the recognition that the verbal units of Christian speech are 'models,' comparable to the thought-models of modern physics. [10] The significance of this appears from John MacIntyre's judge - ment 'that the theory of models succeeds in reinstating the doctrine of analogy in modern theological logic . . . and that analogy is to be interpreted in terms of a theory of models and not *vice versa*.' [11]

The doctrine of analogy is the time-honoured account, going back to Aquinas, of how ordinary language is used to speak intelligibly of a God who is partly like us (because we bear his image) and partly unlike us

---

[8] *Inst.* II. xvii. 2. This thought is picked up in Anglican Article II: 'Christ . . . truly suffered . . . to *reconcile* his Father to us, and to be a sacrifice, not only for original guilt, but also for all actual sins of men.' On propitiation, cf. note 22 below.

[9] For surveys of the present state of play, cf. Ferré's *Language, Logic and God*; Ian G. Barbour, *Myths, Models and Paradigms* (London: SCM, 1974); John Macquarrie, *God-Talk* (London: SCM, 1967).

[10] The pioneer in stating this was Ian T. Ramsey: see his *Religious Language* (London: SCM, 1967); *Models and Mystery* (London: Oxford University Press, 1964); *Christian Discourse* (London: Oxford University Press, 1965). For further discussion of models in theology cf. John MacIntyre, *The Shape of Christology* (London: SCM, 1966), especially pp. 54–81; Thomas Fawcett, *The Symbolic Language of Religion* (London: SCM, 1970) pp. 69–94; Barbour, op. cit.

[11] *The Shape of Christology*, p. 63.

(because he is the infinite Creator while we are finite creatures). [12] All theological models, like the non-descriptive models of the physical sciences, have an analogical character; they are, we might say, analogies with a purpose, thought-patterns which function in a particular way, teaching us to focus one area of reality (relationships with God) by conceiving of it in terms of another, better known area of reality (relationships with each other). Thus they actually inform us about our relationship with God and through the Holy Spirit enable us to unify, clarify and intensify our experience in that relationship.

The last song in *Joseph and the Amazing Technicolor Dreamcoat* assures us that 'any dream will do' to wake the weary into joy. Will any model do to give knowledge of the living God? Historically, Christians have not thought so.

Their characteristic theological method, whether practised clumsily or skilfully, consistently or inconsistently, has been to take biblical models as their God-given starting-point, to base their belief-system on what biblical writers use these models to say, and to let these models operate as 'controls,' both suggesting and delimiting what further, secondary models may be developed in order to explicate these which are primary. As models in physics are hypotheses formed under the suggestive control of empirical evidence to correlate and predict phenomena, so Christian theological models are explanatory constructs formed to help us know, understand and deal with God, the ultimate reality.

From this standpoint, the whole study of Christian theology, biblical, historical and systematic, is the exploring of a three tier hierarchy of models: first, the 'control' models given in Scripture (God, Son of God, kingdom of God, word of God, love of God, glory of God, body of Christ, justification, adoption, redemption, new birth and so forth – in short, all the concepts analysed in Kittel's great *Wörterbuch* and its many *epigoni*); next, dogmatic models which the church crystallized out to define and defend the faith (*homoousion*, Trinity, nature, hypostatic union, double procession of the Spirit, sacrament, the supernatural, etc. – in short, all the concepts usually dealt with in doctrinal textbooks);

---

[12] The idea of analogy is formulated by the *Oxford Dictionary of the Christian Church, s.v.*, as follows: 'A method of predication whereby concepts derived from a familiar object are made applicable to a relatively unknown object in virtue of some similarity between the two otherwise dissimilar objects.' Aquinas' account of analogy is in *Summa Theologica* I. xiii, and can be read in *Words about God*, ed. Ian T. Ramsey (London: SCM, 1971), pp. 36ff. For Thomists, the doctrine of analogy serves to explain how knowledge of creatures gives knowledge of their Creator (natural theology) as well as how biblical imagery gives knowledge of the God of both nature and grace (scriptural theology). For a technical Thomist discussion, concentrating on analogy in natural theology, see E. L. Mascall, *Existence and Analogy* (London: Longmans, 1949) pp. 92–121.

finally, interpretive models lying between Scripture and defined dogma which particular theologians and theological schools developed for stating the faith to contemporaries (penal substitution, verbal inspiration, divinization, Barth's 'Nihil' – *das Nichtige* – and many more).

It is helpful to think of theology in these terms, and of the atonement in particular. Socinus went wrong in this matter first by identifying the biblical model of God's kingship with his own sixteenth-century monar - chy model (a mistake later repeated by Hugo Grotius), second by treating this not-wholly biblical model as his 'control,' and third by failing to acknowledge that the mystery of God is more than any one model, even the best, can express.

We have already noticed that some orthodox writers answering Socinus tended to slip in a similar way. The passion to pack God into a conceptual box of our own making is always strong, but must be resisted. If we bear in mind that all the knowledge we can have of the atonement is of a mystery about which we can only think and speak by means of models, and which remain a mystery when all is said and done, it will keep us from rationalistic pitfalls and thus help our progress considerably.

Bible and Model

Now we come up to our second question, my answer to which has been hinted at already. By what means is knowledge of the mystery of the cross given us? I reply: through the didactic thought-models given in the Bible, which in truth are instruction from God. In other words, I proceed on the basis of the mainstream Christian belief in biblical inspiration, which I have sought to justify elsewhere. [13]

What this belief means, in formula terms, is that the Holy Scriptures of both Testaments have the dual character which the *viva voce* teaching of prophets, apostles and supremely Jesus had: in content, if not in grammatical form, it is both human witness to God and God's witness to himself. The true analogy for inspiration is incarnation, the personal Word of God becoming flesh. As a multiple confession of faith in the God who rules, judges and saves in the space-time continuum which we call world history, the Bible consists of occasional documents, historical, didactic and liturgical, all proclaiming in various ways what God has done, is doing and will do.

Each document and each utterance within that document, like Jesus Christ and each of his utterances, is anchored in a particular historical situation – this particularity marks all the Christian revelation – and to

---

[13] See my *'Fundamentalism' and the Word of God* (London: IVP, 1958), *God has Spoken* (London: Hodder & Stoughton, 1965); 'Inspiration' in *The New Bible Dictionary*, ed. J. D. Douglas et al. (London: IVF, 1962).

discern within these particularities truths from God for universal applica -
tion is the interpreter's major task. His guideline is the knowledge that
God's word for today is found through understanding and reapplying the
word that God spoke long ago in identity (substantial, not grammatical)
with the message of the biblical authors. The way into God's mind
remains via their minds, for their assertions about God embody in
particularized form what he wants to tell us today about himself. In other
words, God *says* in application to us the same things that he originally *said*
in application to those to whom the biblical books were first addressed.

The details of the second application differ from the first in a way that
corresponds to the difference between our situation and that of the first
addressees, but the truths of principle being applied are the same. Divine
speech is itself, of course, a model, but it is a controlling one. It signifies
the reality of mind-to-mind instruction from God to us by verbal means,
and thus teaches us to categorize all other didactic models found in
Scripture, not as hypothesis or hunch, but as revelation.

How do these revealed models become means of God's instruction?
Here, it must regretfully be said, Ian Ramsey, the pioneer exponent of
the model-structure of biblical thinking, fails us. He describes vividly how
these models trigger off religious disclosures and so evoke religious
responses, but instead of equating the beliefs they express with divine
teaching he leaves quite open, and therefore quite obscure, the relation
between the 'disclosures' as intuitions of reality and the thoughts which
the models convey. This means that he lacks criteria for distinguishing
true from false intuitions.

Sometimes he speaks as if all feelings of 'cosmic disclosure' convey
insights that are true and self-authenticating, but one need only mention
the Buddha, Mohammed, Mrs. Mary Baker Eddy, the false prophets
exposed by Jeremiah, Ezekiel and Micaiah in 1 Kings 22, and the
visionaries of Colossians 2:18f., to show that this is not so. Also Ramsey
seems to be without criteria for relating models to each other and
developing from them a coherent belief-system, and he nowhere
considers what the divine-speech model implies. [14]

---

[14] For Ramsey's overall view of models, see the work cited in note 10. On most
theological subjects his opinions, so far as he reveals them, are unexceptionably
middle-of-the-road, but it is noteworthy that in his lecture on 'Atonement
Theology' in *Christian Discourse* (pp. 28ff.) he hails Hastings Randall's Abelardian
treatise *The Idea of Atonement in Christian Theology* (1919) as 'definitive' (p. 89;
no reasons given); limits the 'cosmic disclosure' evoked by the cross to a sense of
'the victorious will of God,' whose plan to maintain a remnant did not fail (pp. 32,
34), and whose love this victory shows (pp. 59f.); rejects the grounding of
justification on substitution or satisfaction as involving 'frontier-clashes with the
language of morals' (p. 40; the old Socinian objection); and criticizes the
exegeting of justification, substitution, satisfaction, reconciliation, redemption,

Must our understanding of how biblical models function be as limited or as loose as Ramsey's is? Not necessarily. Recognition that the biblical witness to God has the logic of models – not isolated, incidentally, but linked together, and qualifying each other in sizeable units of meaning – is compatible with all the views taken in the modern hermeneutical debate.

Central to this debate are two questions. The first is whether the reference-point and subject-matter of biblical witness is just the trans-formed psyche, the 'new being' as such, or whether it does not also, and indeed primarily, refer to saving acts of God and a living divine Saviour that were originally 'there' as datable realities in the space-time continuum of world history, and that owe their transforming power 'here' in Christian lives now to the fact that they were 'there' on the stage of history then. To the extent that the former alternative is embraced, one has to say that the only factual information which the biblical writers commu-nicate is that God's people felt and thought in certain ways at certain times in certain situations.

Then one has to face the question whether the writers thought this was all the factual information they were communicating; if one says no, then one has to justify one's disagreement with them; if one says yes, one has to explain why so much of their witness to Christ has the form of factual narration about him – why, indeed, the 'gospel' as a literary form was ever invented. If, however, one takes the latter alternative, as all sober reason seems to counsel, then the second central question arises: how much distortion of fact is there in the narrating, and how much of guesswork, hunch, and fantasy is there in the interpreting, of the historical realities that were 'there'?

I cannot discuss these massive and complex issues here; suffice it to declare, in relation to this debate, that I am proceeding on the basis that the biblical writers do indeed give true information about certain

---

[14] *(continued)* propitiation and expiation as if these words 'were *not models at all*, but described procedural transactions . . . each describing a species of atonement engineering' (p. 44). Profound confusion appears here. Certainly these words are models, but what they are models of is precisely procedural transactions for achieving atonement, transactions in which the Father and the Son dealt with each other on our behalf. The context of apostolic argument in which these models appear make this unambiguously plain, and to assume, as Ramsey seems to do, that as models they can only have a directly subjective reference to what Bultmann would call a new self-understanding is quite arbitrary. Indeed, Ramsey himself goes on to show that the model-category for biblical concepts does *not* require an exclusively subjective reference, for he dwells on 'love' as a model of *God's* activity (p. 59); and if love can be such a model, why not these other words? It seems evident that Ramsey brought Abelardian-Socinian assumptions to his study of the biblical words, rather than deriving his views from that study.

historical events, public and in principle datable, which have resulted in a Saviour and a salvation being 'there' for sinners to receive by faith; and that the biblical thought models in terms of which these events are presented and explained are *revealed* models, ways of thought that God himself has taught us for the true understanding of what he has done for us and will do in us.

Also, I proceed on the basis that the Holy Spirit who inspired prophetic and apostolic testimony in its written as well as its oral form is now active to teach Christians through it, making them aware of its divine quality overall, its message to themselves, and the presence and potency of God in Christ to whom it points. Since the Spirit has been teaching the church in this way in every age, much of our listening to the Bible in the present will rightly take the form of reviewing theological constructions of the past, testing them by the written word from which they took their rise.

When a particular theological view, professedly Bible-based, has over the centuries proved a mainspring of Christian devotion, faith and love, one approaches it, not indeed uncritically, but with respect, anticipating the discovery that it is substantially right. Our present task is to elucidate and evaluate one historic line of biblical interpretation which has had an incalculable impact on countless lives since it was clarified in the century of the Reformation; it will be strange if it proves to have been entirely wrong.[15]

So much, then, for methodological preliminaries, which have been tedious but necessary; now to our theme directly.

Substitution

The first thing to say about penal substitution has been said already. It is a Christian theological model, based on biblical exegesis, formed to focus a particular awareness of what Jesus did at Calvary to bring us to God. If we wish to speak of the 'doctrine' of penal substitution, we should remember that this model is a dramatic, kerygmatic picturing of divine action, much more like Aulén's 'classic idea' of divine victory (though Aulén never saw this) than it is like the defensive formula-models which we call the Nicene 'doctrine' of the Trinity and the Chalcedonian 'doctrine' of the person of Christ.

Logically, the model is put together in two stages: first, the death of Christ is declared to have been *substitutionary*; then the substitution is

---

[15] Cf. Vincent Taylor's remark, in *The Atonement in New Testament Teaching* (London: Epworth Press, 1940), pp. 301f.: 'The thought of *substitution* is one we have perhaps been more anxious to reject than to assess, yet the immeasurable sense of gratitude with which it is associated . . . is too great a thing to be wanting in a worthy theory of the Atonement.'

characterized and given a specific frame of reference by adding the word *penal*. We shall examine the two stages separately.

Stage one is to declare Christ's death *substitutionary*.

What does this mean? The *Oxford English Dictionary* defines substitution as 'the putting of one person or thing in the place of another.' One oddity of contemporary Christian talk is that many who affirm that Jesus' death was vicarious and representative deny that it was substitutionary; for the *Dictionary* defines both words in substitutionary terms!

Representation is said to mean 'the fact of standing for, or in place of, some other thing or person, esp. with a right or authority to act on their account; *substitution* of one thing or person for another.' And vicarious is defined as 'that takes or supplies the place of another thing or person; *substituted* instead of the proper thing or person.' So here, it seems, is a distinction without a difference.

Substitution is, in fact, a broad idea that applies whenever one person acts to supply another's need, or to discharge his obligation, so that the other no longer has to carry the load himself. As Pannenberg says,

> in social life, substitution is a universal phenomenon . . . Even the structure of vocation, the division of labour, has substitutionary character. One who has a vocation performs this function for those whom he serves. [For] every service has vicarious character by recognizing a need in the person served that apart from the service that person would have to satisfy for himself.[16]

In this broad sense, nobody who wishes to say with Paul that there is a true sense in which 'Christ died for us' (ὑπέρ, on our behalf, for our benefit), and 'Christ redeemed us from the curse of the law, having become a curse for us' (ὑπέρ, again) (Rom. 5:8; Gal. 3:13), and who accepts Christ's assurance that he came 'to give his life a ransom for many' (ἀντί, which means precisely 'in place of,' 'in exchange for'[17]), should hesitate to say that Christ's death was substitutionary. Indeed, if he describes Christ's death as vicarious he is actually saying it.

It is, of course, no secret why people shy off this word. It is because they equate, and know that others equate, substitution in Christology with *penal* substitution. This explains the state of affairs which, writing in 1948, F. W. Camfield described as follows:

> If there is one conclusion which (has) come almost to be taken for granted in enlightened Christian quarters, it is that the idea of substitution has led theology on a wrong track; and that the word 'substitution' must now be dropped from the doctrine of the Atonement as too heavily laden with

---

[16] Wolfhart Pannenberg, *Jesus, God and Man*, tr. Lewis L. Wilkins and Duane A. Priebe (London: SCM, 1968) pp. 268, 259.

[17] See R. E. Davies, 'Christ in our Place – the contribution of the Prepositions,' *Tyndale Bulletin* 21 (1970) pp. 7ff.

misleading and even false connotations. By 'liberal' or 'modernist' theology the idea of substitution is of course rejected out of hand. And even the theology which prides itself on being 'positive' and 'evangelical' and which seeks to maintain lines of communication with the great traditional doctrines of atonement is on the whole disposed to reject it. And this, not merely on the ground that it holds implications which are irrational and morally offensive, but even and specifically on the ground that it is unscriptural. Thus Dr. Vincent Taylor as a result of exhaustive examination of the 'Idea of Atonement in the New Testament' gives it as his conclusion that the idea of substitution has no place in the New Testament writings; that in fact it is opposed to the fundamental teaching of the New Testament; that even St Paul though he sometimes trembles on the edge of substitutionary conceptions nevertheless avoids them. It is difficult to escape the impression that Dr. Vincent Taylor's anxiety to eliminate the idea of substitution from evangelical theology has coloured his interpretation of the New Testament witness. But his conclusions provide a striking indication of the tendency at work in modern evangelical circles. It is felt that nothing has done more to bring the evangelical doctrine of the Atonement into disrepute than the idea of substitution; and therefore something like a sigh of relief makes itself heard when it is suggested that this idea rests on a misunderstanding of the teaching of Scripture.[18]

Today, more than a quarter of a century later, the picture Camfield draws would have to be qualified by reference to the vigorous vindication and use of the substitution idea by such as Pannenberg and Barth.[19] Nonetheless, in British theology the overall situation remains very much as

---

[18] F. W. Camfield, 'The Idea of Substitution in the Doctrine of the Atonement', *SJT* I (1948), pp. 282f., referring to Vincent Taylor, *The Atonement in New Testament Teaching.* Taylor, while allowing that Paul 'in particular, is within a hair's breadth of substitution' (p. 288), and that 'a theologian who retires to a doctrinal fortress guarded by such ordinance as Mark 10:45, Romans 6:10f., 2 Cor. 5:14, 21, Galatians 3:13, and 1 Tim. 2:5f. is more difficult to dislodge than many New Testament students imagine' (p. 289), rejects substitution as implying a redemption 'wrought entirely outside of, and apart from, ourselves so that we have nothing to do but to accept its benefits' (p. 125). He describes Christ's death as a representative sacrifice, involving endurance of sin's penalty plus that archetypal expression of penitence for humanity's wrongdoing which was first conceived by McLeod Campbell and R. C. Moberly. We participate in this sacrifice, Taylor continues, by offering it on our own behalf, which we do by letting it teach us to repent. Taylor admits that from his standpoint there is 'a gap in Pauline teaching. With clear eyes St. Paul marks "the one act of righteousness" in the obedience of Christ (Romans 5:18f.) and the fact that He was "made to be sin on our behalf" (2 Cor. 5:21), but he nowhere speaks of Him as voicing the sorrow and contrition of men in the presence of His Father' (p. 291).

[19] See Pannenberg, op. cit. pp. 258–269; Barth, *Church Dogmatics*, tr. G. W. Bromiley (Edinburgh: T. and T. Clark, 1956) IV. 1, viif., pp. 230ff., pp. 550ff.

Camfield describes. It would, however, clarify discussion if all who hold that Jesus by dying did something for us which we needed to do but could not, would agree that they are regarding Christ's death as substitutionary, and differing only on the nature of the action which Jesus performed in our place and also, perhaps, on the way we enter into the benefit that flows from it. Camfield himself goes on to spell out a non-penal view of substitution.

Broadly speaking, there have been three ways in which Christ's death has been explained in the church. Each reflects a particular view of the nature of God and our plight in sin, and of what is needed to bring us to God in the fellowship of acceptance on his side and faith and love on ours. It is worth glancing at them to see how the idea of substitution fits in with each.

There is, first, the type of account which sees the cross as having its effect entirely on humanity, whether by revealing God's love to us, or by bringing home to us how much God hates our sins, or by setting us a supreme example of godliness, or by blazing a trail to God which we may now follow, or by so involving humankind in Christ's redemptive obedience that the life of God now flows into us, or by all these modes together. It is assumed that our basic need is for motivation Godward and openness to the inflow of divine life; all that is needed to set us in a right relationship with God is a change in us at these two points, and this Christ's death brings about. The forgiveness of our sins is not a separate problem; as soon as we are changed we become forgivable, and are then forgiven at once. This view has little or no room for any thought of substitution, since it goes so far in equating what Christ did for us with what he does to us.

A second type of account sees Christ's death as having its effect primarily on hostile spiritual forces external to us which are held to be imprisoning us in a captivity of which our inveterate moral twistedness is one sign and symptom. The cross is seen as the work of God going forth to battle as our champion, just as David went forth as Israel's champion to fight Goliath. Through the cross these hostile forces, however conceived – whether as sin and death, Satan and his hosts, the demonic in society and its structures, the powers of God's wrath and curse, or anything else – are overcome and nullified, so that Christians are not in bondage to them, but share Christ's triumph over them. The assumption here is that man's plight is created entirely by hostile cosmic forces distinct from God; yet, seeing Jesus as our champion, exponents of this view could still properly call him our substitute, just as all the Israelites who declined Goliath's challenge in 1 Samuel 17:8–11 could properly call David their substitute. Just as a substitute who involves others in the consequences of his action *as if* they had done it themselves is their representative, so a representative discharging the obligations of those whom he represents is their substitute. What this type of account of the cross affirms (though it is not usually put in these terms) is that the conquering Christ, whose victory secured our release, was our representative substitute.

The third type of account denies nothing asserted by the other two views save their assumption that they are complete. It agrees that there is biblical support for all they say, but it goes further. It grounds humanity's plight as victim of sin and Satan in the fact that, for all God's daily goodness to us, as sinners we stand under divine judgement, and our bondage to evil is the start of our sentence, and unless God's rejection of us is turned into acceptance we are lost for ever. On this view, Christ's death had its effect first on God, who was hereby *propitiated* (or, better, who hereby propitiated himself), and only because it had this effect did it become an overthrowing of the powers of darkness and a revealing of God's seeking and saving love. The thought here is that by dying Christ offered to God what the West has called *satisfaction* for sins, satisfaction which God's own character dictated as the only means whereby his 'no' to us could become a 'yes.' Whether this Godward satisfaction is understood as the homage of death itself, or death as the perfecting of holy obedience, or an undergoing of the God-forsakenness of hell, which is God's final judgement on sin, or a perfect confession of man's sins combined with entry into their bitterness by sympathetic identification, or all these things together (and nothing stops us combining them together), the shape of this view remains the same — that by undergoing the cross Jesus expiated our sins, propitiated our Maker, turned God's 'no' to us into a 'yes,' and so saved us. All forms of this view see Jesus as our representative substitute in fact, whether or not they call him that, but only certain versions of it represent his substitution as penal.

This analysis prompts three comments. First, it should be noted that though the two former views regularly set themselves in antithesis to the third, the third takes up into itself all the positive assertions that they make; which raises the question whether any more is at issue here than the impropriety of treating half-truths as the whole truth, and of rejecting a more comprehensive account on the basis of speculative negations about what God's holiness requires as a basis for forgiving sins. Were it allowed that the first two views might be misunderstanding and distorting themselves in this way, the much-disputed claim that a broadly substitutionary view of the cross has always been the mainstream Christian opinion might be seen to have substance in it after all. It is a pity that books on the atonement so often take it for granted that accounts of the cross which have appeared as rivals in historical debate must be treated as intrinsically exclusive. This is always arbitrary, and sometimes quite perverse.

Second, it should be noted that our analysis was simply of views about the death of Christ, so nothing was said about his resurrection. All three types of view usually agree in affirming that the resurrection is an integral part of the gospel; that the gospel proclaims a living, vindicated Saviour whose resurrection as the firstfruits of the new humanity is the basis as well as the pattern for ours is not a matter of dispute between them. It is sometimes pointed out that the second view represents the resurrection of Jesus as an organic element in his victory over the powers of death, whereas the third view does not, and hardly could, represent it as an organic element in the bearing of sin's penalty or the tasting and confessing of its vileness (however the work of Calvary is conceived); and on this basis the third view is sometimes criticized as making the resurrection unnecessary. But this criticism may be met in two ways.

The first reply is that Christ's saving work has two parts, his dealing with his Father on our behalf by offering himself in substitutionary satisfaction for our sins, and his dealing with us on his Father's behalf by bestowing on us through faith the forgiveness which his death secured, and it is as important to distinguish these two parts as it is to hold them together. For a demonstration that part two is now possible because part one is finished, and for the actual implementing of part two, Jesus' resurrection is indeed essential, and so appears as an organic element in his work as a whole.

The second reply is that these two ways of viewing the cross should in any case be synthesized, following the example of Paul in Col. 2:13–15, as being complementary models expressing different elements in the single complex reality which is the mystery of the cross.

Third, it should be noted that not all advocates of the third type of view have been happy to use the word 'substitution.' This has been partly through desire to evade the Socinian criticism that in the penal realm substitution is impossible, and partly for fear that to think of Christ dying for us as our substitute obscures his call to us to die and rise in him and with him, for the moral transforming of us into his holy image. P. T. Forsyth, for example, is one who stresses the vicariousness of Christ's action in his passion as he endured for man's salvation God's personal anger against man's sin; [20] yet he rejects 'substitution' in favour of 'representation' and replaces 'substitution – ary expiation (which, as these words are commonly understood, leaves us too little committed)' by 'solidary reparation,' 'solidary confession and

---

[20] 'He turned the penalty He endured into sacrifice He offered. And the sacrifice He offered was the judgement He accepted. His passive suffering became active obedience, and obedience to a holy doom' (*The Work of Christ* [London: Hodder & Stoughton, 1910] p. 163). In a 2,000–word 'Addendum' Forsyth combats the Ritschlian view, later to be espoused by C. H. Dodd, that the wrath of God is simply the 'automatic recoil of His moral order upon the transgressor . . . as if there were no personal reaction of a Holy God Himself upon the sin, and no infliction of His displeasure upon the sinner' (p. 239). He argues to the position that 'what Christ bore was not simply a sense of the connection between the sinner and the impersonal consequences of sin, but a sense of the sinner's relation to the personal *vis-à-vis* of an angry God. God never left him, but He did refuse Him His face. The communion was not broken, but its light was withdrawn' (p. 243).

praise,' because he wants to stress that we enter into salvation only as we identify with Christ's death to sin and are re-created as the new humanity in him.[21] But, admirable as is Forsyth's wish to stress what is in Romans 6:1–11, avoiding the word substitution can only have the effect of obscuring what is in Romans 3:2 1–28, where Paul describes Christ as 'a propitiation[22] . . . by his blood' (verse 25) in virtue of which God bestows 'the free gift of righteousness' (5:17) upon believing sinners and so 'justifies the ungodly' (4:5). As James Denney said, 'If Christ died the death in which sin had involved us – if in His death He took the responsibility of our sins on Himself – no word is equal to this which falls short of what is meant by calling Him our substitute.'[23] The correct reply to Forsyth would seem to be that before Christ's death can be representative, in Forsyth's sense of setting a pattern of 'confession and praise' to be reproduced in our own self-denial and cross-bearing, it has to be substitutionary in Denney's sense of absorbing God's wrath against our sins; otherwise, our 'confession and praise' in solidarity with Christ becomes itself a ploy for averting that wrath – in other

---

[21] Op. cit., pp. 164, 182, 223, 225f. 'Substitution does not take account of the moral results (of the cross) on the soul' (p. 182, note).

[22] 'Propitiation' (which means quenching God's wrath against sinners) is replaced by 'expiation' (which means removing sins from God's sight) in the RSV and other modern versions. The idea or propitiation includes that of expiation as its means and thus the effect of this change is not to bring in a sacrificial motif that was previously absent, but to cut out a reference to quenching God's anger that was previously thought to be present. The case for 'expiation' was put forward by C. H. Dodd in 1935 and at first gained wide support, but a generation of debate has shown that it 'the linguistic evidence seems to favour "propitiation" ' (Matthew Black, *Romans* New Century Bible [London: Oliphants, 1973], p. 68). See the full coverage of literature cited by Black, and also David Hill *Greek Words and Hebrew Meanings* (London: Cambridge University Press, 1967), pp. 23–48.

[23] Denney, *The Death of Christ*, 2nd. ed., including *The Atonement and the Modern Mind* (London: Hodder & Stoughton, 1911), p. 73. Denney's summary of the meaning of Romans 3:25f. is worth quoting. 'It is Christ set forth in His blood who is a propitiation; that is, it is Christ who died. In dying, as St. Paul conceived it, He made our sin His own; He took it on Himself as the reality which it is in God's sight and to God's law: He became sin, became a curse for us. It is this which gives His death a propitiatory character and power; in other words, which makes it possible for God to be at once righteous and a God who accepts as righteous those who believe in Jesus. . . . I do not know any word which conveys the truth of this if "vicarious" or "substitutionary" does not, nor do I know any interpretation of Christ's death which enables us to regard it as a demonstration of love to sinners, if this vicarious or substitutionary character is denied' (p. 126). Denney's point in the last sentence is that Christ's death only reveals God's love if it accomplished something which we needed, which we could not do for ourselves, and which Christ could not do without dying.

words, a meritorious work, aimed at securing pardon, assuming that in
Christ we save ourselves.

What Denney said about this in 1903 was in fact an answer by
anticipation to Forsyth's formula of 1910. A reviewer of *The Death of
Christ* had argued that 'if we place ourselves at Paul's point of view, we
shall see that to the eye of God the death of Christ presents itself less as
an act which Christ does for the race than as an act which the race does
in Christ.' In *The Atonement and the Modern Mind* Denney quoted these
words and commented on them thus:

> In plain English, Paul teaches less that Christ died for the ungodly, than that
> the ungodly in Christ died for themselves. This brings out the logic of what
> representative means when representative is opposed to substitute.[24] The
> representative is ours, we are in Him, and we are supposed to get over all the
> moral difficulties raised by the idea of substitution just because He is ours, and
> because we are one with Him. But the fundamental fact of the situation is
> that, to begin with, Christ is *not* ours, and we are *not* one with Him . . . we
> are 'without Christ' (χωρίς Χριστου) . . . A representative not produced by
> us, but given to us – not chosen by us, but the elect of God – is not a
> representative at all in the first instance, but a substitute.[25]

So the true position, on the type of view we are exploring, may be put
thus: We identify with Christ against the practice of sin because we have
already identified him as the one who took our place under sentence for
sin. We enter upon the life of repentance because we have learned that
he first endured for us the death of reparation. The Christ into whom we
now accept incorporation is the Christ who previously on the cross
became our propitiation – not, therefore, one in whom we achieve our
reconciliation with God, but one through whom we receive it as a free
gift based on a finished work (cf. Rom. 5:10); and we love him, because
he first loved us and gave himself for us. So substitution, on this view,
really is the basic category; the thought of Christ as our representative,
however construed in detail, cannot be made to mean what substitution
means, and our solidarity with Christ in 'confession and praise,' so far

---

[24] It should be noted that in addition to the rather specialized usage that Denney
has in view, whereby one's 'representative' is the one whose behaviour is taken
as the model for one's own, 'representative' may (and usually does) signify simply
this: that one's status is such that one involves others, for good or ill, in the
consequences of what one does. In this sense, families are represented by fathers,
nations by kings, princes and government ministers, and humanity by Adam and
Christ; and it was as our representative in this sense that Jesus became our
substitute. Cf. pp. 357f. below.

[25] '*The Death of Christ*, p. 304; cf. p. 307, "Union with Christ" (i.e. personal,
moral union by faith) . . . is not a presupposition of Christ's work, it is its fruit.'

from being a concept alternative to that of substitution, is actually a response which presupposes it.

Penal Substitution

Now we move to the second stage in our model-building, and bring in the word 'penal' to characterize the substitution we have in view. To add this 'qualifier,' as Ramsey would call it, is to anchor the model of substitution (not exclusively, but regulatively) within the world of moral law, guilty conscience, and retributive justice. Thus is forged a conceptual instrument for conveying the thought that God remits our sins and accepts our persons into favour not because of any amends we have attempted, but because the penalty which was our due was diverted onto Christ. The notion which the phrase 'penal substitution' expresses is that Jesus Christ our Lord, moved by a love that was determined to do everything necessary to save us, endured and exhausted the destructive divine judgement for which we were otherwise inescapably destined, and so won us forgive - ness, adoption and glory. To affirm penal substitution is to say that believers are in debt to Christ specifically for this, and that this is the mainspring of all their joy, peace and praise both now and for eternity.

The general thought is clear enough, but for our present purpose we need a fuller analysis of its meaning, and here a methodological choice must be made. Should we appeal to particular existing accounts of penal substitution, or construct a composite of our own? At the risk of seeming idiosyncratic (which is, I suppose, the gentleman's way of saying unsound) I plump for the latter course, for the following main reasons.

First, there is no denying that penal substitution sometimes has been, and still sometimes is, asserted in ways which merit the favourite adjective of its critics – 'crude.' As one would expect of that which for more than four centuries has been the mainspring of evangelical piety – 'popular piety,' as Roman Catholics would call it – ways of presenting it have grown up which are devotionally evocative without always being theo - logically rigorous. Moreover, the more theological expositions of it since Socinus have tended to be one-track-minded; constricted in interest by the preoccupations of controversy, and absorbed in the task of proclaim - ing the one vital truth about the cross which others disregarded or denied,

> upholders of the penal theory have sometimes so stressed the thought that Christ bore our penalty that they have found room for nothing else. Rarely have they in theory denied the value of other theories, but sometimes they have in practice ignored them.[26]

---

[26] Leon Morris, *The Cross in The New Testament* (Exeter: Paternoster Press, 1965) p. 401.

Also, as we have seen, much of the more formative and influential discussing of penal substitution was done in the seventeenth century, at a time when Protestant exegesis of Scripture was coloured by an uncriticized and indeed unrecognized natural theology of law, and this has left its mark on many later statements. All this being so, it might be hard to find an account of penal substitution which could safely be taken as standard or as fully representative, and it will certainly be more straightforward if I venture an analysis of my own.

Second, I have already hinted that I think it important for the theory of penal substitution to be evaluated as a model setting forth the meaning of the atonement rather than its mechanics. One result of the work of rationalistic Protestant theologians over three centuries, from the Socinians to the Hegelians, was to nourish the now common assumption that the logical function of a 'theory' in theology is to resolve 'how' problems within an established frame of thought about God and man. In other words, theological theories are like detectives' theories in whodunits; they are hypotheses relating puzzling facts together in such a way that all puzzlement is dispelled (for the convention of 'mystery stories' is that by the last page no mystery should be felt to remain).

Now we have seen that, for discernible historical reasons, penal substitution has sometimes been explicated as a theory of this kind, telling us how divine love and justice could be, and were, 'reconciled' (whatever that means); but a doubt remains as to whether this way of understanding the theme is biblically right. Is the harmonization of God's attributes any part of the information, or is it even the kind of information, that the inspired writers are concerned to give? Gustaf Aulén characterized the 'Christus victor' motif (he would not call it a theory) as a dramatic idea of the atonement rather than a rationale of its mechanics, and contrasted it in this respect with the 'Latin' view, of which penal substitution is one form;[27] but should not penal substitution equally be understood as a dramatic idea, declaring the fact of the atonement kergymatically, i.e. as gospel (good news), just as Aulén's conquest-motif is concerned to do? I believe it should.

Surely the primary issue with which penal substitution is concerned is neither the morality nor the rationality of God's ways, but the remission of my sins; and the primary function of the concept is to correlate my knowledge of being guilty before God with my knowledge that, on the one hand, no question of my ever being judged for my sins can now arise, and, on the other hand, that the risen Christ whom I am called to accept as Lord is none other than Jesus, who secured my immunity from judgement by bearing on the cross the penalty which was my due.

---

[27] *Christus Victor*, p. 175, etc.

The effect of this correlation is not in any sense to 'solve' or dissipate the mystery of the work of God (it is not that sort of mystery!); the effect is simply to define that work with precision, and thus to evoke faith, hope, praise and responsive love to Jesus Christ. So, at least, I think, and therefore I wish my presentation of penal substitution to highlight its character as a kergymatic model; and so I think it best to offer my own analytical definition, which will aim to be both descriptive of what all who have held this view have had in common, and also prescriptive of how the term should be understood in any future discussion.

Third, if the present examination of penal substitution is to be worthwhile, it must present this view in its best light, and I think an eclectic exposition will bring us closest to this goal. The typical modern criticism of older expositions of our theme is that, over and above their being less than fully moral (Socinus' criticism), they are less than fully personal. Thus, for instance, G. W. H. Lampe rejects penal substitution because it assumes that 'God inflicts retributive punishment,' and

> retribution is impersonal; it considers offences in the abstract . . . we ought not to ascribe purely retributive justice to God . . . the Father of mankind does not deal with his children on the basis of deterrence and retribution . . . to hang the criminal is to admit defeat at the level of love . . . It is high time to discard the vestiges of a theory of Atonement that was geared to a conception of punishment which found nothing shocking in the idea that God should crucify sinners or the substitute who took their place. It is time, too, to stop the mouth of the blasphemer who calls it 'sentimentality' to reject the idea of a God of retribution.[28]

Lampe's violent language shows the strength of his conviction that retribution belongs to a sub-personal, non-loving order of relationships, and that penal substitution dishonours the cross by anchoring it here.

James Denney's sense of the contrast between personal relations, which are moral, and legal relations, which tend to be impersonal, external and arbitrary, once drew from him an outburst which in isolation might seem parallel to Lampe's.

> Few things have astonished me more (he wrote) than to be charged with teaching a 'forensic' or 'legal' or 'judicial' doctrine of Atonement . . . There is nothing that I should wish to reprobate more whole-heartedly than the conception which is expressed by these words. To say that the relations of God and man are forensic is to say that they are regulated by statute – that sin is a breach of statute – that the sinner is a criminal – and that God adjudicates

---

[28] G. W. H. Lampe, 'The Atonement: Law and Love,' in *Soundings*, ed. A. R. Vidler (London: Cambridge University Press, 1962), pp. 187ff.

on him by interpreting the statute in its application to his case. Everybody knows that this is a travesty of the truth.[29]

It is noticeable that Denney, the champion of the substitutionary idea, never calls Christ's substitution 'penal'; in his situation, the avoidance must have been deliberate. Yet Denney affirmed these four truths: first, that 'the relations of God and man . . . are personal, but . . . determined by (moral) law'; second, 'that there is in the nature of things a reaction against sin which when it has had its perfect work is final, that this reaction is the divine punishment of sin, and that its finally fatal character is what is meant by Scripture when it says that the wages of sin is death'; third, that 'the inevitable reactions of the divine order against evil are the sin itself coming back in another form and finding out the sinner. They are nothing if not retributive'; and, fourth, 'that while the agony and the Passion were not penal in the sense of coming upon Jesus through a bad conscience, or making Him the personal object of divine wrath, they were penal in the sense that in that dark hour He had to realize to the full the divine reaction against sin in the race . . . and that without doing so He could not have been the Redeemer of that race from sin'.[30] It seems to me that these affirmations point straight to a way of formulating the penal substitution model which is both moral and personal enough to evade all Lampe's strictures and also inclusive of all that the concept means to those who embrace it. But the formulation itself will have to be my own.

So I shall now attempt my analysis of penal substitution as a model of the atonement, under five heads: substitution and retribution; substitution and solidarity; substitution and mystery; substitution and salvation; sub-stitution and divine love. Others who espouse this model must judge whether I analyse it accurately or not.

1. *Substitution and retribution*

Penal substitution, as an idea, presupposes a penalty (*poena*) due to us from God the Judge for wrong done and failure to meet his claims. The

---

[29] Denney, op. cit. pp. 271f.; from *The Atonement and the Modern Mind*. Denney's last sentence overstates. As J. S. Whale says, 'the Christian religion has thought of Christ not only as Victor and as Victim, but also as "Criminal," ' and all three models (Whale calls them metaphors) have biblical justification (*Victor and Victim* [London: Cambridge University Press, 1960], p. 70).

[30] Denney, *The Christian Doctrine of Reconciliation* (London: Hodder & Stoughton, 1917), pp. 187, 214, 208, 273. On pp. 262f. and elsewhere Denney rejects as unintelligible all notions of a quantitative equivalence between Christ's actual sufferings and those which sinners would have to endure under ultimate judge-ment; 'to realise to the full the divine reaction against sin in the race,' whatever it meant, did not mean that.

locus classicus on this is Romans 1:18–3:20, but the thought is everywhere in the New Testament. The judicial context is a moral context too; whereas human judicial systems are not always rooted in moral reality, the Bible treats the worlds of moral reality and of divine judgement as coinciding. Divine judgement means that retribution is entailed by our past upon our present and future existence, and God himself is in charge of this process, ensuring that the objective wrongness and guiltiness of what we have been is always 'there' to touch and wither what we are and shall be. In the words of Emil Brunner, 'Guilt means that our past – that which can never be made good – always constitutes one element in our present situation.'[31] When Lady Macbeth, walking and talking in her sleep, sees blood on her hand, and cannot clean or sweeten it, she witnesses to the order of retribution as all writers of tragedy and surely all reflective men – certainly, those who believe in penal substitution – have come to know it: wrongdoing may be forgotten for a time, as David forgot his sin over Bathsheba and Uriah, but sooner or later it comes back to mind, as David's sin did under Nathan's ministry, and at once our attention is absorbed, our peace and pleasure are gone, and something tells us that we ought to suffer for what we have done. When joined with inklings of God's displeasure, this sense of things is the start of hell. Now it is into this context of awareness that the model of penal substitution is introduced, to focus for us four insights about our situation.

Insight one concerns God: it is that the retributive principle has his sanction, and indeed expresses the holiness, justice and goodness reflected in his law, and that death, spiritual as well as physical, the loss of the life of God as well as that of the body, is the rightful sentence which he has announced against us, and now prepares to inflict.

Insight two concerns ourselves: it is that, standing thus under sentence, we are helpless either to undo the past or to shake off sin in the present, and thus have no way of averting what threatens.

Insight three concerns Jesus Christ: it is that he, the God-man of John 1:18 and Hebrews 1–2, took our place under judgement and received in his own personal experience all the dimensions of the death that was our sentence, whatever these were, so laying the foundation for our pardon and immunity.

> We may not know, we cannot tell
> What pains he had to bear;
> But we believe it was for us
> He hung and suffered there.

---

[31] Brunner, *The Mediator*, tr. O. Wyon (London: Lutterworth Press, 1934), p. 443.

Insight four concerns faith: it is that faith is a matter first and foremost of looking outside and away from oneself to Christ and his cross as the sole ground of present forgiveness and future hope. Faith sees that God's demands remain what they were, and that God's law of retribution, which our conscience declares to be right, has not ceased to operate in his world, nor ever will; but that in our case the law has operated already, so that all our sins, past present and even future, have been covered by Calvary.

So our conscience is pacified by the knowledge that our sins have already been judged and punished, however strange the statement may sound, in the person and death of another. Bunyan's pilgrim before the cross loses his burden, and Toplady can assure himself that

> If thou my pardon hast secured,
> And freely in my room endured
>   The whole of wrath divine,
> Payment God cannot twice demand,
> First from my bleeding surety's hand
>   And then again from mine.

Reasoning thus, faith grasps the reality of God's free gift of righteousness, i.e. the 'rightness' with God that the righteous enjoy (cf. Rom. 5:16f.), and with it the justified man's obligation to live henceforth 'unto' the one who for his sake died and rose again (cf. 2 Cor. 5:14).

This analysis, if correct, shows what job the word 'penal' does in our model. It is there, not to prompt theoretical puzzlement about the transferring of guilt, but to articulate the insight of believers who, as they look at Calvary in the light of the New Testament, are constrained to say, 'Jesus was bearing the judgement I deserved (and deserve), the penalty for my sins, the punishment due to me' – 'he loved me, and gave himself for me' (Gal. 2:20). How it was possible for him to bear their penalty they do not claim to know, any more than they know how it was possible for him to be made man; but that he bore it is the certainty on which all their hopes rest.

2. Substitution and solidarity

Anticipating the rationalistic criticism that guilt is not transferable and the substitution described, if real, would be immoral, our model now invokes Paul's description of the Lord Jesus Christ as the second man and last Adam, who involved us in his sin-bearing as truly as Adam involved us in his sinning (cf. 1 Cor. 15:45ff.; Rom. 5:12ff.). Penal substitution was seen by Luther, the pioneer in stating it, and by those who came after, as grounded in this ontological solidarity, and as being one 'moment' in the larger mystery of what Luther called 'a wonderful exchange'[32] and Dr. Morna Hooker designates 'interchange in Christ.'[33] In this mystery there are four 'moments' to be distinguished. The first is the incarnation when the Son of God came into the human situation, 'born of a woman, born under the law, that he might redeem them which were under the law' (Gal. 4:4f.). The second 'moment' was the cross, where Jesus, as Luther and Calvin put it, carried our identity[34] and

---

[32] Two quotations give Luther's viewpoint here. The first is from his exposition of Psalm 21 (German Bible numbering; in English Bibles, 22): 'This is that mystery which is rich in divine grace to sinners: wherein by a *wonderful exchange* our sins are no longer ours but Christ's: and the righteousness of Christ is not Christ's but ours. He has emptied himself of his righteousness that he might clothe us with it, and fill us with it: and he has taken our evils upon himself that he might deliver us from them . . . in the same manner as he grieved and suffered in our sins, and was confounded, in the same manner we rejoice and glory in his righteousness' (*Werke* [Weimar, 1883] 5.608). The second is from a pastoral letter to George Spenlein: 'Learn Christ and him crucified. Learn to pray to him and, despairing of yourself, say: "Thou Lord Jesus, art my righteousness, but I am thy sin. Thou hast taken upon thyself what is mine and hast given to me what is thine. Thou hast taken upon thyself what thou wast not and hast given to me what I was not" ' (*Letters of Spiritual Counsel*, ed. Theodore C. Tappert, Library of Christian Classics [London: SCM Press, 1955], p. 110.

[33] Article in *Journal of Theological Studies* 22 (1971), pp. 349–361.

[34] Luther puts this dramatically and exuberantly, as was always his way. 'All the prophets did foresee in spirit that Christ should become the greatest transgressor, murderer, adulterer, thief, rebel, blasphemer, etc., that ever was . . . for he, being made a sacrifice for the sins of the whole world, is not now an innocent person and without sins . . . our most merciful Father . . . sent his only Son into the world and laid upon him the sins of all men, saying: Be thou Peter that denier; Paul that persecutor, blasphemer and cruel oppressor; David that adulterer; that sinner which did eat the apple in Paradise; that thief which hanged upon the cross; and, briefly, be thou the person which hath committed the sins of all men; see therefore that thou pay and satisfy for them. Here now cometh the law and saith: I find him a sinner . . . therefore let him die upon the cross . . .' (*Galatians*, ed. Philip S. Watson [London: James Clarke, 1953] pp. 269–271; on Gal. 3:13). Aulén (*Christus Victor*, chapter VI) rightly stresses the dynamism of divine victory in Luther's account of the cross and resurrection, but wrongly ignores the penal substitution in terms of which Christ's victorious work is basically defined. The essence of Christ's victory, according to Luther, is that on the cross as our substitute he effectively purged our sins, so freeing us from Satan's power by overcoming God's curse; if Luther's whole treatment of Gal. 3:13 (pp. 268–282) is read, this becomes very plain. The necessary supplement, and indeed correction, of the impression Aulén leaves is provided by Pannenberg's statement (op. cit., p. 279): 'Luther was probably the first since Paul and his school to have seen

effectively involved us all in his dying – as Paul says, 'one died for all, therefore all died' (2 Cor. 5:14). Nor is this sharing in Christ's death a legal fiction, a form of words to which no reality corresponds; it is part of the objective fact of Christ, the mystery that is 'there' whether we grasp it or not. So now Christ's substitution for us, which is exclusive in the sense of making the work of atonement wholly his and allowing us no share in performing it, is seen to be from another standpoint inclusive of us, inasmuch as ontologically and objectively, in a manner transcending bounds of space and time, Christ has taken us with him into his death and through his death into his resurrection.

Thus knowledge of Christ's death for us as our sin-bearing substitute requires us to see ourselves as dead, risen and alive for evermore in him. We who believe have died – painlessly and invisibly, we might say – in solidarity with him because he died, painfully and publicly, in substitution for us. His death for us brought remission of sins committed 'in' Adam, so that 'in' him we might enjoy God's acceptance; our death 'in' him brings release from the existence we knew 'in' Adam, so that 'in' him we are raised to new life and become new creatures (cf. Rom. 5–6; 2 Cor. 5:17, 21; Col. 2:6–3:4).

The third 'moment' in this interchange comes when, through faith and God's gift of the Spirit, we become 'the righteousness of God' and 'rich' – that is, justified from sin and accepted as heirs of God in and with Christ – by virtue of him who became 'poor' for us in the incarnation and was 'made sin' for us by penal substitution on the cross (cf. 2 Cor. 5:21; 8:9).

And the fourth 'moment' will be when this same Jesus Christ, who was exalted to glory after being humbled to death for us, reappears to 'fashion anew the body of our humiliation, that it may be conformed to the body of his glory' (cf. Phil. 2:5–11; 3:21).

Sometimes it is urged that in relation to this comprehensive mystery of solidarity and interchange, viewed as a whole, Christ the 'pioneer' (ἀρχηγός: Heb. 2:10; 12:2) is best designated the 'representative' and

---

[34] *(continued)* with full clarity that Jesus' death in its genuine sense is to be understood as vicarious penal suffering.' Calvin makes the same point in his more precise way, commenting on Jesus' trial before Pilate. 'When he was arraigned before a judgement-seat, accused and put under pressure by testimony, and sentenced to death by the words of a judge, we know by these records that he played the part (*personam sustinuit*) of a guilty wrongdoer . . . we see the role of sinner and criminal represented in Christ, yet from his shining innocence it becomes obvious that he was burdened with the misdoing of others rather than his own. . . . This is our acquittal, that the guilt which exposed us to punishment was transferred to the head of God's Son . . . At every point he substituted himself in our place (*in vicem nostram ubique se supposuerit*) to pay the price of our redemption' (*Inst.* II. xvi. 5, 7). It is inexplicable that Pannenberg (loc. cit.) should say that Calvin retreated from Luther's insight into penal substitution.

'first-fruits' of the new humanity, rather than being called our substitute. [35] Inasmuch as the interchange theme centres upon our renewal in Christ's image, this point may be readily accepted, provided it is also seen that in relation to the particular mystery of sin-bearing, which is at the heart of the interchange, Christ as victim of the penal process has to be called our substitute, since the purpose and effect of his suffering was precisely to ensure that no such suffering – no God-forsakenness, no dereliction – should remain for us. In the light of earlier discussion [36] we are already entitled to dismiss the proposal to call Christ's death representative rather than substitutionary as both confusing and confused, since it suggests, first, that we chose Christ to act for us, second, that the death we die in him is of the same order as the death he died for us, and third, that by dying in Christ we atone for our sins – all of which are false. Here now is a further reason for rejecting the proposal – namely, that it misses or muffs the point that what Christ bore on the cross was the God-forsakenness of penal judgement, which we shall never have to bear because he accepted it in our place.

The appropriate formulation is that on the cross Jesus' representative relation to us, as the last Adam whose image we are to bear, took the form of substituting for us under judgement, as the suffering servant of God on whom the Lord 'laid the iniquity of us all.' [37] The two ideas, representation and substitution, are complementary, not alternatives, and both are needed here.

---

[35] For 'representative,' cf. M. D. Hooker, op. cit., p. 358, and C. W. H. Lampe, *Reconciliation in Christ* (London: Longmans, 1956) chapter 3; for 'first-fruits,' cf. D. E. H. Whiteley, *The Theology of St. Paul* (Oxford: Blackwell, 1964) pp. 132ff. The preferred usage of these authors seems to reflect both awareness of solidarity between Christ and us and also failure to recognize that what forgiveness rests on is Christ's vicarious sin-bearing, as distinct from the new obedience to which in Dr. Hooker's phrase, we are 'lifted' by Christ's action.

[36] Cf. pp. 102–105.

[37] Isa. 53:6. J. S. Whale observes that this Servant-song 'makes twelve distinct and explicit statements that the Servant suffers the penalty of other men's sins: not only vicarious suffering but penal substitution is the plain meaning of its fourth fifth and sixth verses. These may not be precise statement of Western forensic ideas' – and our earlier argument prompts the comment, a good job too! – 'but they are clearly connected with penalty, inflicted through various forms of punishment which the Servant endured on other men's behalf and in their stead, because the Lord so ordained. This legal or law-court metaphor of atonement may be stated positively or negatively: either as penalty which the Redeemer takes upon himself, or as acquittal which sets the prisoner free. But in either way of stating it the connotation is substitutionary:

In my place condemned he stood;
Sealed my pardon with his blood' (op. cit., p. 69f.)

3. Substitution and mystery

It will by now be clear that those who affirm penal substitution offer this model not as an explanatory analysis of what lay 'behind' Christ's atoning death in the way that the laws of heat provide an explanatory analysis of what lies 'behind' the boiling of a kettle, but rather as a pointer directing attention to various fundamental features of the mystery – that is, according to our earlier definition, the transcendent and not wholly-com - prehensible divine reality – of Christ's atoning death itself, as the New Testament writers declare it. Most prominent among these features are the mysterious divine love which was its source, and of which it is the measure (cf. Rom. 5:8; 1 John 4:8–10; John 15:13); the mysterious necessity for it, evident from Paul's witness in Romans 8:32 that God did not spare his Son, but gave him up to death for us, which shows that, he being he, he could not have saved us at any less cost to himself; the mysterious solidarity in virtue of which Christ could be 'made sin' by the imputing to him of our answerability, and could die for our sins in our place, and we could be 'made righteous' before God through faith by the virtue of his obedience (cf. Rom. 5:17–19; 2 Cor. 5:21); and the mysterious mode of union whereby, without any diminution of our individuality as persons, or his, Christ and we are 'in' each other in such a sense that already we have passed with him through death into risen life. Recognition of these mysteries causes no embarrassment, nor need it; since the cross is undeniably central in the New Testament witness to God's work, it was only to be expected that more dimensions of mystery would be found clustered here than anywhere else. (Indeed, there are more than we listed; for a full statement, the tri-unity of the loving God, the incarnation itself, and God's predestining the free acts of his enemies would also have to come in.) To the question, what does the cross mean in God's plan for human good, a biblical answer is ready to hand, but when we ask how these things can be we find ourselves facing mystery at every point. Rationalistic criticism since Socinus has persistently called in question both the solidarity on which substitution is based and the need for penal satisfaction as a basis for forgiveness. This, however, is 'natural - istic' criticism, which assumes that what humanity could not do or would not require, God will not do or require either. Such criticism is pro - foundly perverse, for it shrinks God the Creator into the image of the human creature and loses sight of the paradoxical quality of the gospel of which the New Testament is so clearly aware. (When we justify the wicked, it is a miscarriage of justice which God hates, but when God justifies the ungodly it is a miracle of grace for us to adore [Prov. 17:15; Rom. 4:5].) The way to stand against naturalistic theology is to keep in view its reductionist method which makes humanity the standard for God; to stress that according to Scripture the Creator and his work are of necessity mysterious to us, even as revealed (to make this point is the proper logical task of the word 'supernatural' in theology); and to remember that what is *above* reason is not necessarily *against* it. As regards the atonement, the appropriate response to the Socinian critique starts by laying down that all our understanding of the cross comes from attending to the biblical witnesses and learning to hear and echo what they say about it; speculative rationalism breeds only misunderstanding, nothing more.

4. Substitution and salvation

So far our analysis has, I think, expressed the beliefs of all who would say that penal substitution is the key to understanding the cross. But now comes a point of uncertainty and division. That Christ's penal substitution for us under divine judgement is the sole meritorious ground on which our relationship with God is restored, and is in this sense decisive for our salvation, is a Reformation point against Rome [38] to which all conservative Protestants hold. But in ordinary everyday contexts, substitution is a definite and precise relationship whereby the specific obligations of one or more persons are taken over and discharged by someone else (as on the memorable occasion when I had to cry off a meeting at two days' notice due to an air strike and found afterwards that Billy Graham had consented to speak as my substitute). Should we not then think of Christ's substitution for us on the cross as a definite, one-to-one relationship between him and each individual sinner? This seems scriptural, for Paul says, 'He loved *me* and gave himself for *me*' (Gal. 2:20). But if Christ specifically took and discharged my penal obligation as a sinner, does it not follow that the cross was decisive for my salvation not only as its sole meritorious ground, but also as guaranteeing that I should be brought to faith, and through faith to eternal life? For is not the faith which receives salvation part of God's gift of salvation, according to what is affirmed in Philippians 1:29 and John 6:44f. and implied in what Paul says of *God calling* and John of *new birth*?[39] And if Christ by his death on my behalf secured reconciliation and righteousness as gifts for me to receive (Rom. 5:11, 17), did not this make it certain that the faith which receives these gifts would also be given me, as a direct consequence of Christ's dying for me? Once this is granted, however, we are shut up to a choice between universalism and some form of the view that Christ died to save only a part of the human race. But if we reject these options, what have we left? The only coherent alternative is to suppose that though God purposed to save every man through the cross, some thwart his purpose by persistent

---

[38] Cf. Anglican Article 11: 'We are accounted righteous before God, only for the merit of our Lord and Saviour Jesus Christ by faith, and not of our own works or deservings.'

[39] Cf. Rom. 1:6, 7; 8:28, 30; 9:11, 24; 1 Cor. 1:9, 24, 26; Gal. 1:15; Eph. 4:4; 1 Thess. 2:12; 5:24; 2 Thess. 2:14; 2 Tim. 1:9; John 1:12f.; 3:3–15; 1 John 5:1.

unbelief; which can only be said if one is ready to maintain that God, after all, does no more than make faith possible, and then in some sense that is decisive for him as well as us leaves it to us to make faith actual. Moreover, any who take this position must redefine substitution in imprecise terms, if indeed they do not drop the term altogether, for they are committing themselves to deny that Christ's vicarious sacrifice ensures anyone's salvation. Also, they have to give up Toplady's position, 'Pay - ment God cannot twice demand, First from my bleeding surety's hand, And then again from mine' – for it is of the essence of their view that some whose sins Christ bore, with saving intent, will ultimately pay the penalty for those same sins in their own persons. So it seems that if we are going to affirm penal substitution for all without exception we must either infer universal salvation or else, to evade this inference, deny the saving efficacy of the substitution for anyone; and if we are going to affirm penal substitution as an effective saving act of God we must either infer universal salvation or else, to evade this inference, restrict the scope of the substitution, making it a substitution for some, not all. [40]

All this is familiar ground to students of the Arminian controversy of the first half of the seventeenth century and of the conservative Reformed tradition since that time; [41] only the presentation is novel, since I have ventured to point up the problem as one of defining Christ's substitution, taking this as the key word for the view we are exploring. In modern usage that indeed is what it is, but only during the past century has it become so; prior to that, all conservative Protestants, at least in the English-speaking world, preferred 'satisfaction' as the label and key word for their doctrine of the cross. [42]

---

[40] 'Unless we believe in the final restoration of all mankind, we cannot have an unlimited atonement. On the premise that some perish eternally we are shut up to one of two alternatives – a limited efficacy or a limited extent; there is no such thing as an unlimited atonement' (John Murray, *The Atonement* [Philadelphia: Presbyterian and Reformed, 1962] p. 27).

[41] Cf. W. Cunningham, *Historical Theology* (London: Banner of Truth, 1960) II. 237–370; C. Hodge, *Systematic Theology* (London: Nelson, 1974) II. 544–562. The classical anti-Arminian polemic on the atonement remains John Owen's *The Death of Death in the Death of Christ* (1648: *Works*, ed. W. Goold [London: Banner of Truth, 1968] X. 139ff.), on the argumentation of which J. McLeod Campbell commented: 'As addressed to those who agreed with him as to the nature of the atonement while differing with him as to the extent of its reference this seems unanswerable' (*The Nature of the Atonement*, 4th ed. [London: Macmillan, 1873], p. 51).

[42] Thus in *The Atonement* (1868) A. A. Hodge, while speaking freely, as his Reformed predecessors did, of Christ as our substitute in a strict sense under God's penal law, complained that in theology the word 'substitution' had no fixed meaning and organized his exposition round the idea of 'satisfaction' which

As I pointed it up, the matter in debate might seem purely verbal, but there is more to it than that. The question is, whether the thought that substitution entails salvation does or does not belong to the convictional 'weave' of Scripture, to which 'penal substitution' as a theological model must conform. There seems little doubt as to the answer. Though the New Testament writers do not discuss the question in anything like this form, nor is their language about the cross always as guarded as language has to be once debate on the problem has begun, they do in fact constantly take for granted that the death of Christ is the act of God which has made certain the salvation of those who are saved. The use made of the categories of ransom, redemption, reconciliation, sacrifice and victory; the many declarations of God's purpose that Christ through the cross should save those given him, the church, his sheep and friends, God's people; the many statements viewing Christ's heavenly intercession and work in men as the outflow of what he did for them by his death; and the uniform view of faith as a means, not of meriting, but of receiving – all these features point unambiguously in one direction. Twice in Romans Paul makes explicit his conviction that Christ's having died 'for' (ὑπέρ) us – that is, us who now believe – guarantees final blessedness. In 5:8f. he says: 'While we were yet sinners, Christ died for us. Much more then, being now justified by his blood, shall we be saved from the wrath through him.' In 8:32 he asks: 'He that spared not his own Son, but delivered him up for us all, how shall he not also with him freely give us all things?' Moreover, Paul and John explicitly depict God's saving work as a unity in which Christ's death fulfils a purpose of election and leads on to what the Puritans called 'application of redemption' – God 'calling' and 'drawing' unbelievers to himself, justifying them from their sins and giving them life as they believe, and finally glorifying them with Christ in his own presence.[43] To be sure, Paul and John insist, as all the New Testament does, that God in the gospel promises life and salvation to *everyone* who believes and calls on Christ (cf. John 3:16; Rom. 10:13); this, indeed, is to them the primary truth, and when the plan of salvation appears in their writings (in John's case, on the lips of our Lord) its logical role is to account for, and give hope of, the phenomenon of sinners responding to God's

---

[42] *(continued)* he claimed was more precise than 'atonement' and was the word 'habitually used by all the Reformers in all the creeds and great classical theological writings of the seventeenth century, both Lutheran and Reformed' (pp. 31ff., 37f.). By contrast the IVF–UCCF basis of faith (1922) speaks of 'redemption from the guilt, penalty and power of sin only through the sacrificial death (as our Representative and Substitute) of Jesus Christ,' not mentioning satisfaction at all, and L. Berkhof's textbook presents Hodge's view, which it accepts entirely, as 'the penal substitutionary or satisfaction doctrine' (*Systematic Theology*, p. 373).
[43] Cf. Rom. 8:28–39; Eph. 1:3–14; 5:25–27; John 6:37–45; 10:11–16, 27–29; 17:6–26.

promise. Thus, through the knowledge that God is resolved to evoke the response he commands, Christians are assured of being kept safe, and evangelists of not labouring in vain. It may be added: is there any good reason for finding difficulty with the notion that the cross *both* justifies the 'free offer' of Christ to all men *and also* guarantees the believing, the accepting and the glorifying of those who respond, when this was precisely what Paul and John affirmed?

At all events, if the use historically made of the penal substitution model is examined, there is no doubt, despite occasional confusions of thought, that part of the intention is to celebrate the decisiveness of the cross as in every sense the procuring cause of salvation.

5. *Substitution and divine love*

The penal substitution model has been criticised for depicting a kind Son placating a fierce Father in order to make him love men, which he did not do before. The criticism is, however, inept, for penal substitution is a Trinitarian model, for which the motivational unity of Father and Son is axiomatic. The New Testament presents God's gift of his Son to die as the supreme expression of his love to men. 'God so loved the world that he gave his only-begotten Son' (John 3:16). 'God is love . . . Herein is love, not that we loved God, but that he loved us, and sent his Son to be the propitiation for our sins' (1 John 4:8–10 KJV). 'God shows his love for us in that while we were yet sinners Christ died for us' (Rom. 5:8). Similarly, the New Testament presents the Son's voluntary acceptance of death as the supreme expression of his love to men. 'He loved me, and gave himself for me' (Gal. 2:20). 'Greater love has no man than this, that a man lay down his life for his friends. You are my friends . . .' (John 15:13f.). And the two loves, the love of Father and Son, are one: a point which the penal substitution model, as used, firmly grasps.

Furthermore, if the true measure of love is how low it stoops to help, and how much in its humility it is ready to do and bear, then it may fairly be claimed that the penal substitutionary model embodies a richer witness to divine love than any other model of atonement, for it sees the Son at his Father's will going lower than any other view ventures to suggest. That death on the cross was a criminal's death, physically as painful as, if not more painful than, any mode of judicial execution that the world has seen; and that Jesus endured it in full consciousness of being innocent before God and man, and yet of being despised and rejected, whether in malicious conceit or in sheer fecklessness, by persons he had loved and tried to save – this is ground common to all views, and tells us already that the love of Jesus, which took him to the cross, brought him appallingly low. But the penal substitution model adds to all this a further dimension of truly unimaginable distress, compared with which every - thing mentioned so far pales into insignificance. This is the dimension indicated by Denney – 'that in that dark hour He had to realise to the full the divine reaction against sin in the race.' Owen stated this formally, abstractly and non-psychologically: Christ, he said, satisfied God's justice

> for all the sins of all those for whom he made satisfaction, by undergoing that same punishment which, by reason of the obligation that was upon them, they were bound to undergo. When I say the same I mean essentially the same in weight and pressure, though not in all accidents of duration and the like.[44]

Jonathan Edwards expressed the thought with tender and noble empathy:

> God dealt with him as if he had been exceedingly angry with him, and as though he had been the object of his dreadful wrath. This made all the sufferings of Christ the more terrible to him, because they were from the hand of his Father, whom he infinitely loved, and whose infinite love he had had eternal experience of. Besides, it was an effect of God's wrath that he forsook Christ. This caused Christ to cry out . . . 'My God, my God, why hast thou forsaken me?' This was infinitely terrible to Christ. Christ's knowledge of the glory of the Father, and his love to the Father, and the sense and experience he had had of the worth of his Father's love to him, made the withholding of the pleasant ideas and manifestations of his Father's love as terrible to him, as the sense and knowledge of his hatred is to the damned, that have no knowledge of God's excellency, no love to him, nor any experience of the infinite sweetness of his love.[45]

---

[44] *Works*, X. 269. To construe Owen's statement of equivalence between what threatened us and what Christ endured in 'quantitative' terms, as if some calculus of penal pain was being applied, would be a misunderstanding, though admittedly one which Owen's constant reliance on the model of payment invites, and against which he did not guard. But Denney's statement expresses what Owen means.

[45] Edwards, *Works*, ed. E. Hickman (London: Banner of Truth, 1975) II. 575. Cf. Luther 'Christ himself suffered the dread and horror of a distressed conscience that tasted eternal wrath'; 'It was not a game, or a joke, or play-acting when he said "Thou hast forsaken me"'; for then he felt himself really forsaken in all things even as a sinner is forsaken' (*Werke*, 5. 602, 605), and Calvin 'He bore in his soul the dreadful torments of a condemned and lost man' (*Inst.* II. xvi. 10). Thus Calvin explained Christ's descent into hell: hell means God-forsakenness, and the descent took place during the hours on the cross. Jesus' cry of dereliction has been variously explained as voicing (a) depressive delusion, (b) genuine perplexity (c) an 'as-if' feeling, (d) trust in God (because Jesus quotes the first words of Psalm 22, which ends with trust triumphant), (e) a repressed thought forcing its way into the open (so that the cry was a Freudian lapse), (f) a truth which Jesus wanted men to know. Surely only the last view can be taken seriously as either exegesis or theology. For a compelling discussion, cf. Leon Morris, op. cit., pp. 42–49.

And the legendary 'Rabbi' Duncan concentrated it all into a single unforgettable sentence, in a famous outburst to one of his classes:

> 'D'ye know what Calvary was? what? what? what?' Then, with tears on his face – 'It was *damnation*; and he took it *lovingly*.'

It is precisely this love that, in the last analysis, penal substitution is all about, and that explains its power in the lives of those who acknowledge it.[46]

What was potentially the most damaging criticism of penal substitution came not from Socinus, but from McLeod Campbell, who argued that by saying that God must punish sin but *need not* act in mercy at all (and in fact does not act in mercy towards all), Reformed exponents of this view reduced God's love to an arbitrary decision which does not reveal his character, but leaves him even in blessing us an enigma to us; 'the unknown God.'[47] The real target of Campbell's criticism is the Scotist model of divine personality with which, rightly or wrongly, he thought Reformed theologians worked; and a sufficient reply, from the standpoint of this lecture, would be that since the Bible says both that Christ's death was a penal substitution for God's people and also that it reveals God's love to sinful men as such, and since the Bible further declares that Christ is the Father's image, so that everything we learn of the Son's love is knowledge of the Father's love also, Campbell's complaint is unreal. But Campbell's criticism, if carried, would be fatal, for any account of the atonement that fails to highlight its character as a revelation of redeeming love stands self-condemned.

The ingredients in the evangelical model of penal substitution are now, I believe, all before us, along with the task it performs. It embodies and expresses insights about the cross which are basic to personal religion, and which I therefore state in personal terms, as follows:

---

[46] C. F. D. Moule is right to say that costly forgiving love which, in the interests of the offender's personhood, requires him to face and meet his responsibility evokes 'a burning desire to make reparation and to share the burdens of the one who forgave him. The original self-concern which, in the process of repentance, is transformed into a concern for the one he has injured makes the penitent eager to lavish on the one who forgives him all that he has and is.' It is certainly right to explicate God's forgiveness of our sins in terms of this model; though whether Moule is also right to define God's justice non-retributively, to eliminate penal satisfaction and to dismiss New Testament references to God's wrath and punishment as atavistic survivals and 'anomalies' is quite another question ('The Theology of Forgiveness,' in *From Fear to Faith: Studies of Suffering and Wholeness*, ed. Norman Autton (London: SPCK, 1971) pp. 61–72, esp. 66f., 72).

[47] Op. cit., p. 55.

(1) God, in Denney's phrase, 'condones nothing,' but judges all sin as it deserves: which Scripture affirms, and my conscience confirms, to be right.

(2) My sins merit ultimate penal suffering and rejection from God's presence (conscience also confirms this), and nothing I do can blot them out.

(3) The penalty due to me for my sins, whatever it was, was paid for me by Jesus Christ, the Son of God, in his death on the cross.

(4) Because this is so, I through faith in him am made 'the righteousness of God in him,' i.e. I am justified; pardon, acceptance and sonship become mine.

(5) Christ's death for me is my sole ground of hope before God. 'If he fulfilled not justice, I must; if he underwent not wrath, I must to eternity.'[48]

(6) My faith in Christ is God's own gift to me, given in virtue of Christ's death for me: i.e. the cross procured it.

(7) Christ's death for me guarantees my preservation to glory.

(8) Christ's death for me is the measure and pledge of the love of the Father and the Son to me.

(9) Christ's death for me calls and constrains me to trust, to worship, to love and to serve.

Thus we see what, according to this model, the cross achieved – and achieves.

Conclusion: The Cross in the Bible

In drawing the threads together, two general questions about the relation of the penal substitutionary model to the biblical data as a whole may be briefly considered.

(1) Are the contents and functioning of this model inconsistent in any way with the faith and religion of the New Testament? Is it degrading to God, or morally offensive, as is sometimes alleged? Our analysis has, I hope, served to show that it is not any of these things. And to have shown that may not be time wasted, for it seems clear that treatments of biblical material on the atonement are often influenced by prejudices of this kind, which produce reluctance to recognize how strong is the evidence for the integral place of substitution in biblical thinking about the cross. [49]

(2) Is our model truly based on the Bible? On this, several quick points may be made.

---

[48] Owen, *Works*, X. 284.

[49] See on this Leon Morris, op. cit., ch. 10, pp. 364–419.

First, full weight must be given to the fact that, as Luther saw, the central question to which the whole New Testament in one way or another is addressed is the question of our relationship, here and hereafter, with our holy Creator: the question, that is, how weak, perverse, estranged and guilty sinners may gain and guard knowledge of God's gracious pardon, acceptance and renewal. It is to this question that Christ is the answer, and that all New Testament interpretation of the cross relates.

Second, full weight must also be given to the fact that all who down the centuries have espoused this model of penal substitution have done so because they thought the Bible taught it, and scholars who for whatever reason take a different view repeatedly acknowledge that there are Bible passages which would most naturally be taken in a penal substitutionary sense. Such passages include Isaiah 53 (where Whale, as we saw, [n. 37] finds penal substitution mentioned twelve times), Galatians 3:13, 2 Corinthians 5:21, 1 Peter 3:18; and there are many analogous to these.

Third, it must be noted that the familiar exegetical arguments which, if accepted, erode the substitutionary view – the arguments, for instance, for a non-personal concept of God's wrath and a non-propitiatory understanding of the ἱλάσχομαι word group, or for the interpreting of bloodshed in the Old Testament sacrifices as the release of life to invigorate rather than the ending of it to expiate – only amount to this: that certain passages may not mean quite what they have appeared to mean to Bible students of earlier generations. But at every point it remains distinctly arguable that the time-honoured view is the true one, after all.

Fourth, it must be noted that there is no shortage of scholars who maintain the integral place of penal substitution in the New Testament witness to the cross. The outstanding contributions of James Denney and Leon Morris have already been mentioned, and they do not stand alone. For further illustration of this point, I subjoin two quotations from Professor A. M. Hunter. I do so without comment; they speak for themselves.

The first quotation is on the teaching of Jesus in the synoptic gospels. Having referred to theories of the atonement 'which deal in "satisfaction" or substitution, or make use of "the sacrificial principle," ' Hunter proceeds:

> It is with this type of theory that the sayings of Jesus seem best to agree. There can be little doubt that Jesus viewed his death as a representative sacrifice for 'the many.' Not only is His thought saturated in Isa. 53 (which is a doctrine of representative suffering), but His words over the cup – indeed, the whole narrative of the Last Supper – almost demand to be interpreted in terms of a sacrifice in whose virtue His followers can share. The idea of substitution which is prominent in Isa. 53 appears in the ransom saying. And it requires

only a little reading between the lines to find in the 'cup' saying, the story of the Agony, and the cry of dereliction, evidence that Christ's sufferings were what, for lack of a better word, we can only call 'penal.'[50]

The second quotation picks up comments on what, by common consent, are Paul's two *loci classici* on the method of atonement, 2 Corinthians 5:21 and Galatians 3:13. On the first, Hunter writes:

> Paul declares that the crucified Christ, on our behalf, took the whole reality of sin upon himself, like the scapegoat: 'For our sake he made him to be sin who knew no sin, so that in him we might become the righteousness of God.' Paul sees the Cross as an act of God's doing in which the Sinless One, for the sake of sinners, somehow experienced the horror of the divine reaction against sin so that there might be condemnation no more.
>
> Gal. 3:13 moves in the same realm of ideas. "Christ redeemed us from the curse of the law, having become a curse for us." ' (I interpose here my own comment, that Paul's aorist participle is explaining the method of redemption, answering the question 'how did Christ redeem us?,' and might equally well therefore be translated '*by becoming* a curse for us'.) The curse is the divine condemnation of sin which leads to death. To this curse we lay exposed; but Christ on his cross identified himself with the doom impending on sinners that, through his act, the curse passes away and we go free.
>
> Such passages show the holy love of God taking awful issue in the Cross with the sin of man. Christ, by God's appointing, dies the sinner's death, and so removes sin. Is there a simpler way of saying this than that Christ bore our sins? We are not fond nowadays of calling Christ's suffering 'penal' or of styling him our 'substitute'; but can we avoid using some such words as these to express Paul's view of the atonement?[51]

Well, can we? And if not, what follows? Can we then justify ourselves in holding a view of the atonement into which penal substitution does not enter? Ought we not to reconsider whether penal substitution is not, after all, the heart of the matter? These are among the questions which our preliminary survey in this lecture has raised. It is to be hoped that they will receive the attention they deserve.

---

[50] A. M. Hunter, *The Words and Works of Jesus* (London: SCM, 1950) p. 100.

[51] A. M. Hunter, *Interpreting Paul's Gospel* (London: SCM, 1954) pp. 31f.

Chapter 9

Sacrifice and Satisfaction

Sacrifice and satisfaction are two concepts with which Scripture teaches us to think of the work of our Saviour I begin my demonstration of this by quoting from the apostle Paul:

> But now a righteousness from God, apart from law, has been made known, to which the Law and the Prophets testify. This righteousness from God comes through faith in Jesus Christ to all who believe. There is no difference, for all have sinned and fall short of the glory of God, and are justified freely by his grace through the redemption that came by Christ Jesus. God presented him as a sacrifice of atonement, through faith in his blood. He did this to demonstrate his justice, because in his forbearance he had left the sins committed beforehand unpunished – he did it to demonstrate his justice at the present time, so as to be just and the one who justifies the man who has faith in Jesus.[1]

A Work of God

I invite you to notice three things straightaway.

First, *the atonement is the work of God*. This paragraph comes at the conclusion of a long section[2] in which Paul has been dwelling on the righteous judgement of God as our judge at the last day. His thought is crystallized when he says, 'Because of your stubbornness and unrepentant heart, you are storing up wrath against yourself for the day of God's wrath, when his righteous judgement will be revealed.' We notice the two phrases together: 'day of . . . wrath' and 'righteous judgement revealed.' Wrath is not a fitful, petulant, childish thing in God. Wrath is the attribute expressed in righteous judgement. It is holiness rejecting sin.

SACRIFICE AND SATISFACTION was originally published in in *Our Saviour God* ed. J. M. Boice (Grand Rapids: Baker Book House, 1981), pp. 125–137. Reprinted by permission.
[1] Rom. 3:21–26.
[2] Rom. 1:18–3:20.

At the end of this first great doctrinal section Paul reached the conclusion that the law of God exposes sin and guilt everywhere and brings all under condemnation. The whole world is held accountable to God; and by the works of the law (that is, by human works) no one will be justified in God's sight, for through the law comes knowledge of sin. This is a universal fact and the universal problem.

'But now,' Paul says, beginning a new subject, 'righteousness from God is revealed in a different way from the way of judgement on wrongdoing.' The phrase 'righteousness from [of] God' at the beginning of verse 21 still means God's quality of doing right in every thing he does; however, the issue of *this* display of God's righteousness is not our condemnation but its opposite, our justification. It sounds fantastic, too good to be true. But Paul goes on to explain that this is exactly what he means. This revelation of the righteousness of God is a disclosure of God in action, setting sinners right with himself, justifying them (to use the word that he introduces in verse 24 and again in verse 26).

The second thing I ask you to notice from this passage is that *the atonement has the nature of sacrifice*. Look again at verse 25. It tells us that God set forth his Son as 'a propitiation by his blood' (KJV). 'Blood' is New Testament shorthand, pointing to animal sacrifice as a type of the death of Christ and to Christ's death as coming in the category of sacrifice. 'Blood' tells us that sacrifice is the clue we need for interpreting the nature of the atonement.

What does the sight of blood do to you? Some people find that it turns their stomachs and makes them feel quite faint. If you are one of those, you would have had a hard time in temple and tabernacle worship in ancient Israel, for much blood was spilled in the course of that worship. Some of the sacrifices offered to God were foodstuffs of different kinds – cereal offerings (the meal offerings) and liquid offerings (the drink offerings). But most of the offerings were of animals that were ceremonially slaughtered.

The worshiper would draw near with his perfect victim. He would lay his hand on the animal's head and kill it. The priest would then draw and collect the blood and pour it out on one of the altars of God, ordinarily the altar of burnt offering, though on the Day of Atonement blood had to be poured out on the altar of incense too. [3] Thus was sacrifice made. It was specifically stated in the Old Testament rituals that sin offerings and guilt offerings must take this form: an animal killed, the blood drained, and the blood thrown out at the base of the altars, as prescribed.

Romans 3:25 is not the only place where Paul speaks of Christ's death in this sacrificial shorthand. In Romans 5:9 he says, 'We have now been justified by his blood.' In Ephesians 1:7 he says, 'In him we have redemption

---

[3] Exod. 30:10.

through his blood.' In Colossians 1:20, speaking of reconciliation, he says that the Lord Jesus Christ made peace 'through his blood.' Each time the word *blood* occurs, it is theological shorthand expressing the thought of sacrifice for sin.

The other New Testament writers speak of the blood of Christ in just the same way. Hebrews does so in far more texts than we can mention here: Hebrews 9:11–14 is one example. 1 Peter 1:19 reminds us that we were redeemed by 'the precious blood of Christ, a lamb without blemish or defect.' 1 John 1:7 tells us that 'the blood of Jesus, his Son, purifies us from every sin.' As a literal idea it makes our imagination boggle – red blood, yet cleansing! Yes, but the theological meaning is right; Christ's blood, that is, his atoning sacrifice, does cleanse from sin. Again, in Revelation the blood of Christ is referred to with the same sacrificial significance: 'To him who loves us and has freed us from our sins by his blood . . . to him be glory and power' (1:5–6). 'You are worthy to take the scroll and to open its seals, because you were slain, and with your blood you purchased men for God' (5:9). In all these texts the atonement of Christ has the nature of sacrifice.

Third, *the atonement displays God's righteousness*. Righteousness is that quality in God whereby he always does what is right, the quality whereby he maintains and meets the claims of the past in the present, giving to every man man his due. That was Aristotle's definition of man's right - eousness, and it is the fundamental biblical view of the righteousness of God also. God gives man his due.

This makes the righteousness of God in judgement very easy to understand, but it makes the righteousness of God in justifying the sinner appear at first inexplicable because it sounds wrong. It is marvellous good news. But surely, we say, it is not right that God, the just judge, should justify the ungodly, as Paul in Romans 4:5 actually says he does. Can it be right for God to behave this way? That is the question to which Paul is addressing himself in the compressed words of Romans 3:25–26. And he is telling us here that it really is right. It has become right. It has become the only right thing for God to do in virtue of his having sent his Son to be our sin-bearer.

This aspect of righteousness, whereby claims are met, was described in Roman law as 'satisfaction' (*satisfactio*), which means 'doing enough (*satisfacere*) to meet the claims that are there.' Paul is saying that God justifies us in a way that fully meets the claims that are there. So since the time of the great Anselm, the Christian church has rejoiced to use this word *satisfaction* as a term expressing the real significance of the sacrifice of Christ. As Anselm expounded satisfaction, it was a matter of satisfying God's outraged honour, and that indeed is part of the truth. But when Luther came along, he broadened the idea of satisfaction to what he found in the Bible, and he made the right and true point that the satisfaction of Jesus Christ restores God's glory through Christ's enduring all penal retribution for sin. The satisfaction of Christ glorifies God the Father and wins salvation for the sinner by being a satisfaction of God's justice. That is the thought Paul is expressing in Romans 3:25–26.

Paul tells us that God set forth his Son to be a propitiation by his blood. This, says Paul, was 'to demonstrate his justice, because in his forbearance he had left the sins committed beforehand unpunished.' He had indeed justified sinners. He had been doing it throughout the whole Old Testament period. But he had been doing it on no more substantial a basis than the offering of animal sacrifice.

Anyone who thought about things might well raise the question, 'How can the death of an animal put away the sin of a man?' There was no answer to that question once it was raised. So right up to the death of the Lord Jesus a great question mark hung over God's grace in forgiving sins. Men praised God for the mercy, but they could not see its basis in righteousness. But now you can see it, says Paul. Now it is made plain. The redemption that is in Christ Jesus covered that. It had retrospective efficacy; but not only that, it has efficacy in the present and for the future also. For Paul goes on to say, 'He did it to demonstrate his justice at the present time, so as to be just and the one who justifies the man who has faith in Jesus' (v.26).

In other words, through the redemption that is in Christ Jesus justice is done. Sin is punished as it deserves. But it is punished in the person of a substitute. Now we can see how it is that God's justification is just. Now we can see how God's justification of sinners is itself justified. God has shown his righteousness. He has satisfied himself; rendering the satisfac - tion that was due his own holiness. And so men may go free. God propitiated himself, we may say. God both gave and received satisfaction through the death of Christ.

This is why the word satisfaction has become a precious word to the people of God down the centuries – as, for instance, in the prescribed communion service in the prayer book of my own church:

> Almighty God, our heavenly Father, who of thy tender mercy didst give thine only Son Jesus Christ to die upon the cross for our salvation, who made there, by his one oblation of himself once offered, a full, perfect and sufficient sacrifice, oblation and satisfaction for the sins of the whole world.

Or as in the Heidelberg Catechism:

> My only comfort in life and death is that I belong to my faithful Saviour Jesus Christ, who with his precious blood has fully satisfied for all my sins

Thus Paul presents to us the realities of sacrifice and satisfaction

Atonement

Scholars dispute among themselves whether the deepest thought in the sacrificial rituals which God gave to his people in Old Testament times is: 1) a gift to God, 2) communion with God, or 3) making atonement before God. All three thoughts are there, of course. When the burnt offering was given to God and the whole carcass was consumed, clearly the thought of a gift was present. Again, when in the making of the peace offerings a meal took place in the sanctuary, clearly the thought of communion with God was present. But I do not think there can be any doubt that the deepest and most fundamental thought is of atonement.

In explaining the sacrificial system to his people in Old Testament times, God made this very plain by the things he told them. In Leviticus 17:11 we find him saying as the explanation of a prohibition that he has just given against the eating of blood, 'The life of a creature is in the blood, and I have given it to you to make atonement for yourselves on the altar; it is the blood that makes atonement for one's life.' The thought is that where sin has taken place, death must follow. 'That soul that sins, it shall die' is the basic form of that principle. In the sacrificial system, however, the man has sinned but the animal dies instead.

Some scholars have wondered whether the thought is that the blood makes atonement for sin by in some way releasing a life-force which re-animates and re-energizes the sinner's relationship with God, which sin has somehow broken. That is pure fancy. There is no evidence to back such an idea.

Every scriptural analogy and the whole attitude throughout the Old Testament to these animal sacrifices shows that the shedding of blood means the pouring out of life in a death of which the shed blood is witness. It is to exhibit death that the blood is presented at the altar. This alone is the basis on which God promised forgiveness of sin to his Old Testament people when they transgressed. So this alone is the meaning of blood-shedding in sacrifice. It is the laying down of life in death which atones.

Substitution

But now notice that the significance of sacrifice is not merely the laying down of life in death as such. It is the surrendering of life in *substitution* for the guilty, death-deserving party. This is the key reality, the very essence of what was going on in the sacrificial ritual and the very essence of what was going on when our Lord Jesus Christ died on Calvary nineteen-and-a-half centuries ago.

Here again we are using a word which the church has learned to love. True, it does not occur in the Bible any more than *satisfaction* does, but it is used and loved because it is the word that fits. It is the word that describes the essence of this sacrificial transaction.

Think of the ritual of those Old Testament sacrifices and you will see this plainly. The sinner comes with his sacrifice, and what does he do? He puts his hand on the animal's head and then kills it. Could any action make more evident that this is a substitutionary death, that the animal is dying on behalf of its owner who brought it and who puts his hand on its head in order to establish the link between it and him? This has been challenged, but it is too obvious to be denied.

Again, there is the annual ritual of the scapegoat, which taught the same lesson even more vividly. This is the ritual of the Day of Atonement, when comprehensive atonement is achieved for all the sins of the people during the previous year. What happens? It is laid out for us in Leviticus 16. In this ritual the high priest, having first offered a sin-offering to make atonement for himself, takes two goats. He is to put his hands on the head of one of them and 'confess over it all the wickedness and rebellion of the Israelites – all their sins – and put them on the goat's head. He shall send the goat away into the desert in the care of a man appointed for the task. The goat will carry on itself all their sins to a solitary place' (Lev. 16:21–22). What is the meaning of this ritual? It is a dramatization of what happens when the animal is killed and the blood is poured out at the base of the altar as a sign that life has been taken. The scapegoat is a picture of the removing of sin.

This is made plain by what happens to the second goat. The second goat is the one that really counts. The action with the scapegoat is only a picture of what happens through the second goat. The second goat is killed and offered as a sin-offering in the normal way. Thus atonement was made for the people of Israel. The banishing of the scapegoat into the wilderness was an illustrative device to make plain to God's people that their sin really has been taken away.

When the writer to the Hebrews speaks of Christ achieving what the Day of Atonement typified – our perfect and permanent cleansing from sin – he focuses not on the goat that went away into the wilderness but on the animal that was offered in sacrifice once a year by the high priest.

When Christ came as high priest of the good things that are already here, he went through the greater and more perfect tabernacle that is not man-made, that is to say, not a part of this creation. He did not enter by means of the blood of goats and calves; but he entered the Most Holy Place once for all by his own blood, having obtained eternal redemption. The blood of goats and bulls and the ashes of a heifer sprinkled on those who are ceremonially unclean sanctify them so that they are outwardly clean. How much more, then, will the blood of Christ, who through the eternal Spirit offered himself unblemished to God, cleanse our consciences from acts that lead to death, so that we may serve the living God![4]

There is the blood of Christ fulfilling the whole pattern of the Day of Atonement ritual.

Do we need further confirmation of this? If we do, we can find it. In Isaiah 53 it is stated explicitly (v.10) that God is making his servant's soul an offering for sin. In verses 4–6 we are told what that means: 'He was stricken by God, smitten . . . and afflicted . . . pierced . . . crushed.' Yes, but 'he was pierced for *our transgressions*, he was crushed for *our iniquities*; the punishment *that brought us peace* was upon him, and by his wounds *we* are healed. We all, like sheep, have gone astray, each of us has turned to his own way; and the LORD has laid on him *the iniquity of us all*.' That is what it means to say that his soul is made an offering for sin. It is substitution.

In Paul, who says many things about the atonement and pictures it in many different ways, I see a certain hierarchy of concept. Paul says, 'May I never boast except in the cross of our Lord Jesus Christ.' [5] We might ask Paul, 'Why do you thus glory and rejoice in Jesus' shameful execution?' Paul would reply

Because the cross was a sacrifice and that sacrifice means redemption; it means redemption, that is, purchase out of bondage, because it means reconciliation, the restoring of relations of peace with God; it means reconciliation because it means propitiation (by his death Christ has quenched God's wrath, so making peace); and it was a work of propitiation because it was a work of substitution under judgement. Only so could it cover sin, quench wrath, make peace, and set us free from penal bondage and jeopardy.

In other writings, Paul makes substitution the essence of his explanation of the cross. For instance, in Galatians 3:13–14 Paul writes, 'Christ redeemed us from the curse of the law [the expression of the holiness of God in threatened judgement].' And how did he do it? That is what the next clause tells us. It ought really to be translated: 'Christ redeemed us from the curse of the law by becoming a curse for us . . . that the blessing given to Abraham might come to the Gentiles.' The blessing of Abraham is the gift of righteousness, as he has already said in this paragraph. Christ redeemed us from the curse of the law by becoming that curse in our place, so that we sinners might be pardoned and set right with God.

Martin Luther got the message and spelled it out in his commentary on Galatians as vividly as ever it has been spelled out by anyone. He comments thus on Galatians 3:13:

---

[4] Heb. 9:11–14.
[5] Gal. 6:14.

All the prophets did foresee in spirit that Christ should become the greatest transgressor, murderer, adulterer, thief, rebel, blasphemer, etc., that ever was or could be in all the world. For he, being made a sacrifice for the sins of the whole world, is not now an innocent person and without sins . . . but a sinner.

He is, of course, talking about the imputing of our wrongdoing to Christ as our substitute. He continues,

Our most merciful Father . . . sent his only Son into the world and laid upon him . . . the sins of all men, saying: Be thou Peter that denier; Paul that persecutor, blasphemer and cruel oppressor; David that adulterer; that sinner which did eat the apple in Paradise; that thief which hanged upon the cross; and briefly, be thou the person which hath committed the sins of all men; see therefore that thou pay and satisfy for them. Here now cometh the law and saith: I find him a sinner . . . therefore let him die upon the cross. And so he setteth upon him and killeth him. By this means the whole world is purged and cleansed from all sins.[6]

Has anyone ever stated the glorious truth of Christ's substitutionary death for sinners in a more vivid and clearer way than Luther?

Again, Colossians 2:14 is a glowing verse, full of imagery, in which Paul explains how he can assert so confidently that God has forgiven us all our trespasses. This is how he has done it, says Paul: 'Having cancelled the written code, with its regulations, that was against us and that stood opposed to us; he took it away, nailing it to the cross.' Think that one out. The bond is the IOU by which God binds us. It is nothing other than the requirement of his law, which we are bound to meet under pain of damnation. If one fails to settle an IOU, one is in trouble, and that is the trouble we were in. We owe to God perfect obedience to his law. But we had failed to obey the law, and so the bond had become our death warrant. It was under the curse of the law that we stood, there and nowhere else. But now, says Paul, God has cancelled the bond 'that was against us . . . nailing it to the cross [of Christ].'

Look at the cross with the eye of faith, says Paul, and you will see that the superscription of the Saviour's accusation does not read, 'This is the king of the Jews.' Oh, the eye of sense will see that, for that is what Pilate wrote, as the four Gospels record. But the eye of faith sees a different charge written there. The stated cause of sentence and execution which the eye of faith sees is the bond that was our death warrant, which demanded our death for nonobedience. That is why Christ was there. That is why he hung on the cross. He was paying the penalty incurred by our unpaid debt of obedience.

---

[6] Martin Luther, *A Commentary on St. Paul's Epistle to the Galatians* (Grand Rapids: Baker, 1979 rep.) pp. 269, 272.

In verse 15 Paul tells us more of what we should be seeing as in faith we gaze at Calvary. We should realize, he says, that on the cross Christ 'disarmed the powers and authorities [shook them off him, as one shakes off a garment that one is discarding, and] . . . made a public spectacle of them, triumphing over them.' The principalities and powers, Satan and his hosts, were concerned at all costs to see that Jesus' venture of putting away our sin should fail. They tempted him to abandon the way of the cross and go another way. We do not know in what form the powers of hell assaulted him on the cross, though it is plain from this text as well as others that they did. But on the cross Jesus defeated them for all time.

Looking at the cross with the eye of sense you might think you were looking at a wretched failure, a good man dying as the result of a miscarriage of justice. You might see it as a shocking scandal and a sad end to his ministry. But look at the cross with the eye of faith, says Paul, and what you see is victory. You see the Saviour triumphing over his enemies and defeating them once and for all, by enduring our punishment and so guaranteeing our final deliverance from Satan's sway.

Now look at what Paul says in 2 Corinthians 5:21. How is it that God in Christ is reconciling the world to himself? By not imputing men's trespasses to them. And how is it that he does not impute men's trespasses to them? By virtue of the fact that he imputes them to the Lord Jesus so that Jesus pays for them in our stead. 'God made him who had no sin to be sin for us [not by committing sin, but by having our sins reckoned to his account], so that in him we might become the righteousness of God.' Substitution! That is the message.

In our preaching we cast around for illustrations of this, and it is good that we do. None are perfect, but they help. For instance, there is the story P. T. Forsyth tells of Schamyl, the Tartar general, who found that some member of his army was leaking secrets to the enemy and who threatened many lashes with the whip once the culprit was discovered. Schamyl had been taking his whole household with him on his campaign, and it turned out that it was his own mother who had been leaking the secrets. Schamyl immediately shut himself up in his tent, and nobody saw him for two days. Then someone ventured to make his way into the tent to see what was going on. He found Schamyl lashing himself.

Again, we tell the story of the Argyll Highlander recorded by Ernest Gordon in *Through the Valley of the Kwai*, a book which tells of that nightmarish business in the last war where prisoners were used to build a Japanese military railroad through Southeast Asia. The shovels were counted at the end of the day's work. One day the Japanese guard reckoned that there was one missing and that this must mean that some member of the work party had stolen his shovel and traded it to the Thais. Nobody admitted to doing this. The guard became furious and started yelling, 'All die! All die!' He actually raised his rifle and pointed it at random at the men in the line. The Argyll soldier then stepped forward and said, 'I did it.' The guard went up to him, raised his rifle and beat the man's head in, killing him. When they got the shovels back to their headquarters in the camp, they were counted again and there was no shovel missing. But a man had given his life for his brethren.

These stories bring us part of the way along the road of illustrating the reality of substitution which the New Testament has spelled out.

God So Loved

The cross of Christ is a revelation of the love of God, for it reveals what that love is prepared to suffer for the one loved. I believe that the presentation of the death of Christ as substitution exhibits the love of the cross more richly, fully, gloriously, and glowingly than does any other presentation. It gets us nearer to the heart of that love than any of the other pictures that the New Testament contains.

Again, Luther saw it and gloried in the fact that the man who knows Christ can be assured of such love. He once wrote to a friend,

> Learn Christ and him crucified. Learn to pray to him, and despairing of yourself to say this, 'Lord Jesus, you are my righteousness, I am your sin. You have taken upon yourself what is mine and given me what is yours. You have made me what I was not. You have taken to yourself what you were not.

There has been an exchange, a great and wonderful exchange. Luther actually used that phrase, a 'wonderful exchange.' He knew that the Son of God has taken all our guilt and set upon us all his righteousness. Was there ever such love?

Rabbi Duncan was a great Reformed teacher in New College, Edinburgh, a hundred years ago. In one of his famous excursions in his classes, where he would move off from the Hebrew he was supposed to be teaching to theological reflections on this or that, he threw out the following question: 'Do you know what Calvary was? What? What? What?' He said it like that, jerky, pressing his question. 'Do you know what Calvary was?' Then, having waited a little and having walked up and down in front of them in silence, he looked at them again and said, 'I'll tell you what Calvary was. It was *damnation*, and he took it *lovingly*.' The students in his class reported that there were tears in his eyes as he said it. And well there might be. '*Damnation*, and he took it *lovingly*!'

Calvin's understanding of the clause of the creed which says 'He descended into hell' was that it related to the three hours of darkness on the cross, when the Son knew himself forsaken of his Father because he was bearing the world's sin. Probably that is not what the creed originally meant, but it is a good exposition of the truth about the cross. What love!

Deep, rich, and full peace of conscience comes only when you know that your sins have been, not simply disregarded, but judged, judged to the full and paid for to the full by the Son of God in your place. This is expressed perfectly in a beautiful hymn by Augustus M. Toplady, a hymn to which he gave the title 'Faith Reviving.' Here is the troubled Christian finding again his peace.

> From whence this fear and unbelief?
> Has not the Father put to grief
>   His spotless Son for me?
> And will the righteous Judge of men
> Condemn me for that load of sin
>   Which, Lord, was charged on thee?
>
> Complete atonement thou hast made
> And to the utmost farthing paid
>   Whate'er thy people owed.
> Nor can God's wrath on me take place
> When sheltered 'neath thy righteousness
>   And covered by thy blood.
>
> If thou my pardon hast secured
> And freely in my room endured
>   The whole of wrath divine,
> Payment God cannot twice demand
> First from my bleeding surety's hand
>   And then again from mine.
>
> Return, my soul, unto thy rest,
> The sorrows of thy great High Priest
>   Have bought thy liberty.
> Trust in his efficacious blood,
> Nor fear thy banishment from God
>   Since Jesus died for thee!

If you want to know what it means to say that Christ died for us, that hymn tells you.

Richard Hooker, that great Anglican theologian of the sixteenth century, wrote this at the end of his *Learned Sermon on Justification*.

Let men count it folly, or frenzy, or whatsoever. We care for no knowledge, no wisdom in the world but this, that man has sinned and God has suffered, that God has been made the sin of man and man is made the righteousness of God.

My sin has been judged already, the penalty has been paid. 'Payment God cannot twice demand, first from my bleeding surety's hand and then again from mine.' This is the height of joy and glory, of thanksgiving, of almost overwhelming delight to which scriptural meditations on Christ's death as sacrifice and satisfaction lead us. 'Thanks be to God for his indescribable gift' (2 Cor. 9:15).

Chapter 10

Justification: Introductory Essay

Martin Luther described the doctrine of justification by faith as *articulus stantis vel cadentis ecclesiae* – the article of faith that decides whether the church is standing or falling. By this he meant that when this doctrine is understood, believed, and preached, as it was in New Testament times, the church stands in the grace of God and is alive; but where it is neglected, overlaid, or denied, as it was in medieval Catholicism, the church falls from grace and its life drains away, leaving it in a state of darkness and death. The reason why the Reformation happened, and Protestant churches came into being, was that Luther and his fellow Reformers believed that Papal Rome had apostatised from the gospel so completely in this respect that no faithful Christian could with a good conscience continue within her ranks.

Justification by faith has traditionally, and rightly, been regarded as one of the two basic and controlling principles of Reformation theology. The authority of Scripture was the *formal* principle of that theology, determin-ing its method and providing its touchstone of truth; justification by faith was its material principle, determining its substance. In fact, these two principles belong inseparably together, for no theology that seeks simply to follow the Bible can help concerning itself with what is demonstrably the essence of the biblical message. The fullest statement of the gospel that the Bible contains is found in the epistle to the Romans, and Romans minus justification by faith would be like *Hamlet* without the Prince.

A further fact to weigh is that justification by faith has been the central theme of the preaching in every movement of revival and religious awakening within Protestantism from the Reformation to the present day. The essential thing that happens in every true revival is that the Holy Spirit teaches the church afresh the reality of justification by faith, both as a truth and as a living experience. This could be demonstrated historically from the records of revivals that we have; and it would be

JUSTIFICATION: INTRODUCTORY ESSAY was originally published in Buchanan, James *The Doctrine of Justification: An Outline of its History in the Church and of its Exposition from Scripture* (London: Banner of Truth Trust, 1961), pp. 1–9. Reprinted by permission.

theologically correct to define revival simply as God the Spirit doing this work in a situation where previously the church had lapsed, if not from the formal profession of justification by faith, at least from any living apprehension of it.

This being so, it is a fact of ominous significance that Buchanan's classic volume, now a century old, is the most recent full-scale study of justification by faith that English-speaking Protestantism (to look no further) has produced. If we may judge by the size of its literary output, there has never been an age of such feverish theological activity as the past hundred years; yet amid all its multifarious theological concerns it did not produce a single book of any size on the doctrine of justification. If all we knew of the church during the past century was that it had neglected the subject of justification in this way, we should already be in a position to conclude that this has been a century of religious apostasy and decline. It is worth our while to try and see what has caused this neglect, and what are the effects of it within Protestant communities today; and then we may discern what has to be done for our situation to be remedied.

But first we ought to observe how far-reaching such neglect is, and how much we stand to lose by it. For the doctrine of justification by faith is like Atlas: it bears a world on its shoulders, the entire evangelical knowledge of saving grace. The doctrines of election, of effectual calling, regeneration, and repentance, of adoption, of prayer, of the church, the ministry, and the sacraments, have all to be interpreted and understood in the light of justification by faith. Thus, the Bible teaches that God elected men in eternity in order that in due time they might be justified through faith in Christ. He renews their hearts under the Word, and draws them to Christ by effectual calling, in order that he might justify them upon their believing. Their adoption as God's sons is consequent on their justification; indeed, it is no more than the positive aspect of God's justifying sentence. Their practice of prayer, of daily repentance, and of good works – their whole life of faith – springs from the knowledge of God's justifying grace. The church is to be thought of as the congregation of the faithful, the fellowship of justified sinners, and the preaching of the Word and ministry of the sacraments are to be understood as means of grace only in the sense that they are means through which God works the birth and growth of justifying faith. A right view of these things is not possible without a right understanding of justification; so that when justification falls, all true knowledge of the grace of God in human life falls with it, and then, as Luther said, the church itself falls. A society like the Church of Rome, which is committed by its official creed to pervert the doctrine of justification, has sentenced itself to a distorted understanding of salvation at every point. Nor can these distortions ever be corrected till the Roman doctrine of justification is put right. And something similar happens when Protestants let the thought of justification drop out of their minds: the true knowledge of salvation drops out with it, and cannot be restored till the truth of justification is back in its proper place. When Atlas falls, everything that rested on his shoulders comes crashing down too.

How has it happened, then, we ask, that so vital a doctrine has come to be neglected in the way that it is today?

The answer is not far to seek. Just as Atlas, with his mighty load to carry, could not hover in mid-air, but needed firm ground to stand on, so does the doctrine of justification by faith. It rests on certain basic presuppositions, and cannot continue without them. Just as the church cannot stand without the gospel of justification, so that gospel cannot stand where its presuppo - sitions are not granted. They are three: the divine authority of Holy Scripture, the divine wrath against human sin, and the substitutionary satisfaction of Christ. The church that loses its grip on these truths, loses its grip on the doctrine of justification, and to that extent on the gospel itself. And this is what has largely happened in Protestantism today.

Let us look at this in detail. Take the three doctrines in order.

(i) The divine authority of the Bible

To Reformation theologians – among whom we count the Puritans, the early Evangelicals, and theologians like Buchanan – what Scripture said, God said. To them, all Scripture had the character claimed for itself by biblical prophecy – the character, that is, of being the utterance of God spoken through human lips. The voice that spoke was human, but the words spoken were divine. So with the Bible: the pen and style were human, but the words written were God's. The Scriptures were both humanity's word and God's word; not just humanity bearing witness to God, but God bearing witness to himself. Accordingly, theologians of the Reformation type took the biblical doctrine of sin and salvation exactly as it stood. They traced out the thoughts of Paul, and John, and Peter, and the rest of those who expounded it, with loving care, knowing that hereby they were thinking God's thoughts after him. So that, when they found the Bible teaching that God's relationship with humankind is regulated by his law, and only those whom his law does not condemn can enjoy fellowship with him, they believed it. And when they found that the heart of the New Testament gospel is the doctrine of justification and forgiveness of sins, which shows sinners the way to get right with God's law, they made this gospel the heart of their own message.

But modern Protestants have ceased to do this, because they have jettisoned the historic understanding of the inspiration and authority of Holy Scripture. It has become usual to analyse inspiration naturalisti - cally, reducing it to mere religious insight. Modern theology balks at equating the words of the Bible with the words of God, and fights shy of asserting that, because these words are inspired, they are therefore inerrant and divinely authoritative. Scripture is allowed a relative authority, based on the supposition that its authors, being men of insight, probably say much that is right; but this is in effect to deny to Scripture the authority which properly belongs to the words of a God who cannot lie. This modern view expressly allows for the possibility that sometimes the biblical writers, being children of their age, had their minds so narrowed by conditioning factors in their environment that, albeit unwittingly, they twisted and mis-stated God's truth. And when any particular biblical idea cuts across what people today like to think, modern Protestants are fatally prone to conclude that this is a case in point, where the Bible saw things crooked, but we today, differently conditioned, can see them straight.

So here. Modern people, like many pre-Christian pagans, likes to think of themselves as sons of God by creation, born into the divine family and objects of God's endless paternal care. The thought appeals, for it is both flattering and comforting; it seems to give us a claim on God's love straight away. Protestants of today (whose habit it is to take pride in being modern) are accordingly disinclined to take seriously the uniform biblical insistence that God's dealing with humanity are regulated by law, and that God's universal relation to humankind is not that of Father, but of Lawgiver and Judge. They grant that this thought meant much to Paul, because of his rabbinic conditioning, and to the Reformers, because legal concepts so dominated the Renaissance culture of their day, but, these Protestants say, forensic imagery is really quite out of place for expressing the nature of the personal, paternal relationship which binds God to his human crea - tures. The law-court is a poor metaphor for the Father's house. Paul was not at his best when talking about justification. We, in our advanced state of enlightenment, can now see that God's dealings with his creatures are not, strictly speaking, legal at all. Thus modern Protestantism really denies the validity of all the forensic terms in which the Bible explains to us our relationship with God.

The modern Protestant, therefore, is willing to see humanity as a wandering child, a lost prodigal needing to find a way home to the heavenly Father, but, generally speaking, is not willing to see humanity as a guilty criminal before the Judge of all the earth. The Bible doctrine of justification, however, is the answer to the question of the convicted lawbreaker: how can I get right with God's law? How can I be just with God? Those who refuse to see their situation in these terms will not, therefore, take much interest in the doctrine. Nobody can raise much interest in the answer to a question which, so far as they are concerned, never arises. Thus modern Protestantism, by its refusal to think of humanity's relationship with God in the basic biblical terms, has knocked away the foundation of the gospel of justification, making it seem simply irrelevant to humanity's basic need.

The second doctrine which the gospel of justification presupposes is

(ii) *The divine wrath against human sin*

Just as modern Protestants are reluctant to believe that humankind has to deal with God, not as a Father, but as a Judge, so they are commonly unwilling to believe that there is in God a holy antipathy against sin, a righteous hatred of evil, which prompts him to exact just retribution when his law is broken. They are not, therefore, prepared to take seriously the biblical witness that humanity in sin stands under the wrath of God. Some dismiss the wrath of God as another of Paul's lapses; others reduce it to an impersonal principle of evil coming home (sometimes) to roost: few will allow that wrath is God's personal reaction to sin, so that by sinning we make God our enemy. But Reformation theologians have always believed this; first, because the Bible teaches it, and, second, because they have felt something of the wrath of God in their own convicted and defiled consciences. And they have preached it; and thus they have in past days laid the foundation for proclaiming justification. But where there is an unwillingness to allow that sinners stand under the judicial wrath of God, there is no foundation for the preaching of deliverance from that wrath – which is what the gospel of justification is about. Thus in a second way modern Protestantism undercuts that gospel, and robs it of relevance for humanity's relationship with God.

The third presupposition is

(iii) *The substitutionary satisfaction of Christ*

It is no accident that at the time of the Reformation the penal and substitutionary character of the death of Christ, and the doctrine of justification by faith, came to be appreciated together. For in the Bible they belong together. Justification is grounded on the sin-bearing work of the Lamb of God. It is the second, completing stage in the great double transaction whereby Christ was made sin and believing sinners are made 'the righteousness of God in him' (2 Cor. 5:21). Salvation in the Bible is by substitution and exchange: the imputing of men's sins to Christ, and the imputing of Christ's righteousness to sinners. By this means, the law, and the God whose law it is, are satisfied, and the guilty are justly declared immune from punishment. Justice is done, and mercy is made triumphant in the doing of it. The imputing of righteousness to sinners in justification, and the imputing of their sins to Christ on Calvary, thus belong together; and if, in the manner of so much modern Protestantism, the penal interpretation of the Cross is rejected, then there is no ground on which the imputing of righteousness can rest. And a groundless imputation of righteousness to sinners would be a mere legal fiction, an arbitrary pretence on God's part, an overturning of the moral order of the universe, and a violation of the law which expresses his own holy nature; in short, would be a flat impossibility, which it would be blasphemous even to contemplate. No; if the penal character of Christ's death be denied, the right conclusion to draw is that God has never justified any sinner, nor ever will. Thus modern Protestantism, by rejecting penal substitution, is guilty of under - mining the gospel of justification by faith in yet a third way. For justification cannot be preached in a way that is even reverent when that which alone makes moral sense of it is denied. No wonder, therefore, that the subject of justification is so widely neglected at the present time.

What must we do to reinstate it in our pulpits and our churches? We must preach it in its biblical setting; we must re-establish its presupposi - tions. We must reaffirm the authority of Scripture, as truth from the mouth of God. We must reaffirm the inflexible righteousness of God as a Judge, and the terrible reality of his wrath against sin, as Scripture depicts these things. And we must set forth against this black background the great exchange between Christ and his members, the saving transaction which justification completes.

The good news of Christ in our place, and we in his, is still God's word to the world: it is through the foolishness (as men call it) of this message, and this message alone, that God is pleased to save them that believe: The value of Buchanan's book today is that it will help us to understand this message better, and so to preach it in the full and comprehensive way in which the modern world needs to hear it.

It only remains to say a word about the author himself. Buchanan was born at Paisley in 1804, and ordained in 1827. In 1828 he commenced a very successful ministry at North Leith, where he gained a great reputation as an earnest, eloquent, evangelical preacher. Two years after the Disrup - tion, in 1845, he was appointed to the Chair of Apologetics at New College, Edinburgh, and in 1847 he succeeded Chalmers as Professor of Systematic Theology. He retired in 1868, and died two years later.

He was a prolific and popular writer: his first book, *Comfort in Affliction* (1837), sold nearly 30,000 copies. His two most valuable works were *The Office and Work of the Holy Spirit* (1842), an exposition which still merits study, and *The Doctrine of Justification*, the Cunningham Lectures for 1866. The Dictionary of National Biography says of him: 'Though not eminent for his powers of original thought, Buchanan had a remarkable faculty for collecting what was valuable in the researches and arguments of others, and presenting it in clear form and lucid language.' *The Doctrine of Justification* bears this out. Its teaching is not original, either in intention or in fact. All that Buchanan aims to do is to clarify and re-state the historic doctrine of the Westminster Confession and the great seventeenth- century Reformed divines; to show how the church had arrived at it; and how some had deviated from it; and to gather up the best that generations of devout evangelical students had thought and said by way of exposition of it. He fulfilled his task in a most masterly way, as the reader will discover. He was essentially a preacher, and preachers tend to be wordy on paper, so that one has to bear with a measure of prolixity and a style that sometimes sags; but it is easy to forgive him that when his analysis of justification in relation to the whole divine economy is so supremely good. It is doubtful whether a better exposition of it exists. And his preacher's style imparts a warmth to his writing which we do not find in (say) the lawyer-like Cunningham, and which is very refreshing. There is no doubt that this is still the best textbook on its subject, from the standpoint of the classic covenant theology, that the student can find.

Chapter 11

The Love of God: Universal and Particular

On Knowing Love

It was, I think, Voltaire who first observed that ever since God made humanity in his own image humanity has been trying to return the compliment. Whoever said it, it is true, and many theological mistakes have been made through likening the God of infinite power, holiness, goodness, and wisdom to finite and fallen humanity.

The KISS formula – 'keep it simple, stupid!' – is current wisecracking wisdom. But the idea behind the formula, namely, that the notion that seems simplest will always be soundest, has been around in theology since at least the third century, when Sabellians and Arians 'simplified' the truth of the Trinity in a way that actually denied it (the former turning God into a quick-change artist playing three roles, the latter turning the divine Son and Spirit into two high-class creatures). Many more theological mistakes have come from embracing simplistic naiveties that at the time felt comfortable to the mind.

The idea of the grace of God that prompts this chapter seems to involve error of both kinds, as we shall see. Since however my goal here is positive exposition with the minimum of controversy, I focus first not on disputable opinions, but on basic questions of definition and method.

My title affirms that God's love is a reality. All Christian teaching says this. But what is love? Asking that question must be our starting point, for 'love,' both as a noun and as a verb, is among the most misused words in the English language. And although God's love is our prime concern we must begin by noting how modern Westerners use the word of each other, for it is here that the worst confusions arise.

'Love' as a term, because of its historic Christian associations, still carries in what was once Christendom glowing overtones of nobility and grandeur. Certainly, the mutual devotion of lovers, and the self-sacrificing

THE LOVE OF GOD: UNIVERSAL AND PARTICULAR was originally published in *The Grace of God, the Bondage of the Will*, ed. Thomas R. Schriener and Bruce A. Ware (Grand Rapids: Baker Book House, 1995) pp. 413–428. Reprinted by permission.

paths of parenthood and friendship can be noble indeed. But in current use 'love' has become virtually synonymous with liking and wanting something or someone, and there is nothing necessarily noble or grand about that. 'I love chocolate,' 'I love sunsets,' 'I love jazz,' 'I love redheads,' 'I love sex' – such states of liking and wanting are so many egocentric highroads to self-gratifying self-indulgence. When persons are the objects of our likes and wants, then manipulation, exploitation, and abuse are likely to result, alternating with unprincipled indulgence of the other person's whims on the principle, it seems, of doing to others as you would like them to do to you. Parents 'loving' their children by giving them everything they ever want is an obvious example. Thus, what we call our love for people often does them harm. Sometimes it is assumed that God's love, if real, would itself take the form of unprincipled indulgence of our whims, and then the fact that comforts we pray for are not always given is treated as proving a lack either of love or of power on God's part. Such are the confusions that have to be sorted out.

In *The Four Loves* C. S. Lewis distinguished *agape* (the New Testament Greek word for God's love and Christian love) from *storge* (the feeling of affection or fondness); *eros* (the feeling of desire and need for some person or thing that is felt to be attractive, especially in sexual or aesthetic contexts); and *philia* (the attitude of friendliness to one who is friendly to you). Each of these three is a blend of animal instinct, personal taste, appreciative awareness, and self-gratifying impulse, and in this all three differ radically from *agape*.

What is *agape*? Human *agape* is a way (1 Cor. 13:1) – that is, a path of action – of which four things are true. First, it has as its purpose doing good to others, and so in some sense making those others great. *Agape* Godward, triggered by gratitude for grace, makes God great by exalting him in praise, thanksgiving, and obedience. *Agape* manward, neighbour love as Scripture calls it, makes fellow humans great by serving not their professed wants, but their observed real needs. Thus, marital *agape* seeks fulfilment for the spouse and parental *agape* seeks maturity for the children. Second, *agape* is measured not by sweetness of talk or strength of feeling, but by what it does, and more specifically by what of its own it gives, for the fulfilling of its purpose. Third, *agape* does not wait to be courted, nor does it limit itself to those who at once appreciate it, but it takes the initiative in giving help where help is required, and finds its joy in bringing others benefit. The question of who deserves to be helped is not raised; *agape* means doing good to the needy, not to the meritorious, and to the needy however undeserving they might be. Fourth, *agape* is precise about its object. The famous *Peanuts* quote, 'I love the human race – it's people I can't stand,' is precisely not *agape*. *Agape* focuses on particular people with particular needs, and prays and works to deliver them from evil. In all of this it is directly modelled on the love of God revealed in the gospel.

Knowing God's Love: The Method

Basic to Christianity is the conviction that we learn what love is from watching God in action – supremely, from watching God in the person of the Father's incarnate Son, Jesus Christ, as he lives, gives, suffers, and dies to achieve our redemption. We do the watching through Bible study, following the narratives of the Gospels and the explanations in the Epistles. The point is often made that before Christianity arrived the *agape* word-group was unspecific, was rarely used, and signified no more than contentment with something, so that by defining it in terms of the love shown forth in Christ the apostles made it a new thing – love of a kind that the world never dreamed of before. This is right, and we must never let ourselves think of *agape* in any terms not validated by the redemptive work of Jesus.

But to understand correctly what the New Testament says about this love of God we must set it in the frame of the total biblical witness to God, and that means observing the following perspectival guidelines.

Remember *the sovereignty of the divine Creator*. Older Reformed theology, organizing the teaching of the canonical Scriptures, called the different aspects of God's being his attributes, some communicable and others incommunicable. The former, so called because in our sanctification they begin to be reproduced in us, were commonly listed as wisdom, truth, goodness (meaning grace, mercy, and long-suffering love), holiness, and righteousness; highlighting God's personhood, they together answered the question How does God behave? The latter, commonly listed as self-existence (aseity), immutability, infinity, eternity, and simplicity (meaning inner integration), highlighted God's transcendence; combining as an answer to the question How does God exist? They underlined at every point the contrast between the majestic self-sustaining omnipotence of the divine life and the creaturely dependence, weakness, and sinful disorder of ours. God's sovereignty, in which the perfection of his powers operates to express the perfection of his moral character, straddles this classification, for it is essentially personal action on an altogether transcendent plane. God 'rules in the world and his will is the final cause of all things, including specifically creation and preservation (Ps. 95:6; Rev. 4:11), human govern - ment (Pr. 21:1; Dn. 4:35), the salvation of God's people (Rom. 8:29f.; Eph. 1:4, 11), the sufferings of Christ (Lk. 22:42; Acts 2:23), man's life and destiny (Acts 18:21; Rom. 15:32), and even the smallest details of life (Matt. 10:29). God reigns in his universe.'[1] The love of God is thus sovereign love, and must always be acknowledged as such.

Remember *the trinity of the divine Lord*. Within the one God's complex being are three personal centers ('centers' is not perhaps an ideal word,

---

[1] Bruce Milne, *Know the Truth* (Downers Grove, Ill.: InterVarsity Press, 1982) p. 66.

but we have none better). Each is 'I' to himself and 'you' to the other two. By God's own naming they are the Father, the Son, and the Holy Spirit. God is a society, a community of mutual love, and a team: he is they and they are he, if such language may be allowed. [2] Speaking epistemologically, the truth of the Trinity became known only through the life and words of the incarnate Son who came from the Father and prayed to the Father, and who when returning to the Father promised that the Spirit would be sent as his deputy; but speaking ontologically, the fact of God's triunity is eternal. The love of God is thus triune love, and should always be thought of in that way.

Remember *the unity of the divine character*. God in Scripture regularly uses the word *holy* with a global meaning, to bring together and hold together in our minds both the metaphysical perfections and the moral glories characterizing the triune Lord, who in all his words and deeds is unchangeably wise, just, pure, good, and true. Every time he says he is holy or calls himself the Holy One of Israel, the adjective carries this full weight of meaning. In this broad sense, therefore, holiness is the attribute displayed in all God's attributes; and thus the love of God is holy love, and must ever be viewed so, in explicit relation to the other aspects of God's being.

Remember *the analogy of the divine self-description*. This point follows from the last. God who gave us language prompted his penmen in Scripture to speak of him in nouns, verbs, and adjectives taken from the common human stock of language, just as he did himself when speaking through the prophets and through his Son, Jesus Christ. But because all these words ordinarily refer to finite and fallen human beings, when they are used of God they must be partially redefined: the core of the meaning will remain, but all associations or implications that suggest human finitude and fallenness must be eliminated, and the core meaning must be set in the frame of God's perfection and purity. It is evident that the Bible writers were mentally doing this all the time, in a way that had become second nature to them, and in interpreting their writings we must follow this out. So the love of God is not identical with, but analogous to, what is noblest in human love, and the precise terms of the analogical adjust - ment our minds must make at this point have to be learned from the rest of the teaching about God that the Bible gives. What was said about *agape* has already alerted us to the major difference there is between God's love and man's.

Remember *the epistemology of the divine instruction*. God through his Spirit interprets the Bible to us, that is, enables us to understand the writers' meaning and apply their points to ourselves, and so to apprehend

---

[2] cf. Matt. 28:19; John 14:15–26; 2 Cor. 13:14; Eph. 1:3–14; 2:18–22; Rev. 1:4–5; etc. Though the apostles developed no trinitarian vocabulary, trinitarian thinking pervades the entire New Testament.

what he, the divine Author, wishes to teach us from the inspired text. But the Bible is a set of more or less occasional writings, in which things dealt with in detail are clearer than those to which only passing reference is made. Knowing that sin has twisted our minds, just as it has twisted our moral sensibilities, and both at a deeper level than we can track, we should not let ourselves speculate beyond what Scripture clearly teaches, and should be willing to settle for ignorance (*docta ignorantia*, well-taught ignorance, as it has been called) rather than indulge our theological fancies.

Also, we should take 'what Scripture clearly teaches' to mean 'what exegesis shows that the Bible writers wanted their readers to gather from their words' – not what those words might seem to be saying when recontextualized in a latter-day dogmatic frame. So our understanding of the love of God must be limited by what the Bible's homiletical flowings of thought actually yield. We should confine ourselves to this, and eschew extrapolations beyond it.

A model of this kind of conscientious theological discretion, and one that bears directly on our present subject, is Anglican Article 17 (1571), 'Of Predestination and Election.' In Reformation days, as since, treat-ments of God's love in election were often given shape, overshadowed, and indeed preempted by wrangles of an abstract sort about God's sovereignty in reprobation. But in the New Testament, most notably in Romans 8:28–11:36 and Ephesians 1:3–14, election is a pastoral theme, spelled out for believers' encouragement, reassurance, support, and wor-ship. That is exactly how Article 17 treats it, by drawing out in direct echoes of Scripture the comfort of election, by bypassing debates about reprobation, and by directing unbelievers, seekers, and saints alike to the 'whosoever will' promises and mandates of the gospel, which chart the way of life. Because methodologically the article is such a good example of observing biblical parameters, and also because its contents bear directly on what we must deal with next, it is here reproduced in full, in hope that the quaintness of the wording will not obscure the quality of the thinking.

Anglican Article 17 Of Predestination and Election

> Predestination to Life is the everlasting purpose of God, whereby, before the foundations of the world were laid, he hath constantly [firmly] decreed by his counsel secret to us, to deliver from curse and damnation those whom he hath chosen in Christ out of mankind, and to bring them by Christ to everlasting salvation, as vessels made to honour. Wherefore, they which be endued with so excellent a benefit of God be called according to God's purpose by his Spirit working in due season; they through Grace obey the calling; they be justified freely; they be made sons of God by adoption; they be made like the image of his only-begotten Son Jesus Christ; they walk religiously in good works; and at length, by God's mercy, they attain to everlasting felicity.

As the godly consideration of Predestination and our Election in Christ is full of sweet, pleasant, and unspeakable comfort to godly persons, and such as feel in themselves the working of the Spirit of Christ, mortifying the works of the flesh and their earthly members, and drawing up their mind to high and heavenly things, as well because it doth greatly establish and confirm their faith of eternal Salvation to be enjoyed through Christ, as because it doth fervently kindle their love towards God: So, for curious and carnal persons, lacking the Spirit of Christ, to have continually before their eyes the sentence of God's predestination [i.e., the thought of it] is a most dangerous downfall, whereby the Devil doth thrust them either into desperation or into wretchlessness [recklessness] of most unclean living no less perilous than desperation.

Furthermore, we must receive God's promises in such wise as they be generally set forth to us in holy Scripture; and, in our doings that Will of God is to be followed which we have expressly declared unto us in the Word of God.

Calvinism, like Arminianism, is a word that means somewhat different things to different people. The present chapter has its place in an anti-Arminian symposium to which writers from various Christian traditions have contributed. I should like to observe here that the essence of my Calvinism, so-called (I do not refuse the label), is found in Anglican Article 17.

Knowing God's Love: The Biblical Witness

The love of God is a great and wide-ranging biblical theme on which one could dilate at length, but for our purposes the scriptural testimony may be summarized as follows.

God's love is spoken of by means of a varied and overlapping vocabulary. Goodness (glorious generosity), love itself (generous goodness in active expression), mercy (generous goodness relieving the needy), grace (mercy contrary to merit and despite demerit), and loving-kindness (KJV) or steadfast love (RSV) (generous goodness in covenantal faithfulness) are the main terms used. The often-echoed self-description whereby God expounds his name (Yahweh, the LORD) to Moses on Sinai crystallizes these ideas: 'The LORD, the LORD, the compassionate and gracious God, slow to anger, abounding in love and faithfulness, maintaining love to thousands, and forgiving wickedness, rebellion and sin.' [3] The New Testament gauges divine *agape* by the staggering gift of God's Son to suffer for mankind's salvation, [4] and thus deepens all these ideas beyond what Old Testament minds could conceive.

[3] Exod. 34:6–7.
[4] cf. Rom. 5:7–8.

God's love is revealed in his providential care for the creatures he made. 'The LORD is good to all; he has compassion on all he has made. . . . The eyes of all look to you, and you give them their food at the proper time. You open your hand and satisfy the desires of every living thing.'[5]

God's love is revealed in the universal invitations of the gospel, whereby sinful humans are invited to turn in faith and repentance to the living Christ who died for sins and are promised pardon and life if they do. 'God so loved the world that he gave his one and only Son, that whoever believes in him shall not perish but have eternal life.'[6] 'God is love (*agape*). This is how God showed his love among us: He sent his one and only Son into the world that we might live through him. This is love: not that we loved God, but that he loved us and sent his Son as an atoning sacrifice for our sins.'[7] And God in the gospel expresses a bona fide wish that all may hear, and that all who hear may believe and be saved.[8] This is love in active expression.

God's love is revealed when 'because of his great love for us'[9] he brings the spiritually dead to life in Christ and with Christ under the ministry of the gospel,[10] uniting us to Christ in co-resurrection for everlasting life and joy.[11] 'Dead' evidently signifies total unresponsiveness to God, total unawareness of his love, and total lack of the life he gives: no metaphor for spiritual inability and destitution could be stronger. What Paul speaks of here is the work of grace that elsewhere he describes as God 'calling' – that is, actually bringing unbelievers to faith by his Spirit so that they respond to the invitation given and trust in Christ to save them, 'Those he called, he also justified'[12] – and no one is justified who has not come to faith.[13] Other New Testament passages designate this same work of grace, whereby God makes us Christians, as new creation,[14] and as regeneration or new birth.[15] No declarations that we do not become Christians without creative prevenient grace could be clearer. Passages like John 6:37–39; 17:2, 6, 9, 24; Romans 8:29; Ephesians 1:3–12;

---

[5] Ps. 145:9, 15–16; cf. Ps. 104:21; Matt. 5:45; 6:26; Acts 14:17.

[6] John 3:16; cf. Rom. 10:11–13; Rev. 22:17.

[7] 1 John 4:8–10.

[8] 1 Tim. 2:3–6; cf. 4:9–10.

[9] 1 John 4:8.

[10] Eph. 2:1, 4–5.

[11] vv.6–7.

[12] Rom. 8:30.

[13] For further instances of this Pauline usage see Rom. 9:24; 1 Cor. 1:9, 26; Gal. 1:15; 1 Thess. 2:12; 2 Thess. 2:14; 2 Tim. 1:9.

[14] 2 Cor. 5:17; Gal. 6:15.

[15] John 1:12–13; 3:3–8; Tit. 3:5; James 1:18; 1 Pet. 1:23; 1 John 2:28; 3:9; 4:7; 5:1, 4.

2 Thessalonians 2:13 show that this grace is given according to a pretem –
poral divine plan, whereby its present recipients were chosen as sinners
to be saved.

So it appears, first, that God loves all in some ways (everyone whom
he creates, sinners though they are, receives many undeserved good gifts
in daily providence), and, second, that he loves some in all ways (that is,
in addition to the gifts of daily providence he brings them to faith, to new
life, and to glory according to his predestinating purpose). This is the clear
witness of the entire Bible.

Knowing God's Love: The Theological Models

The Reformation was an Augustinian revival. Its great discovery, the
doctrine of justification by faith, was fitted into a robust Augustinian and
Pauline doctrine of grace, according to which fallen humans are totally
unable to respond in repentance, faith, and love to God, until prevenient
grace – that is, the regenerating Holy Spirit – inwardly renews them. That
is, God 'calls' them in Paul's special sense of the word. The doctrine that
the God who calls thereby shows love to the called that goes beyond the
love he shows to others, and that this love is gratuitous and as such
amazing, being the opposite of what they deserved, was taken in stride.
But such teaching is strong meat, too strong for some stomachs, and as in
Augustine's day it produced the reaction of semi-Pelagianism, so in the
late sixteenth century it produced the reaction of Arminianism, an
adjustment of the Calvinist thesis about God's saving love and man's moral
responsibility. Our next task is to compare these two models of the saving
love of God.

Historically, Arminianism has affirmed, in the words of W. R. Bagnall,
'conditional in opposition to absolute predestination, and general in
opposition to particular redemption.'[16] This verbal antithesis is not in fact
as simple or as clear as it sounds, for changing the adjective involves
redefining the noun. What Bagnall should have said is that Calvinism
affirms a predestination from which conditionality is excluded and a
redemption to which particularity is essential, and Arminianism denies
both. To Calvinism predestination is essentially God's unconditional
decision about the destiny of individual sinners; to Arminianism it is
essentially God's unconditional decision to provide means of grace to
sinners, decisions about individuals' destiny being secondary and conse –
quent upon foresight (or as Clark H. Pinnock, who denies God's
foresight, would presumably say, discovery) of what use they make of
those means of grace. To mainstream Calvinism, predestination of persons

---

[16] W. R. Bagnall, in *Writings of Arminius*, trans. James Nichols and W. R. Bagnall
(Grand Rapids: Baker, 1956), I.3.

means the foreordaining of both their doings, including their response to the gospel, and their consequent destinies; to mainstream Arminianism, it means a foreordaining of destinies based on doings foreseen or discerned but not foreordained. Arminianism affirms that God predestined Christ to be the world's Saviour, and repentance and faith to be the way of salvation, and the gift of universal sufficient grace to make saving response to Christ possible for everyone everywhere, but denies that any person is predestined to believe.

On the generic Calvinist view, election, which is a predestinating act on God's part, means the sovereign choice of particular sinners to be saved by Jesus Christ through faith, and redemption, the first step in working out God's predestining purpose, is an achievement that actually guarantees salvation – calling, pardon, adoption, preservation, final glory – for all the elect. In the generic Arminian view, however, what the death of Christ secured was a possibility of salvation for sinners generally, a possibility that, so far as God is concerned, might never have been actualized in a single case; and the electing of individuals to salvation is God noting in advance who will believe and so qualify for glory, as a matter of contingent (not foreordained) fact. Whereas to Calvinism election is God's resolve to save, for Arminianism salvation rests neither on God's election nor on Christ's cross, but on each person's own co-operation with grace, which is something that God does not himself guarantee.

Biblically, the difference between these two conceptions of how God in love relates to fallen human beings may be pinpointed thus. Armini - anism characteristically treats our Lord's parable of the supper to which further guests were invited in place of those who never came [17] as picturing the whole truth about the love of God in the gospel. On this view, when you have compared God's relation to fallen humans with that of a dignitary who urges needy folk to come and enjoy his bounty, you have said it all. Calvinism, however, does not stop here, but characteristically links the picture of the supper with that of the Shepherd [18] who has his sheep given to him to care for, [19] who lays down his life for them, [20] and who guarantees that all of them will hear his voice, follow him, [21] and be kept by him from perishing forever. [22] In other words, Calvinism holds that divine love does not stop short at graciously inviting, but that the triune God takes gracious action to ensure that the elect respond. On this view, both the Christ who saves and the faith that embraces him as Saviour are God's gifts, and the latter is as much a foreordained reality as is the

---

[17] Luke 14:16–24; cf. Matt. 22:1–10.

[18] John 10:11–18, 24–29.

[19] vv.14, 16, 27; cf. 6:37–40.

[20] John 10:15.

[21] vv.16, 27.

[22] v.28.

former. Arminians praise God for his love in providing a Saviour to whom all may come to find life; Calvinists do that too, and then go on to praise God for actually bringing them to the Saviour's feet.

So the basic difference between the two positions is not, as is sometimes thought, that Arminianism follows Scripture while Calvinism follows logic, nor that Arminianism knows the compassionate love of God while Calvinists know only his sovereign power; nor that Armini - anism affirms a connection between persevering in faith and obedience as a means and reaching heaven as an end that Calvinism's 'once saved – always saved' slogan actually denies; nor that Arminianism discerns a bona fide free offer of Christ in the gospel that Calvinism fails to discern and take seriously; nor that Arminianism acknowledges human moral respon - sibility before God while Calvinism reduces our race to robots. No, the difference is this: that Calvinism recognizes a dimension of the saving love of God against which Arminianism has reacted and which it now denies, namely, God's sovereignty in bringing to faith and keeping in faith all those who are actually saved. Arminianism gives Christians much to thank God for, but Calvinism gives them more.

Arminians appear in public as persons supremely concerned to do justice to the love of God, the glory of Christ, the moral responsibility of man, and the call to Christian holiness. The reason why they maintain universal redemption; human ability, whether by nature or by grace, for independent response to the gospel; and the conditional character of election is that they think these assertions necessary as means to their avowed end. What they rarely see is that in all this they are not affirming what Calvinism denies so much as denying what Calvinism affirms. Everyone in the Reformed mainstream will insist that Christ the Saviour is freely offered – indeed, freely offers himself – to sinners in and through the gospel; and that since God gives us all free agency (that is, voluntary decision-making power) we are indeed answerable to him for what we do, first, about universal general revelation, and then about the law and the gospel when and as these are presented to us; and that only those who persevere in their Christian pilgrimage ever reach the heavenly city. But Calvinism at the same time affirms the total perversity, depravity, and inability of fallen human beings, which results in them naturally and continually using their free agency to say no to God, and the absolute sovereignty of the regenerating God who effectually calls and draws them into newness of life in Christ. Calvinism magnifies the Augustinian principle that God himself graciously gives all that in the gospel he requires and commands, and the reactive rationalism of Arminianism in all its forms denies this to a degree. The Arminian idea is simpler, for it does not involve so full or radical an acknowledgement of the mystery of God's ways, and it assimilates God more closely to the image of man, making him appear like a gentle giant who is also a great persuader and a resourceful maneuverer, although he is sometimes frustrated and disappointed. But if the measure of love is what it really gives to the really needy and undeserving, then the love of God as Calvinists know it is a much greater thing than the Arminians imagine, and is much diminished by the Arminian model of God and his ways with mankind.[23]

Knowing God's Love: The Nature and the Extent of the Atonement

That the atoning death of Jesus Christ is the supreme achievement and demonstration of God's love is Christian common ground, on which both Calvinists and Arminians take their stand. Disagreement begins, however, when the cross is fitted into the larger theological frame that each embraces. The Reformed way, as marked out by Luther and Calvin (who, be it said, not all Calvinists think spoke the last word about the cross), was to celebrate the atonement in an inclusive rhetoric that aimed to highlight the availability to all of pardon through Calvary, and the sufficiency of Christ's blood to cleanse the foulest from sin. The Reform - ers then highlighted the particularity of God's love to his elect in their treatment of the calling, justifying, preserving, and glorifying of Chris - tians. As we have already seen that both the universal availability of Christ and his benefits and the particularity of effectual calling are set forth in Scripture as expressions of God's love, the Reformers cannot at this point be seriously faulted. Later, however, when Lutheran and Arminian revisionists began to turn the apparent universality of the atonement against the idea of personal salvation as a fruit of God's sovereign election, Reformed theologians searched the Scriptures again; and, facing the view that Christ died for everyone equally, thus making salvation possible for all though guaranteeing it for none, they focused the question that Louis Berkhof with his unfailing pedestrian clarity states in the following way:

> The question . . . is not (a) whether the satisfaction rendered by Christ was in itself sufficient for the salvation of all men, since this is admitted by all; (b) whether the saving benefits are actually applied to every man, for the great majority of those who teach a universal atonement do not believe that all are actually saved; (c) whether the *bona fide* offer of salvation is made to all who hear the gospel, on the condition of repentance and faith, since the Reformed Church does not call this in question; nor (d) whether any of the fruits of the death of Christ accrue to the benefit of the non-elect in virtue of their close

---

[23] Some of the material in this paragraph is adapted from J. I. Packer, 'Armini-anisms,' in *Through Christ's Word: A Festschrift for Dr. Philip E. Hughes* , ed. W. Robert Godfrey and Jesse L. Boyd (Phillipsburg, N.J.: Presbyterian and Reformed, 1985) pp. 121–48. (Reprinted in Vol. 4 of this collection.)

association with the people of God, since this is explicitly taught by many Reformed scholars. On the other hand, the question does relate to the design of the atonement. Did the Father in sending Christ, and did Christ in coming into the world, to make atonement for sin, *do this with the design or for the purpose of saving only the elect or all men?*[24]

And their answer, in brief, was that Scripture, when searched, shows clearly enough that Christ died at the Father's will with the specific purpose of saving the elect.

John Owen's *The Death of Death in the Death of Christ* (Latin title, *Sanguis Jesu Salus Electorum*, the blood of Jesus the salvation of the elect), a polemical work published in 1648,[25] seems to show conclusively that biblical statements about the cross, viewed in context, are characteristically particularist. Christ is said to have died for his sheep,[26] his church,[27] God's elect,[28] 'many'[29], his own people,[30] 'us' who now believe,[31] and among them 'me';[32] and the language of Christ 'dying for' others (*hyper* or *anti* in the Greek) proves on examination regularly to imply that those others are or will be saved. The atonement thus appears as an effective propitiatory transaction that actually redeemed – that is, secured redemption for – those particular persons for whom Jesus on the cross became the God-appointed substitute.[33] Since the Bible rules out all thought of universal salvation, yet depicts the cross as effective for the salvation of those for whom it was endured, 'particular' or 'definite' redemption must be the true concept. Sometimes, for the sake of the T–U–L–I–P acronym,[34] Calvinists have spoken of limited atonement, but Roger Nicole counsels against this.

> The language of limited atonement describes inadequately and unfairly the view which is held by Reformed people. The problem is that it seems to place emphasis upon limits. It seems to take away from the beauty, glory and fullness of the work of Christ. We seem to say that it does not go quite as far as it

---

[24] Louis Berkhof, *Systematic Theology*, 4th ed. (Grand Rapids: Eerdmans, 1949) pp. 393–94.

[25] John Owen, *Works* (Edinburgh: Banner of Truth, 1967), X. 193–28.

[26] John 10:11, 15.

[27] Eph. 5:25.

[28] Rom. 8:32–35.

[29] Matt. 20:28.

[30] Matt. 1:21.

[31] Tit. 2:14, etc.

[32] Gal. 2:20.

[33] cf. Gal. 3:13; Eph. 1:7; Col. 2:14.

[34] T(otal Depravity) – U(nconditional election) – L(imited atonement) – I(rresistible grace) – P(erseverance of the saints). It works only in English.

could or should go . . . what we need to say is that the atonement is definite, that it is related to a particular people whom God has chosen. This helps us psychologically. Because if you say, 'I believe in limited atonement,' the one who disagrees with you will say, 'I believe in *unlimited* atonement.' He appears to be the one who exalts the greatness of the grace of Christ . . . Why put ourselves at a disadvantage? On that account, I will gladly send the tulips flying! You see, I am not Dutch; I am Swiss, and I do not care so much about the tulips. I do not care about acronyms. I care about the precious faith of the Reformed church . . . and I do not think that 'limited atonement' represents me. I want to say 'definite atonement' or 'particular redemption,' and I would encourage other people to do so also.[35]

Surely this is wise advice. I wish I had taken it earlier in life.

In 1959 I wrote a longish introduction to a reprint of Owen's treatise, as a kind of hors d'oeuvres to the study of the work itself. Though the essay was not originally intended to be read apart from Owen, I let it be reprinted as a separate pamphlet, and eventually reprinted it separately myself as a chapter in *A Quest for Godliness*.[36] (When you can't beat 'em, join 'em.) Terry Miethe, discussing it,[37] evidently did not think it necessary to read Owen's treatise, where the actual argumentation is contained, and faulted me for outlining in my introduction assertions about Calvinism that it would take a book or two to make good.[38] Miethe's whole discussion is unsatisfying; he regularly confuses his readers by not distinguishing his own idea of divine sovereignty and election, and of human freedom, from that of Calvinists generally and myself in particular; he fails to engage with the best exponents of the position he controverts; he presents arguments inexactly; he writes constantly as if what is at issue is the availability of Christ to all who turn to him, something that was never in dispute; he treats echoes of biblical phrase - ology in sixteenth-century Anglican formularies as the Church of England

---

[35] Roger Nicole, 'Particular Redemption,' in *Our Saviour God*, ed. James Montgomery Boice (Grand Rapids: Baker, 1980) pp. 168–69.

[36] (Wheaton: Crossway, 1990) pp. 125–48.

[37] Terry Miethe, 'The Universal Power of the Atonement,' in *The Grace of God, the Will of Man: A Case for Arminianism*, ed. Clark H. Pinnock (Grand Rapids: Zondervan, 1989) pp. 71–96. 'I was asked by my editor and publisher to "address" Packer's introduction,' p. 95, note 44.

[38] Ibid., pp. 87–88. 'This is a clear example of a simple assertion, which in logic amounts to nothing more than the fallacy of *petitio principii* (begging the question).' The same might with equal justice, or injustice, be said of Miethe's own statement. Miethe adduces a professional logician, Irving M. Copi, to explain what begging the question means (see p. 95, note 43). From the Copi quote it is clear that when no inferential argument is being attempted, as in the Packer passage that Miethe is discussing, no question is or can be begged.

taking sides in a seventeenth-century debate; and he claims to be defend –
ing the view that 'the redemptive events in the life of Jesus provided a
salvation so extensive and so broad as to potentially include the whole of
humanity past, present and future!'[39] But he never tells us how this
salvation might reach humanity past, or persons who do not encounter
the gospel in the present. Again, he writes: 'Man's natural inability to
believe (it has been shown) is not taught, at least in Ephesians 2:8 [who
ever thought it was?], and (I would argue) not in the rest of Scripture
either'[40] – which makes one wonder how he would handle John 6:43–44;
Romans 8:7–8; and 1 Corinthians 2:14. Understanding is not advanced
by such discussions.

Knowing God's Love: Gratitude and Joy

We have seen that the measure of *agape* is its giving, and that our holy
sovereign triune self-revealed Creator-God shows *agape* to all his rational
creatures in some ways and to some in all ways; that is, not only in
providential provision but also saving them from sin for eternal glory. We
have seen that there is a gospel addressed to all, which the church is charged
to take to all, that proclaims a Saviour who is there for all in the power of
his atoning death and risen life; and we have seen that through this gospel
a pattern of sovereign grace in effectual calling, justification, sanctification,
and glorification is being worked out in life after life. We may now say that
to know that nothing ever 'will be able to separate us from the love of God
that is in Christ Jesus our Lord'[41] is the height of Christian assurance, and
to that 'to know this love that surpasses knowledge – that you may be filled
to the measure of all the fullness of God'[42] is the acme of Christian progress,
and that these are the twin peaks of true Christian living in this world.

In all the Christian's knowledge of God's gracious giving Luther's *pro
me* – the 'for me' of Galatians 2:20 – is central. To know that from eternity
my Maker, foreseeing my sin, foreloved me and resolved to save me,
though it would be at the cost of Cavalry; to know that the divine Son
was appointed from eternity to be my Saviour, and that in love he became
man for me and died for me and now lives to intercede for me and will
one day come in person to take me home; to know that the Lord 'who
loved me and gave himself for me'[43] and who 'came and preached peace'

---

[39] Ibid., p. 72; quoting from Donald Lake, 'He Died for All: The Universal
Dimensions of the Atonement,' in *Grace Unlimited*, ed. Clark H. Pinnock
(Minneapolis: Bethany Fellowship 1975) p. 31.

[40] Ibid., p. 86.

[41] Rom. 8:39.

[42] Eph. 3:18–19.

[43] Gal. 2:20.

to me through his messengers[44] has by his Spirit raised me from spiritual death to life-giving union and communion with himself, and has prom - ised to hold me fast and never let me go – this is knowledge that brings overwhelming gratitude and joy. As Luther himself put it in his answer to Erasmus, 'now that God has taken my salvation out of the control of my own will, and put it under the control of His, and promised to save me, not according to my working or running, but according to his own grace and mercy, I have the comfortable certainty that he is faithful and will not lie to me, and that He is also great and powerful, so that no devils or opposition can break Him or pluck me from Him. "No one," He says, "shall pluck them out of my hand, because my Father which gave them to me is greater than all."[45] Thus it is that, if not all, yet some, indeed many, are saved. . . . Furthermore, I have the comfortable certainty that I please God, not by reason of the merit of my works, but by reason of His merciful favour promised to me; so that, if I work too little, or badly, He does not impute it to me, but with fatherly compassion pardons me and makes me better. This is the glorying of all the saints in their God.'[46] Such glorying is in truth mainstream biblical Christianity – an immeas - urably richer reality than can ever emerge from any account of the love of God that stops short at general goodwill and that drops the personal, individualizing *pro me* of sovereign grace.

'Thank God for his gift that is too wonderful for words!'[47] May all God's people come to appreciate it! In heaven we all most certainly will, and it is a sad thing that any in this world should take up with a theology that in any measure deprives them of this cognitive foretaste of heaven here and now. I pray that our loving God will show the full glory of his love, in its particularity as well as its universality, to us all.

---

[44] Eph. 2:17.

[45] John 10:28–29.

[46] Martin Luther, *The Bondage of the Will*, trans. J. I. Packer and O. R. Johnston (London: James Clarke; Old Tappan, N.J.: Revell, 1957) p. 314.

[47] 2 Cor. 9:15 CEV.

Chapter 12

'Good Pagans' and God's Kingdom

Non-Christians regularly object to the teaching that those who have never heard the gospel may be condemned to hell. Many Christians don't like it either. In fact, universalism – the belief that every one, sooner or later, will be reconciled to God and saved by him – has in this century quietly become part of the orthodoxy of many Christian thinkers and groups. But if all people will eventually be saved, why should they sacrifice to become Christians in this life? Why, indeed, should we endure hardship to evangelize them?

The problem of individual *human destinies* has always pressed hard upon thoughtful Christians who take the Bible seriously, for Scripture affirms these three things:

1.   The *reality* of hell as a state of eternal destructive punishment in which God's judicial retribution for sin is directly experienced.
2.   The *certainty* of hell for all who choose it by rejecting Jesus Christ and his offer of eternal life.
3.   The *justice* of hell as a fit divine infliction upon humanity for our lawless and cruel deeds.

It was, to be sure, hell-deserving sinners whom Jesus came to save, and all who put their trust in him may know themselves forgiven, justified, and accepted forever – and thus delivered from the wrath to come. But what of those who lack this living faith? Those who are not just hypocrites in the church, about whose destiny Christ is very clear, but 'good pagans' who lived before the Incarnation, or who through no fault of their own never heard the Christian message, or who met it only in an incomplete and distorted form? Or what about those who lived in places (modern Albania, for instance) where Christianity was a capital offence, or who suffered from ethno-nationalistic or socio-cultural conditioning against

---

'GOOD PAGANS' AND GOD'S KINGDOM was originally published in *Christianity Today*, January 17, 1986. Reprinted by permission.

the faith, or who were so resentful of Christians for hurting them in one way or another that they were never emotionally free for serious thought about Christian truth? Are they all necessarily lost?

Mixed Answers

To this question Christians have given mixed answers:

- Some have maintained that all unbelievers go to hell because, being sinners like everyone else, they deserve to. The indictment is unanswerable, but is the conclusion inescapable? Not all have thought so.
- A number of Christian thinkers have opened the door a crack – sometimes, indeed, more than a crack – to find a place for 'good pagans' in God's kingdom. The church's earliest defenders of the faith saw Greek philosophy as a God-taught preparation for the gospel among the Gentiles. They affirmed the salvation of Socrates, Plato, and their ilk through faith in the revelation they received of the preincarnate Word. This view still has its defenders.
- Many have urged the hope of universal salvation of infants through Christ's cross – moving on from Augustine's and Dante's idea that unbaptized children who died would miss heaven but would be spared the pains of hell.
- The official Roman Catholic view was that there is no salvation outside the Roman communion and apart from its sacramental life. But the Council of Trent's statement that believers in the truth who, for whatever reason, cannot be baptized may yet be saved through 'baptism of desire' (i.e., desire for baptism) has been further developed by Vatican II:

> Those who, while guiltlessly ignorant of Christ's gospel and of his Church, sincerely seek God and are brought by the influence of grace to perform his will as known by the dictates of conscience, can achieve eternal salvation.

The phrase 'guiltlessly ignorant' points to ignorance that is invincible – that is, dominant and incurable, yet due wholly to conditioning, not to negligence or ill will or any intention, direct or remote, to disobey God. This notion was originally devised to explain how Protestants could be saved. But it is now used to affirm the possibility of salvation in any religion.[1]

---

[1] One Protestant thinker hospitable to this idea was C. S. Lewis. In *The Last Battle*, Aslan says he views as offered to himself all service sincerely rendered to the false god Tash. Some Catholic theologians base their confidence of universal salvation on this line of thought.

- Among Protestants, some Arminians hold that grace sufficient for salvation is given to everyone without exception, those who do not hear the gospel no less than those who do, so that everyone's salvation is in principle possible.
- Some Calvinists have guessed that God regenerates a certain number of unevangelized adults, bringing them to repentance and faith through general revelation alone.
- More recently, Karl Barth taught that in Christ crucified, all human - kind was reprobated and condemned, and in Christ risen, all humankind is elected and justified. This has given a great fillip to explicit universalism – a conclusion that Barth himself seems to have avoided only by will power.[2]

Pressure Points

The problem of the nonbeliever's destiny is acutely felt at present in the Western churches. There are at least three reasons for this:

Pastorally, pressure is felt because post-Christian pluralism and anti-Christian alternatives are always on our doorstep. We rub shoulders with people of other, ethnic faiths; with people who are 'into' cults; with disillusioned ex-Christians; with hostile scientific humanists.

In the mainline churches we find a Pandora's box full of mutated, not to say mutilated, Christianities: products of liberal randomness and radical reaction, of hermeneutical indiscipline, and sometimes, one fears, of sheer incompetence. Among evangelicals there remains something of a con - sensus on essentials, but evangelicals seem to be a quarter or less of the professing Christians in America and the Commonwealth, and outside evangelical circles one hears little more than what Eeyore called a 'confused noise.' How much of the faith of the Scriptures, we wonder, do those nurtured amid the confusion ever come to know?

Nor is this all. The public media, the national education systems, and the literary establishments are resolutely secular, which means that men, women, and children – especially children – are being powerfully conditioned against biblical Christianity. What should we say of the non-belief found among the victims of this ideological juggernaut? They did not create the secular ideology. It created them, moulding them to its own sub-Christian shape.

To generous Christian hearts it seems nightmarish that unbelief resulting from the collapse of Christian culture round a person's head

---

[2] Not all theologians, however, are as strong-willed as Barth. In much of today's Protestantism, belief in universal salvation, as the fruit and measure of Christ's redemptive victory, has become the standard view.

could ruin that person's soul. The problem presses. What does the Bible say?

Theologically, pressure is felt because Christianity faces an upsurge of Islam and other great ethnic religions – all of which resent and reject Christianity's exclusive claim to be final truth from God for all humanity. As the world's population explodes, the percentage of our race that gives allegiance to Christianity keeps shrinking. This not only makes trium - phalism impossible, but it also makes the universal significance of Jesus Christ seem problematical to many.

One response is the claim that Christ may be perceived, or posited, in existing ethnic faiths. In other words, these faiths should be understood as being already in essence what Christianity itself is. This solves the problem of relating Christianity to other faiths by the device of deft definition. But it flies in the face of the fact that the closer one looks at ethnic religions, the more different from Christianity, both in ends proposed and in means to them, they are found to be. It leaves us with a new set of questions:

Should ordinary adherents of ethnic religions (who deny the Trinity, the Incarnation, the Atonement, and salvation by grace through faith whenever these tenets are put to them) be counted as 'anonymous Christians'? Though they may be invincibly and therefore excusably ignorant, can we say that they are thus (because of their sincerity) being saved by the Christ whom, if they have heard of him at all, they reject? If so, why evangelize them? What is the point of asking anyone to change religions, if all religions are at bottom Christianity in disguise?

What does a Hindu or Muslim gain by becoming a Christian? Nothing, it seems, that they really did not have before. But shall we then discount the testimony of Hindu and Muslim converts that their conver - sion was a passage from death to life? Shall we conclude that the old liberal and theosophic notion of all religions climbing the same mountain and meeting at the top is true after all? The questions press. Again we ask, what does the Bible say?

Strategically, pressure is felt because Protestantism is radically split about mission. *Mission* is shorthand for the task that the church is sent into the world to do in Christ's name, for love of God and neighbour. Two views clash as to what mission involves:

One view stands in line with the patristic, counter-Reformation Roman Catholic, and last-century Protestant missionary movements. It urges that the mandate is, first, to evangelize and plant churches; second, to relieve need at all levels, giving visibility and credibility to the good news of the Saviour who makes us care for others; and third, to Christianize pagan cultures.

The view of some moderns, however, defines the mission as, first, to seek justice, peace, and prosperity in communities where these are lacking; second, to engage in dialogue with non-Christian religions in order to understand them and show them respect; and third, to nurture Christians and extend the church if time and circumstances permit – which, it is acknowledged, they may not.

The first view has now the Lausanne Covenant as its charter. The second reflects what was put forward by the WCC sponsored conference at Bangkok on Salvation Today. Which set of priorities is right? What does the Bible say?

Ultimate Optimism

Subordinating evangelism to socio-political concerns makes sense only if universalism is true. The universalist idea that all people will eventually be saved by grace is a comforting belief. It relieves anxiety about the destiny of pagans, atheists, devotees of non-Christian religions, victims of post-Christian secularity – the millions of adults who never hear the gospel and the millions of children who die before they can understand it. All sensitive Christians would like to embrace universalism; it would get us off a very painful hook. Let us see what can be said in its favour.

Modern universalism's basic idea is not that no one deserves to be damned, but that everyone will eventually be brought in humble gratitude to accept the acceptance with God that Christ's redemptive death won for them. Though hell is real, it will ultimately have no tenants.

Roman Catholic universalists hold that man's natural inclination toward goodness and God continues despite the Fall. It is sustained by universal grace and constitutes implicit faith – an openness to God through which Christ and his salvation will in due course, here or hereafter, be received even by Judas (a good test case by which to measure universalist reasoning).

Protestant universalists often say explicitly that those who leave this world in unbelief enter hell, but then exit, having been brought to their senses, encountered Christ, and embraced him while there. The essential claim is that hell does for the faithless what the Roman Catholic purgatory does for believers: it fits them for the enjoyment of heaven.

Universalism is the ultimate optimism, of grace, outstripping any form of mainstream Protestantism, Calvinist or Arminian. For universalists, hell is never the ultimate state. It is a stage on the journey home. Through post-mortem encounter with Christ (a second chance for some, a first chance for others). God sovereignly calls and saves everyone out of what the New Testament calls 'eternal punishment' and 'eternal destruction.' [3] No one is finally lost. Hell ends up empty.

---

[3] Matt. 25:46; 2 Thess. 1:9, where *destruction* certainly means, not annihilation, but a state of conscious ruin.

Counter-Arguments

How is this view of hell's empty landscape supported? No biblical passage unambiguously asserts universal final salvation. Universalism is in fact a logical speculation that discounts the evident meaning of some New Testament passages in favour of what is claimed to be the overall thrust of New Testament thinking: that God's retributive justice toward men is always a disciplinary expression of redeeming love.

It would be nice to believe that, but Scripture nowhere suggests it when speaking of divine judgement, and the counter-arguments seem overwhelmingly cogent:

1. Does not universalism ignore the constant biblical stress on the *decisiveness* and *finality* of this life's decisions for the determining of eternal destiny? Can this emphasis be evaded? Surely not.

2. Does not universalism condemn Christ himself, who warned men to flee hell at all costs, as having been either *incompetent* (ignorant that all were finally going to be saved) or *immoral* (knowing but concealing it, so as to bluff people into the kingdom through fear)? Can this dilemma be overcome? Surely not.

3. Does not the universalist idea of sovereign grace saving all non-believers after death raise new problems? If God's ability to bring all humans to faith eventually is posited, why would he not do it in this life in every case where the gospel is known? But if it is beyond God's power to convert all who know the gospel here, on what grounds can we be sure that he will be able to do it hereafter? Can any universalist's doctrine of God be made fully coherent? Surely not.

4. Does not the thoughtful Christian conscience reject universalism, just because one cannot apply it to oneself? 'I dare not say to myself that if I forfeit the opportunity this life affords I shall ever have another; and therefore I dare not say so to another man,' wrote James Denney. Is there any way around this? Surely not.

Universalism, therefore, will not work. This life's decisions must be deemed to be in every case decisive. And thus, proclaiming the gospel to our fallen, guilty, and hell-bent fellows must be the first service we owe them in light of their first and basic need. The proclamation must have the priority that the older, the historic catholic, mission strategy gave it. 'I am under obligation both to Greeks and to barbarians . . . to preach the gospel,' wrote Paul.

> For 'every one who calls upon the name of the Lord will be saved.' But how are men to call upon him . . . of whom they have never heard? . . . Faith comes from what is heard, and what is heard comes by the preaching of Christ.[4]

---

[4] Rom. 1:14–15; 10:13–14, 17, citing Joel 2:32.

Light for All

But could God, in particular cases, work with and through the light of general revelation – light that comes to every human being – to evoke repentance and faith, and thus to bring about the salvation of some to whom no verbal message about God forgiving sins has ever come?

The question is prompted by Peter's statement: 'In every nation anyone who fears him and does right is acceptable.'[5] It is supported by Paul's assertion: '[God] did not leave himself without witness.'[6] Add to that his strong declaration of general revelation from God to all mankind in Romans 1:18–2:16.

Consider the acknowledgement and worship of Israel's God by Melchizedek, Jethro, Job, Abimelech, Baalam, Naaman, the sailors in Jonah's boat, Cyrus, and Nebuchadnezzar. Compare John's description of the preincarnate Word as "the true light that enlightens every man'[7] with his analysis of the sinner's judgment as flight from the light, while 'he who does what is true comes to the light.'[8] That God will judge us all according to what we have done with the light we were given, and that this is supremely just on his part, I take for granted.

In *Christianity and World Religions*, Sir Norman Anderson states the question as it relates to non-Christian worshippers: 'Might it not be true of the follower of some other religion that the God of all mercy had worked in his heart by his Spirit, bringing him in some measure to realize his sin and need for forgiveness, and enabling him, in his twilight as it were, to throw himself on God's mercy?'

The answer seems to be yes, it might be true, as it may well have been true for at least some of the Old Testament characters. If ever it is true, such worshipers will learn in heaven that they were saved by Christ's death and that their hearts were renewed by the Holy Spirit, and they will join the glorified church in endless praise of the sovereign grace of God. Christians since the second century have hoped so, and perhaps Socrates and Plato are in this happy state even now – who knows?

But we have no warrant to expect that God will act thus in any single case where the gospel is not known or understood. Therefore our missionary obligation is not one whit diminished by our entertaining this possibility. Nor will this idea make the anti-Christian thrust and conse - quent spiritual danger of non-Christian religions seem to us any less than it did before.

---

[5] Acts 10:35.
[6] Acts 14:17.
[7] John 1:9; cf. v.4.
[8] John 3:19–21.

If we are wise, we shall not spend much time mulling over this notion. Our job, after all, is to spread the gospel, not to guess what might happen to those to whom it never comes. Dealing with them is God's business: he is just, and also merciful, and when we learn, as one day we shall, how he has treated them we shall have no cause to complain. Meantime, let us keep before our minds humankind's universal need of forgiveness and new birth, and the graciousness of the 'whosoever will' invitations of the gospel. And let us redouble our efforts to make known the Christ who saves to the uttermost all who come to God by him.

Chapter 13

The Problem of Universalism Today

By universalism I mean the expressed hope, indeed the professed cer -
tainty, that all people, past, present and future, from Adam right up to the
end of time, will be found at the last in the Kingdom and the enjoying
God. It is the doctrine for which the Greek name is *apokatastasis* − 'the
restoration.' It is based upon another sort of universalism about which
there is no dispute, which we will take as our starting point for thinking
about this restoration hope.

   The universalism which we all accept is that set of qualities which
constitute New Testament Christianity a faith for the whole world,
making the universal claim based upon belief in one Creator, one
humanity, one final judgment, and one Redeemer. You remember how
Paul at Athens affirmed the reality of the one God, and the one humanity,
and the one destiny for the whole world, namely, to stand before God to
be judged − 'he has appointed a day in which he will judge the world by
that man whom he has ordained.'

   That sounds ominous, but good news now follows, though Paul was
howled down by the Areopagus before he could deliver it. The universal
Christian claim upon humankind is based on redemption − on the
doctrine, that is, that there is one Saviour of the whole world, and one
atoning transaction in virtue of which forgiveness is freely offered to
everybody. One thinks of Romans 5, the Adam-Christ parallel; one
thinks of, 'God in Christ was reconciling the world to himself,' [1] and of,
'Behold the Lamb of God who takes away the sin of the world.' [2]

   From this the New Testament writers draw the corollary conclusion
that there is in fact only one people of God − the universal Christian
church. The seed of Abraham has become a world-wide community of
Jews and Gentiles who have received Jesus Christ, and become Abraham's
heirs in him. And the Christian claim is that no other faith can stand beside

---

THE PROBLEM OF UNIVERSALISM TODAY was originally a transcribed
address published in *Theolog Review*, Nov. 1969, Vol. 5, No. 3, pp. 16–24.
Reprinted by permission, expanded with further editing.

[1]   2 Cor. 5:19.

[2]   John 1:29.

Christianity: by making an inclusive claim, demanding response from all people in the world, the gospel makes an exclusive claim, insisting that all other faiths must be abandoned in order to worship God as we should and honour Christ as we ought.

'The gospel,' says Paul, 'is the power of God unto salvation to everyone that believes.'[3] There is universalism for you! But to respond to the gospel, means as he said to the Thessalonians, 'to turn from idols to serve the living and true God.' There is a universal mission committed to the church to take the gospel to the ends of the earth. 'Go and make disciples of all nations,' said our Lord.[4] The message preached is the call of God to the whole earth, and by right of both creation and redemption God claims a response from every person to whom the message comes.

Now this sort of universalism which makes Christianity into a world religion is not in dispute; and we take it, as I said, as our starting point. The question for us is whether any of this implies a doctrine of universal salvation, the restoration of literally everyone to the fellowship with God for which Adam was made and from which he fell.

The title of this paper speaks of universalism as a problem today. Why is it specially a problem? There are four reasons:

1. *Universalism is rapidly advancing throughout Protestantism*

This is a new situation. Universalism was first broached by the Alexan - drian theologian Origen; who looked forward to even the devil being saved; and Origen's notion was condemned in the sixth century. That condemnation was thought conclusive throughout Christendom for centuries: universalism was regarded as a condemned eccentricity. In the days of the Reformation, some of the Anabaptists took it up and the reformers repeated the patristic condemnation against them. This is how things were in Protestantism until the 19th century.

Then in the 19th century the status of universalism began to change. The father of German liberalism, Schleiermacher, and many liberals following him, and English divines like the Anglican Andrew Jukes and the Baptist Samuel Cox, the Scotsman Thomas Erskine, and others, began seriously to argue universalism. Poets began to express the univeralist hope in their verses; Browning, Tennyson, Coventry Patmore, and in North America Whittier and Walt Whitman, come to mind as examples.

By the twentieth century universalism had established itself as a respected position, and in our time we see it literally carrying all before it. I think it would be true to say that the majority of theologians and world church strategists active today are at least sympathetic and in many cases actually committed, to universalist teaching. I quote the late Bishop John Robinson:

---

[3] Romans 1:16.
[4] Matt. 28:18.

It is impossible to ignore a consensus of contemporary names such as Nicholas Berdyaer, the Russian Orthodox; William Temple, Anglican; John Baillie, Church of Scotland; C. H. Dodd, Congregationalist; Charles Raven, another Anglican; Herbert Farmer, an English Presbyterian, all of whom have come out more or less in favour of this doctrine.[5]

Robinson's own name can be added to the list; so can the American Nels Ferré, and John Hick, and of the Swiss theologians Michaelis and Karl Barth, who if he did not actually commit himself to universalism, was clearly very sympathetic towards it. Universalism it seems has come to stay. It is going to be advocated throughout our lifetime by very able people. We cannot ignore this. What should we think about it? What are we going to say when challenged by it?

2. The theological claim of universalism is momentous

The claim is that this teaching alone does justice to the love of God and the victory of the Cross and the thrust of the Bible. Whereas, so it is claimed, any belief in the eternal loss, eternal torment, of any of God's rational creatures makes God out to be, at the least, a failure and perhaps even a devil. This kind of thing is constantly affirmed by universalist theologians. It is a tremendously far-reaching claim and one that we cannot disregard. Is this really true? If not, why not?

3. The pastoral implications of universalism are far-reaching

If all people are, in the title of a 19th century tract, 'Doomed to be Saved,' then it follows that the decisiveness of decisions made in this life, and the urgency of evangelism here in this life, immediately, are undermined. Other ways of loving your neighbour here in this life may now be considered as perhaps more important than seeking to win him or her to Christ. And it is no accident that keenness on the social gospel, so-called, and universalist theology have gone hand in hand. As Golthold Müller wrote, 'almost all leading religious socialists have appeared as universalists in their theology.' This is true, from F. D. Maurice – a wishful universalist of the last century to J. A. T. Robinson, who was a thorough-going socialist and a thorough-going universalist throughout his career.

You can see what the missionary implications of this teaching are going to be. What is the main job of Christian missionary witness? To win men to Christian faith? Or to do something else for them? Universalism prompts the latter view.

In evangelical history there have been repeated movements of the Spirit, movements of missionary and evangelistic advance, which have

---

[5] J. A. T. Robinson, *In the End, God* (London, 1950).

had at their heart earnest prayer offered by good Christian souls, in terms of their belief that without Christ, men and women are lost. This is not a question of how they preached; it is a question of how they prayed. Were they right to pray that way? Such prayer was, literally, the powerhouse of the evangelical awakening in the 18th century and of the 19th century missionary movement, and of the passion for worldwide evangelism ever since. Was it off centre? – Uninstructed prayer? – Foolish and stupid prayer? Or did it reflect a true insight into how things were?

4. Its personal appeal is strong

I know that the historic evangelical attitude has been to regard universal - ism with what one book speaks of as 'something akin to hatred.' Evangelicals have said how morally weakening this doctrine is and how spiritually deadening it is. They have equated it with the first lie, the devil's lie in the garden of Eden, 'you shall surely not die.' They have seen it as a modern version of the first piece of armour the devil puts on Mansoul in Bunyan's 'Holy War,' namely, 'the hope of doing well at the last what life soever you have lived.' This is what universalism is in practice, evangelicals have said. It is a deadly thing. It is false hope.

In these days of expanding world population when there are literally millions who have never heard of Christ, and great political forces are now ranged in battle array to ensure that they never will hear of Christ, it is difficult for a person to be glib about a rejection of universalism. We would, all of us, in our hearts, like to be universalists; we find that the doctrine of eternal punishment for some is a very uncomfortable truth to live with and sometimes we find ourselves wishing that it was not there. Many pastors have, I think, succumbed to the temptation to live and preach and act as if it were not there. We ourselves will be exposed to the same temptation. Is it the ostrich temptation? – simply hide our head and not face God's facts? Or might it be that, after all, we may properly in this day and age jettison the doctrine of eternal punishment and take up universalism after all. Will the Bible let us do that?

The Case for Universalism

1. The Biblical Picture

Universalism is a thesis about human destiny argued, at least by its modern exponents, from the Bible itself. Now we know what the Bible has to say about the destiny of the believer. The Bible is very clear and emphatic about the Christian's hope.

'There is now no condemnation to them that are in Christ Jesus.'

'Neither life nor death nor anything in creation can separate us from the love that is in Christ Jesus our Lord.'

'Where I am, there shall my servant be.'

As Richard Baxter wrote long ago:

> My knowledge of that life is small,
> the eye of faith is dim;
> But it's enough that Christ knows all;
> And I shall be with him.

That is the Christian hope in a nutshell.

Our question is about those who go through life and leave this world as unbelievers: those whom Paul describes in Ephesians 2:12 as being 'without God and without hope in the world.' The New Testament seems very clear at first sight about the hopeless condition both in this world and in the world to come.

Remember how in Romans, Paul draws out and dwells on the wretchedness of unbelievers, how they are under the law, obliged to perform God's requirements perfectly, and are exposed to judgement if they break the law; and they are also under sin, so that they lack in themselves the power to keep the law. All people, Jews and Gentiles, says Paul, are under sin,[6] and face God's judgment for their disobedience. This is worked out in Romans 1–2. The principle of judgment is retribution; everyone's track record in relation to God in this life comes back to them as their eternal destiny; fixed and shaped by their own past choices. Such is Paul's point when he says in 2 Cor. 5:10 that at the judgment seat of Christ we 'receive the things done in the body, whether good or evil.'

Now we see the meaning of the wrath of God: it signifies his retributive judgment upon those who have transgressed his law. This means that unbelievers are subjected to death; being under law and under sin, they are inescapably under wrath and under death. Death has reigned, and reigns still, over all people who have live without Christ. 'The wages of sin is death,'[7] and death in the New Testament does not mean annihilation or extinction, but rather what is already means in the Old Testament, separation from that which is essential to your fulfilling your own destiny. Physical death, the separating of oneself from one's body, is a sign of the deeper death – separation from God.

When scripture speaks, as it does, of a *living death*; the thought is not biological, but the thought is of a spiritual relationship that has gone

---

[6] Rom. 3:9.
[7] Rom. 3:23.

wrong. 'And she that liveth in sin is dead while she lives.'[8] (Paul, in the
Pastorals.) 'You were dead in trespasses and sin' – the death in this case is
a broken relationship with God, which means that something essential
for which you were made is missing from you – you are separated from
your own true and complete life. That is death here, and that will be the
essence of death hereafter.

In Romans 8, Paul says 'to be carnally minded is death' (here and
now), and he says 'Then if you live after the flesh you shall die' (that is
in the future).[9] But the essence of death in both texts is the same:
non-relationship with God.

According to Oliver Quick, Regius Professor of Theology at Oxford,[10]
there are two texts which are quite explicit for continued existence in the
experience of retribution beyond this life. The first is Matt. 25:47, at the
end of the parable of the sheep and the goats. The one group, those hailed
as blessed by the Father, go away into eternal life (*zoe aionios*), and the others
go away into *aionios kolasis*, translated in our Bibles 'eternal punishment.'

What does *aionios* mean here? Well, we know that the basic meaning
of *aionios* in the New Testament is, related to the world to come as
contrasted with the present order of things. Thus it stands for fixity and
finality, and so comes to denote endlessness, just because the age to come
is the last age: and thus both the life and the punishment must be held to
be 'eternal' in the old naive sense of 'endlessly-continuous.'

The second text that Quick quotes is the picture text at the end of
Revelation 20:10, 15 which refers to the lake of fire, where the beast and
the false prophet are, and where those who are rejected at the great white
throne of judgement will also be. The torment there goes on for ever and
ever, says the writer of Revelation. The torment presumably is the
knowledge of one's own ill-desert and God's displeasure, and of the good
that one has lost. This is the witness of the New Testament.

This was the doctrine of the synagogue and the apocalyptic writings
in the days of the New Testament and for a century before. It was
endorsed by Jesus Christ throughout his ministry. W. G. T. Shedd, the
last-century Presbyterian divine, says very forthrightly, 'Jesus Christ is the
person who is responsible for the doctrine of eternal perdition.'[11] And you
remember some of the fearsome pictorial language which he used and
which, *prima facie*, is expressing precisely this idea: the weeping and
gnashing of teeth, the outer darkness, the worm not dying and the fire

---

[8] 1 Tim. 5:6.

[9] Rom. 8:6, 13.

[10] O. C. Quick, *The Gospel of the New World* (London: Nisbet, 1944) 116. 'The
strain of anti-unniversalist teaching in the New Testament can hardly be regarded
by an impartial mind as other than conclusive' (p. 115).

[11] W. G. T. Shedd, *Dogmatic Theology* (Edinburgh: T. & T. Clark, 1889), II, p.
680.

not being quenched. His use of the picture of Gehenna, the valley of Hinnom, outside of Jerusalem where rubbish was burned, as a picture of the final destiny of some, and his reference to the great gulf fixed between the places where Dives and Lazarus were, point the same way.

One has to ask, soberly I hope, and reverently, how could the Lord have made the fact of eternal punishment for the impenitent clearer than he did? What more could he have said to make it clear if passages like this do not make it clear? It is, to be sure, a fearful doctrine but it is there in the gospels, and we must take it as seriously as we take any other elements of our Lord's teaching.

It is observable that the New Testament is not in the least troubled about eternal retribution, as if it were. Rather, the insistence all the way through is that the final punishment of the impenitent is right, and is a manifestation of God's glorious justice, and something for which the people of God should praise him. Read the exposition of the principle in Rom. 2:5f., where Paul speaks explicitly of 'the righteous judgement of God'; and the way in which the judgment on Babylon is regarded (in Rev. 18:20 and 19:2) as a matter for which God should be praised. Compare also the Old Testament where saints and Psalmists rejoice at the righteous judgment of God. The source of joy that seems to be uppermost in their mind is the knowledge that God is vindicated, and his righteous - ness has triumphed at last. If we find it hard to identify with, we must ask ourselves why, and where the difficulty comes. Certainly this is the biblical view.

2. The Universalist Response

Now, what does the universalist say in response to all this? There were some in the last century who based their universalist belief on a flat denial of this biblical teaching as some sort of mistake, and substituted in its place the belief that, since the divine character is one of total benevolence, all people would be restored to fellowship with God immediately upon death. But that is not the way in which today's thoughtful universalists put their belief; they put it, rather, in the form of a speculation about what happens after death.

They say that for all those who die out of Christ, there is a second chance. Universalism is one of the many types of 'second chance' speculations. And, say the universalists, hereby setting themselves apart from other exponents of the 'second chance' idea, they are sure that the second chance is going to be accepted in every single case. God's confrontation of the impenitent after death with the issues of the gospel, which either they did not hear or they rejected in this life, is sooner or later going to be successful: there is going to be a universal positive response.

Hell is real, say the universalists, but it is temporary. It is not the ultimate state for anyone, it is only the penultimate state. E. Brunner, expounding this doctrine (he never finally committed himself to it) speaks of hell as 'a pedagogic cleansing process.'[12] Hell in this view is a means of grace: it is a rough place, a place of correction, a place where people come to their senses. It is a kind of purgatory for those whom the Church of Rome would not allow into purgatory.

This is a doctrine of salvation through, and out of, the state which the New Testament refers to in one place as 'perdition,' in another place as 'eternal destruction,' and in another as 'eternal punishment.' It is an unqualified and unlimited optimism of grace. Sin is a reality, hell is a reality: but God's grace is going to triumph in the end!

3. Arguments Justifying This Thesis

The positive arguments put forward fall into two classes: first, exegetical, second, theological. Taking the exegetical argument first, there are, universalists say, three classes of texts in the New Testament which point this way. 1) Those which predict the actual salvation of all people. [13] 2) Those texts announcing God's will to save all people; [14] 3) Those that assert that through the achievement of Christ on the cross God stands here and now in such a relation to all people that salvation must come to them eventually. [15]

Are these texts conclusive as props of the position they are produced to prove? One cannot say so, for the following three reasons. 1) All these texts are juxtaposed with texts in the documents from which they are drawn which refer specifically to the prospect of some perishing through unbelief. And unless we assume that the writers did not know their own minds, we have to conclude that they cannot in the texts quoted, really have meant to affirm universal final salvation. 3) Let us note the fact that there is no Scripture for any form of the second probation theory. You certainly cannot argue it from that mysterious text 1 Peter 3:19, telling us how, quickened in the Spirit, Christ went and preached to the spirits in prison 'who were disobedient in the days of Noah.' Whatever that means, it is a reference to a message taken to a particular, limited group of spirits in prison. And the fact that the group is so limited is a strong argument against there being in Peter's mind any suggestion of a universal publishing of the gospel to people beyond the grave.

The attempt to establish the doctrine of universalism by exegetical means must be held to have failed. As long ago as 1908, Robert Mackintosh, whose position might be regarded as wishful universalism, wrote, 'The question is generally argued as one of New Testament

---

[12] Emil Brunner, *Eternal Hope* (London: Lutterworth Press, 1954) p. 183.

[13] John 12:32; Acts 3:21; Eph. 1:10; Rom. 5:18; Phil. 2:9–11; 1 Cor. 15:22–28.

[14] 2 Peter 3:9; 1 Tim. 2:4.

[15] 2 Cor. 5:19; 1 John 2:2; Heb. 2:9; Titus 2:11; Col. 1:20.

interpretation, but the present writer does not think that hopeful. He sees no ground for challenging the old doctrine on exegetical lines.'[16] And most modern universalists would agree with that. Therefore, they base their universalist speculation on a different foundation.

They seek to present it as an irresistible theological inference from certain things in the New Testament; an inference so irresistible and certain as to warrant our discounting certain other things in the New Testament. It is, in other words, a hermeneutical speculation, bound up with the belief that the Bible is not entirely consistent. Leaving that aside for the moment (though I should want to contest the idea at some point), let us see how they argue this line of thinking in theological terms.

God, they say, is love. This is the real centre of the New Testament revelation; love must have the last word, and love in the Scriptures is sovereign love; therefore the love of God must imply an effective intention to save all his rational creatures. Nels Ferré, the American, expounds this in terms of the old liberal thought of the universal fatherhood of God – 'God has no permanent problem children.'[17]

Bishop Robinson, in his pre-*Honest to God* days, argued that the only way of holding to the New Testament insistence that love is the last word to be spoken of God, is to be quite frank in interpreting what the Scriptures say about his retributive justice as a function of his redeeming love. He rejects the idea that God's loving purpose could triumph if any were lost on the grounds that such thinking 'cannot preserve the absolute identity of divine love and justice.'[18] For Robinson, you have to under-stand God's justice as a function and activity of his love furthering his purpose of love, i.e. correction leading to the response of repentance and the final enjoyment of heaven.

Does the New Testament anywhere lead us to believe that justice and love are identical? I would not have thought so. But Robinson insists on it.

The second line of theological arguing starts from the fact that the cross was a decisive victory. The very essence of the victory, so they say, consists in the fact that the cross effectively saved all humanity. And they understand faith as simply a matter of coming to acknowledge the fact that you were saved; faith is the opening of blind eyes so that people acknowledge what they already are – sinners in a state of salvation and grace.

But, is this the teaching of the New Testament? The New Testament, to me, seems to be saying that no one is actually saved, no one is actually

---

[16] See Hastings' *Dictionary of Christ and the Gospels* (Edinburgh: T. & T. Clark, 1908) II. 785.

[17] Nels Ferré, *The Christian Understanding of God* (London: SCM Press, 1952) p. 229.

[18] J. A. T. Robinson, *In the End, God* (London: James Clarke, 1950) p. 104.

in Christ, until they have actually believed into Christ. This is the doctrine of Eph. 2:12f.: 'Before you came to Christ, you were without hope.' The New Testament seems to be very clear then where there is no actual belief, there is no actual salvation, no state of grace in any sense at all. Compare John 3:16 and 36, which make this very explicit. Likewise, 'Whosoever calls upon the name of the Lord shall be saved,' sounds a very different doctrine from the universalists' awakening to faith. Again, compare Hebrews 10:39: 'We are not of them that draw back, but have faith unto the saving of the same.'

Now there is a positive, cogent and conclusive argument against universalism, which I will strengthen as I close. I simply ask, does not the New Testament actually insist on the decisiveness of this life? What did our Lord mean when He threatened the Jews with the prospect of dying in their sins,[19] as being the ultimate disaster? What did he mean in the parable of Dives and Lazarus where he included the detail about the great gulf fixed between the two men?

What did he mean when he spoke of one group going away into eternal life, and the other group going away into eternal punishment, the judge - ment being passed in each case on the basis of what they had done in this life? What did he mean when he spoke of Judas in this way in Matt. 26:24, '. . . good it were for the man if he had not been born'? Universalism is a doctrine of the salvation of Judas. Could our Lord have used these words if he had expected the salvation of Judas? And what does the rest of the New Testament mean when it speaks in similar terms: Gal. 6:7, Heb. 9:27, etc.? What are we going to make of these passages? And there are many more like them. Are they not pressing upon us the decisiveness of this life?

The conclusion of the matter must be that of James Denney, writing on this subject more than sixty years ago – 'I dare not say to myself that if I forfeit the opportunity this life offers, I shall ever have another, and therefore I dare not say so to another man.'[20] Preachers, can you get around that? It would simply be dishonest to encourage in others a hope I dare not rely on myself.

So I don't find myself able to be a universalist, even though not being one is uncomfortable, and the thought of some being lost troubles and grieves the heart. I find myself obliged to stick to the old view that the choices and decisions of this life are truly decisive, and to evangelize and to preach the gospel in these terms and as an expression of this conviction.

This is where my argument leads me; and these are my reasons for judging that universalist speculation at the present time is a very great evil, calculated to blight a ministry, and as the older evangelicals used to think, 'guaranteed to ruin souls.'

---

[19] John 8:21, 24.

[20] James Denney, *Studies in Theology* (London: Hodder & Stoughton, 1902) p. 244.

Chapter 14

Evangelicals and the Way of Salvation

New Challenges to the Gospel: Universalism and Justification by Faith

I

Whether in this land of pitchers, plates, diamonds and strikes I can make a point by talking of English cricket I do not know. But I am going to try.

Half-way through the afternoon of Monday, July 20, 1981, in Leeds, Yorkshire, England were in trouble. It was the fourth day of the third of six five-day test matches against Australia. The first had been lost, the second drawn, and this, the third, now seemed doomed. The seventh player in England's second innings had just been dismissed with the score at 135; this was still 92 runs behind Australia's first inning total of 401, and only three more English men remained to bat, while Australia had an entire second innings still to come. In cricket the batsmen (whom you may call strikers if you prefer) operate in pairs, and as the new man walked to the wicket, his partner, Ian Botham, who had so far scored 23, went to meet him.

The following dialogue then took place, in the idiom that you might call sportsman's swagger. Botham: 'You don't fancy hanging around on this wicket for a day and a half, do you?' New batsman: 'No way.' Botham: 'Right; come on, let's give it some humpty.' Which they did, hitting the ball all over the field to such good effect that, incredibly, England's score rose to 356, with Botham making 149, before the last man was out. Australia was then dismissed for less than the 129 runs needed to win, and an apparently inevitable defeat had been turned into a famous victory, vividly illustrating the truth that attack is the best form of defence.[1]

EVANGELICALS AND THE WAY OF SALVATION was originally published in *Evangelical Affirmations*, ed. C. F. H. Henry and Kenneth Kantzer (Grand Rapids: Zondervan, 1990), pp. 107–136. Reprinted by permission.

[1] Ian Botham, *The Incredible Tests* (London: Pelham, 1981), p. 65.

I tell you that story so as to tune you in to the fact that, as I see it, the subject area that I have been given requires that, like Botham, I too give it a bit of humpty, and attack. Truths that seem to me vital are threatened, and to reaffirm them effectively I shall have to hit out – not only at non-evangelicals, but at some of my evangelical brothers too. I have no wish to hurt anyone's feelings, but I must take a risk on that, for my judgment is that on matters so grave only forthright statement can be appropriate or adequate. So prepare for strong words.

II

First, I would like to make clear where I come from. I speak out of a heritage that is several centuries old, namely the theological approach that is rooted in the two tenets once singled out by Melanchthon as the foundation-principles of the Reformation.

The first foundation-principle is the formal one, namely the authority of the Scriptures, or, more fully, the sufficiency for all questions of faith, life, and action of the authoritative, God-breathed, self-interpreting biblical canon, which the Holy Spirit opens our minds and enlightens our hearts to understand. The second foundation-principle, the substantial one, is justification by faith only, or more fully, our entire and final acceptance by God, here and now, on Christ's account, through the faith that in self-despair and a sense of guilt, shame, weakness, and spiritual hunger looks to Jesus Christ in conscious trust to worship and serve him as our sin-bearing Saviour. I shall shortly focus attention on the second of these principles, but I see need at the outset to state my methodology in a clear and sharp-edged way, for I think it is a lack of clarity here that produces the erosions of belief elsewhere on which I have to comment.

I begin, then, by affirming, with Reformed theology generally, that acceptance of all that Scripture teaches, and a refusal either to add to it or subtract from it in our thinking about God, and the absolutizing of it as our interpretative framework for understanding everything else, is categorically necessary, for two reasons.

The first reason is that the fallen human mind, biased and warped as it is, more or less, by the universal anti-God syndrome called sin, fails to form and own and retain within itself true notions about the Creator drawn from general revelation, whether in the order and course of the world, our own created makeup, or the workings of natural conscience. God's general revelation of himself, though genuinely given to all, is correctly received by none. Scripture makes this point by speaking of our human minds as *darkened* and *blinded*, and of our hearts as *hardened*.[2]

---

[2] See Romans 1:21; Eph. 4:18.

The second reason is that regenerate believers, to whom the Spirit interprets the Scriptures, are nonetheless still prone to lapse intellectually into the world's ways of thinking, just as sometimes they lapse morally into the world's ways of behaving, and so they need constant critical correction and redirection by the Word of God. The reality of spiritual darkness in all minds was recognized by none of the subjectivist theolo - gians of the Enlightenment and the Romantic movement, whatever spot on the spectrum that links rationalism and mysticism each occupied; and nowadays it is hard to get even evangelicals to take it seriously. But the Bible acting as judge and guide is a cognitive necessity for benighted sinners like ourselves, and evangelicals no less than others must learn to suspect themselves when they find themselves embracing innovations and modifications of view that reflect in a direct way the secular culture around them.

To fall victim to secular philosophy and ideology has been a charac - teristic Protestant vice for three centuries, and it is one from which evangelicals are by no means free. To be an avowed Bible-believer is no guarantee that one's interpretation of the Bible will always be right, or that secularist distortions will never invade one's mind to discolour one's thoughts. We affirm this, pontifically enough, with regard to (for instance) Jehovah's Witnesses; we need humbly to remember that we face the same danger also.

How then may we avoid subjectivist eccentricity in our own biblical interpretation? The first necessity is precision in handling texts. The canon that God in his wisdom gave us is a miscellany of occasional writings, each anchored in a particular socio-cultural milieu and requiring grammatical-historical exegesis.

To discover what each passage meant as a message about God written on his behalf to a particular envisaged readership must be our first step. But then, in order to determine what meaning God has for us in this historical material, we must go on to an *a posteriori* theological analysis and application according to the analogy of Scripture. By theological analysis, I mean seeing what truths about God and his world the passage teaches, or assumes, or illustrates. By theological application, I mean reflecting on how these truths impact our lives today.

When I say that this analysis and application must be *a posteriori*, I mean that nothing must be read into texts that cannot be read out of them. When I say that it must be faithful, I mean that nothing taught by any text may be disregarded or left unapplied. When I speak of the analogy of Scripture, I am referring to the traditional procedures of letting one part of Scripture throw light on another that deals with the same subject, and of maintaining internal theological coherence by interpreting am - biguous passages in harmony with unambiguous ones, and of allowing things that define themselves as primary and central to provide a frame of reference and a perspective for looking at those that are secondary and peripheral.[3]

By observing these principles we may with the help of God's Spirit rise via the teaching of each author in his own situation to perceive the teaching of God himself as it bears on us in our situation. But if we allow ourselves, as so many do, to discount specific teachings of Scripture as being out of line with the Bible's main thrust, or to think it possible that God's penmen did not always manage to express what they intended to say, or to suppose that while God kept them right on major matters he left them free to go wrong on details, we may expect, I think – and here, *pace* Jack Rogers and Donald McKim, I have nearly five centuries of responsible evangelical opinion with me – to be constantly going astray on matters of importance.[4] The instances of relativistic and impressionistic slippage that we shall discuss now might well be cases in point.

---

[3] The idea of the analogy of Scripture assumes that the extent of the biblical canon is fixed and known. In the contemporary context this assumption, which many Protestant liberals query and which Roman Catholics claim presupposes the infallibility of the canonizing church, requires exposition and defence, which is not possible here. Materials which in my judgement make possible a convincing defence of the 66-book Protestant canon as fixed and certain in its God-givenness are contained in Roger Beckwith, *The Old Testament Canon of the New Testament Church* (London: SPCK and Grand Rapids: Eerdmans, 1985); F. F. Bruce, *The Canon of Scripture* (Downers Grove: Inter-Varsity Press, 1988); Bruce Metzger, *The Canon of the New Testament* (Oxford: Clarendon Press, 1987); H. N. Ridderbos, *The Authority of the New Testament Scriptures* (Philadelphia: Presbyterian and Reformed, 1963 2nd rev. ed., *Redemptive History and the New Testament Scriptures*, 1988); Karl Barth, *Church Dogmatics* I.ii. (Edinburgh: T. & T. Clark, 1956), chapter 3, pp. 457–740; G. C. Berkouwer, *Holy Scripture* (Grand Rapids: Eerdmans, 1975), chapter 3, pp. 67–104; A. B. du Toit, 'The Canon of the New Testament,' in *Guide to the New Testament*, vol. 1, ed. A. B. du Toit (Pretoria: N. G. Transvaal, 1979); David G. Dunbar, 'The Biblical Canon,' in *Hermeneutics, Authority, and Canon*, ed. D. A. Carson and John D. Woodbridge (Grand Rapids: Zondervan, 1986), pp. 295–360. See also Lee M. McDonald, *The Formation of the Christian Biblical Canon*, revised edition (Peabody: Hendrickson, 1995).

[4] In the *Authority and Interpretation of the Bible*, (San Francisco: Harper and Row, 1979), Rogers and McKim maintain that authentic, healthy Christian theology has always recognized, implicitly if not explicitly, that God so accommodated himself to the humanity of the Bible writers as to produce for us a Bible that, while functioning as a safe guide for faith and life, contains various sorts of mistakes on matters of factual detail. This thesis in historical theology with its implications for healthy bibliology today and tomorrow is effectively countered by John D. Woodbridge in *Biblical Authority: A Critique of the Rogers-McKim Proposal* (Grand Rapids: Zondervan, 1982).

III

Evangelicals have always seen the question of salvation as one of supreme importance, and their witness to the way of salvation as the most precious gift they bring to the rest of the church. This conviction rests not on the memory of the conversion of Paul or Augustine or Luther or Wesley or Whitefield or any other evangelical hero, but on the emphasis with which the Bible itself highlights salvation as its central theme. The Scriptures – or perhaps I should say, preachers like Christ, Peter, Paul, Isaiah, and Ezekiel, as recorded in the Scriptures – clearly regard ordinary human beings as lost, and accordingly call on them to repent, turn or return to God, come to Christ, put faith in him, and so find the pardon, peace, and newness of life that they need.

The main concepts that the New Testament uses to delineate this salvation are reconciliation, redemption, and propitiation, all won for us by the sacrificial death of Christ; forgiveness, remission of sins, justification, adoption; regeneration or renovation (that is, new birth); the indwelling of the Holy Spirit as God's seal of ownership within us; sanctification; and glorification. By contrast the chief notions that are used to describe the condition of those who do not believe in Jesus Christ, whether they have heard the gospel or not, are spiritual deadness, darkness of mind, delusion with regard to God, gods, and supernatural powers generally, moral delinquency bringing guilt and shame, and a destiny of certain distress. Paul speaks of 'the day of God's wrath, when his righteous judgement will be revealed, and God will give to each person according to what he has done. To those who by persistence in doing good seek glory, honour and immortality, he will give eternal life. But for those who are self-seeking, and who reject the truth and follow evil, there will be wrath and anger' (Romans 2:5–8). Thus, those who are not Christ's are perishing, and need to be saved. Historic evangelicalism, with some differences, I grant, of nuance in exposition and of evangelistic practice, but with great solidarity of substance, as the literature from Luther on attests, has constantly affirmed these things. Modern evangelicalism will stand revealed as a degenerate plant if it does not just as constantly do the same.

There are, however, strong tendencies at work today that press evangelicals to revise these views. I shall deal with four such tendencies, which in *ad hominem* form may be stated as follows:

1. The question of salvation is less *urgent* than evangelicals have thought. This contention raises the issue of universalism, and the destiny of those who never heard the gospel.

2. The question of salvation is less *agonizing* than evangelicals have thought. This contention raises the issue of conditional immortality, and the annihilation of unbelievers following the last judgement.

3. Justification by faith is a less *central* doctrine than evangelicals have thought. It is contended that for Paul, its chief expositor, justification was

only significant for anti-Jewish polemic, and the heart of his gospel was elsewhere.

4. Faith is a less *substantial* reality than evangelicals thought. Some dissolve away its cognitive substance, treating it simply as an existential commitment to a behaviour pattern like that which the gospels ascribe to Jesus, while denying that it assumes or requires any specific beliefs about Jesus' deity, saviourhood, or even (in Tillich's case) historicity. Others dissolve away every element in faith except its cognitive substance, treating it as simply the mind's grateful acknowledgement that Jesus, the incarnate Son of God, died for one's sins. On that view, cheap grace as denounced by Bonhoeffer is gospel truth after all; easy-believism is the true way of salvation, just as the Western religious world on the fringe of the churches wishes to think, and antinomianism really is the true Christian life.

We will review these proposed revisions of historic evangelical soteriology in order, though spending most time on the first (the big one!).

IV

The basis of the first revision, whereby the urgency of the question of salvation is destroyed, is the belief that some form of universalism is true. By universalism I mean, not Christianity's claim to be a faith for all humankind as distinct from a tribal or ethnic religion, but belief that, as the late C. H. Dodd somewhere put it, 'as every human being lies under God's judgement, so every human being is ultimately destined, in God's mercy, to eternal life.'

This is *apokatastasis* (restoration) according to Origen, the doctrine of the guaranteed future salvation of all humankind, including Judas, the thieving hypocrite of whom Jesus himself said: 'Woe to that man who betrays the Son of Man! It would be better for him if he had not been born' (Matt. 26:24). Universalists, however, must respectfully decline to endorse Jesus' judgement here, at least in its obvious meaning, since they themselves expect Judas to be saved.

Universalism, which was condemned in the sixth century and quies - cent till the nineteenth, is currently popular, and on the march, among both Protestants and Roman Catholics. Its motivations are complex. A last-century story pinpoints two of them. The question was asked: What is the difference between Unitarians and Universalists? The answer given was: The Unitarians believe that God is too good to damn anyone; the Universalists believe that man is too good for God to damn.

Today, only the most thoughtless sentimentalist could maintain that humanity is too good for God to damn, for all the facts about human nature that the twentieth century can claim to have uncovered highlight our moral flaws. Many, however, press with zeal the momentous claim that only a doctrine of universal salvation does justice to the reality of God's love for humankind, and of Christ's victory won on the cross, and of the praiseworthiness of God who has providentially permitted so much inhumanity in human relations, so much unfruitful suffering, and so much waste of good, in the course of world history. [5] Other motivations towards universalism operate too.

The monist or pantheist conception of God's relation to the world makes it necessary that the eschatological consummation whereby, as Paul puts it, God 'heads up' all things in Christ (Eph. 1:10), with every knee bowing at the name of Jesus and God himself becoming 'all in all' (1 Cor. 15:28) should involve every rational being relating harmoniously to the God of love in responsive loving rapport. This is the characteristic view of process theology, the fag-end of Anglo-Saxon liberalism, which, though uncertain whether the consummation can ever actually happen (because its God is so far from being omnipotent and sovereign over his world), is quite certain that the responsive love of every rational soul to God is part of the definition of it.

Without universal reconciliation to God the consummation would not be a consummation: that is the argument. So among the theologians it is the supposed demands of eschatology, as well as of Christology, soteriology, theodicy, and doxology, that prompt universalist opinion.

It is not only at the level of reflective theology that motivations to universalism have emerged in our day. Pastoral motivations operate too. H. O. J. Brown identifies as a

> motive to universalism a sense of the futility and failure of the Christian enterprise. It is not on the mission field that universalism is strongest, despite its obvious emotional appeal to those with unconverted loved ones. Nor is it in North America, where evangelism and renewal are prominent if not dominant features of the Christian scene.

---

[5] For the thesis that divine love points to universalism, see J. A. T. Robinson, *In the End God* (London: James Clarke, 1950; 2nd edition, London: Fontana, 1968) and Nels Ferré, *The Christian Understanding of God* (London: SCM, 1952), pp. 219ff. For the idea that the victory of Christ on the cross and in the resurrection entails universalism, see G. C. Berkouwer's critique, *The Triumph of Grace in the Theology of Karl Barth* (Grand Rapids: Eerdmans and London: Paternoster, 1956), pp. 262–96, 361–68. For the view that theodicy requires us to posit universalism, see John Hick, *Evil and the God of Love* (London: Fontana, 1968), and Nels Ferré, *Evil and the Christian Faith* (New York: Harper, 1947). There are useful brief reviews of universalist thinking in Stephen H. Travis, *Christian Hope and the Future* (Downers Grove: Inter-Varsity Press, 1980), pp. 124ff, and in *Themelios* 4.2, Jan. 1979, articles by R. J. Bauckham, N. T. Wright, E. A. Blum, and B. J. Nicholls.

It is in Europe, among the theologians, preachers, and people especially of the state-supported churches, who observe that most of Western Europe ignores Christ and has no higher value than hedonistic self-fulfilment. Because they are not winning others to Christ, but are being ignored, some people like to say, 'It doesn't really matter; everybody will be saved in the end' – a confession of failure, a sort of baptizing of our own powerlessness.[6]

And this rationalizing reaction (as I believe it to be) to gross evangelistic and pastoral failure will, as Brown notes, itself operate as a cause of further failure in the future, because 'if one thinks this way, there is scant motive to seek to bring people to conversion or renewal.' If all are, as the title of a 19th century tract put it, 'Doomed to be Saved,' then the heat is off so far as evangelism is concerned, and it will be proper to give other ways of loving your neighbour a permanent priority over evangelizing him. It is no accident, I think, that universalism and Christian socialism have long walked hand in hand, nor that the theological thought of the World Council of Churches, which has in effect redefined mission as the necessary quest for socio-politico-economic *shalom* (peace and plenty), with church-planting evangelism as an additional option if circumstances, time, and energy allow it to be fitted in, has a pronouncedly universalistic cast.

No evangelical, I think, need hesitate to admit that in his heart of hearts he would like universalism to be true. Who can take pleasure in the thought of people being eternally lost? If you want to see folk damned, there is something wrong with you! Universalism is thus a comfortable doctrine in a way that alternatives are not. But wishful thinking, based on a craving for comfort and a reluctance to believe that some of God's truth might be tragic, is no sure index of reality.

Yesterday's evangelicals felt the attraction of universalism, I am sure, just as poignantly as we do, but they denounced the doctrine as morally weakening and spiritually deadening. They equated it with the world's first falsehood, the devil's declaration in Eden, 'you will not surely die.' They saw it as the modern version of the first piece of armour that the devil puts on Mansoul in Bunyan's *Holy War*, namely 'the hope of doing well at the last what life soever you have lived.' And they preached and prayed as they believed – especially, it seems, prayed.

Evangelicals know that the power behind the eighteenth century revivals and the great nineteenth century missionary movement was prayer, and that the prayer was made out of hearts agonizing over the prospect of all who leave this world without Christ being lost. Was such prayer misconceived? uninstructed? foolish? wrong-headed? Evangelicals who value their heritage must ponder that question, recognizing that if universalism is true, all that missionary passion and praying was founded

---

[6] H. O. J. Brown, 'Will Everyone be Saved?' *Pastoral Renewal*, June 1987, p. 13.

on a monstrous mistake. Could so much evangelical piety have been so far astray?

But universalism, like all other matters of doctrine, is ultimately a biblical question, and the evangelical way to assess it is by reference, not to our heritage, but to the Bible. So I shall now attempt a biblical response to the universalist thesis.

The universalist task is to circumvent the seemingly solid New Testament witness to the fate of the unbelievers, who are declared to be under sin, law, wrath and death (so says Romans 3:9, 19; 1:18; 5:17), alienated from God and without hope (so says Eph. 2:12), facing exclusion from God's presence as punishment for their non-subjection to as much of the law and the gospel as they knew (Romans 1:18–2:16). Jesus himself is strong on the horrific consequences of rejecting him: as W. G. T. Shedd said a century ago, 'Jesus Christ is the person who is responsible for the doctrine of eternal perdition.'[7]

Granted that Jesus' references to weeping and grinding teeth, outer-darkness, worm and fire, Gehenna, and the great gulf fixed are imagery, the imagery clearly stands for a terrible retribution. Nor, be it said, do Bible writers find a moral problem in catastrophic retribution; instead, they see such retribution as solving the moral problem of evil being allowed to run loose in God's good world, because retribution vindicates God's righteousness as judge of all the earth (see Rev. 19:1–5). How can universalism be affirmed on a biblical basis, we ask, in the face of all this?

Here the ways divide. Roman Catholic universalists refuse to believe that any human beings fail to receive grace that moves them to seek God inwardly here and now, or that any form of religion in this world fails to bring its faithful adherents the salvation that Christians know through Christ. Serious attempts to find biblical support for such speculations are, however, lacking. Protestant universalists usually fol - low a different route, arguing that those who leave this world in unbelief do indeed go to hell, but in due course come out of it, having been brought to their senses, and so to a positive response to Christ, through the harrowing torment they have tasted. Hell thus does for unbelievers what Rome thinks purgatory does for believers – that is, it fits them for heaven.

So Protestant universalism appears as a doctrine of salvation out of what the New Testament calls 'eternal destruction,' 'eternal punishment,' and 'perdition,' through some kind of post-mortem encounter with Christ and his offer of mercy (a 'second chance' for some, a 'first chance' for others). This view is a speculation that differs from other 'second-chance' speculations by its categorical confidence that the post-mortem invitation to turn to Christ will succeed in every single case. Debating responses leap to mind: if as a Calvinist one posits God's sovereign ability

---

[7] W. G. T. Shedd, *Dogmatic Theology* (Edinburgh: T & T Clark, 1889), II. 680.

to call all men effectually to himself after death, the question arises as to why in that case he does not do it here, while if as an Arminian one thinks it beyond God's power to bring all men to faith here, the question arises as to how in that case he will be able to do it there. But is there biblical warrant for universalist speculation? There does not appear to be. Exe - getical arguments fail, for no text certainly and unambiguously asserts universal final salvation, and those that verbally admit of such a construc - tion are more naturally taken in a more restricted sense, as the standard commentaries do in fact take them. [8] And there are Bible-based counter- arguments, some of which I shall now briefly deploy, casting them into question form.

(1) Does not universalism deny the sufficiency of Scripture? What warrant have we for embracing any speculation that lacks explicit biblical support, and basing our attitudes and actions directly upon it?

(2) Does not universalism ignore something that Scripture stresses, namely the unqualified decisiveness of this life's decisions for our eternal destiny? What point is Jesus making when he warns the unbelieving Jews that they will die in their sins (John 8:21), and speaks of the great gulf fixed between two sorts of people, the godly and the ungodly, after death (Luke 16:26), and declares that speaking against the Holy Spirit will not be forgiven either here or hereafter (Matt. 12:32)? What point is Paul making when he declares that spiritually one reaps what one sows, either eternal life or destruction (Gal. 6:7f.), and that at Christ's judgement seat each person will 'receive what is due him for the things done while in the body, whether good or bad' (2 Cor. 5:10)? Hebrews 2:1f.; 3:8–4:11; 6:4–8; 10:26–31; 12:15–17, 25, and Revelation 14:9–11; 20:6, 10, 14f., 27; 21:8, 14f., would also come into the argument at this juncture.

(3) Does not universalism imply that the preaching of Christ and the apostles, who warned people to flee from the judgment of hell-fire by repentance here and now, is either inept or immoral? If the preachers did not themselves know that all were finally to be saved, their preaching was inept (and so today's universalists are wiser than Christ); if they knew it but concealed it, so as to bluff people into the kingdom by using the fear motive, their preaching was immoral (and so today's universalist preachers can be more righteous than Christ). Is either alternative

---

[8] The texts in question are John 12:32; Acts 3:21; Romans 5:18f.; 11:32; 1 Cor. 15:22–28; 2 Cor. 5:19; Eph. 1:10; Col. 1:20ff; Phil. 2:9–11; Heb. 2:9; Tit. 2:11; 1 Tim. 2:4; 1 John 2:2; 2 Peter 3:9. In Hastings' *Dictionary of Christ and the Gospels* (Edinburgh: T & T Clark, 1908), II. 785, Robert Mackintosh, himself a wishful universalist, observed: 'The question (sc., of universalism) is generally argued as one of New Testament interpretation. The present writer does not think that hopeful. He sees no ground for challenging the old doctrine on exegetical lines.' Nothing that has been offered during the past eighty years seems to invalidate that verdict.

acceptable? 'We must preach hell,' wrote Nels Ferré, 'as having a school and a door in it.'[9] But why did not Jesus preach hell that way? The question presses; and if no satisfactory answer to it can be found, can universalism be right?

(4) Is not universalism rejected by each Christian's own conscience? Charity and wishful thinking may make us want to affirm a universalism that embraces everyone else, but would we be able to envisage our own spiritual pilgrimage in the terms in which we would then be envisaging theirs? Surely there is no answer to the dictum of James Denney: 'I dare not say to myself that if I forfeit the opportunity this life affords I shall ever have another, and therefore I dare not say so to another man.'[10] To hand others a lifebelt to which I could not entrust myself is neither compassionate nor humble, but at best thoughtless and at worst cynical. But is not this where universalism would lead me?

But if, under pressure from such questions, we stop our ears to the universalist siren song, how shall we then rebut the claim that in this world of sin and pain, where it seems that in every Christian era most people die without knowing the gospel and most who hear it are unmoved by it, universalist belief is needed to do justice to the biblical themes of God's love, Christ's victory at Calvary, and divine competence in world-management? Is there any viable theodicy – any way, that is, of showing God to be gloriously in the right, and thus worthy of our praise – other than that of process theology, which sees God as intending universal salvation but does not know if he can bring it off, or of universalism, which rests its theodicy on the certainty that he can and will? Is it right to affirm, as some have done, that the only alternative to embracing one or other of these views is to surrender the real goodness of God's character? No, for there is a further option in theodicy; it is the option that evangelical theology has historically embraced, and that direct biblical exegesis without extrapolation and speculation actually establishes. It can be set out like this.

(1) The sin that God mysteriously chooses to permit and humans madly choose to commit so offends God, and so robs people of value in his sight, that retribution for the impenitent becomes the natural reaction whereby he expresses his holy nature. This self-vindicating judicial righteousness is glorious, and calls for praise.

(2) Mysteriously again, God chooses to extend mercy to the penitent – mercy at which general revelation hints, and which the gospel shows to be based on costly blood atonement and defines in generous promises of justification, regeneration, and glorification. This marvellous mercy is glorious, and calls for praise.

---

[9] Ferré, *The Christian Understanding of God*, p. 241.

[10] James Denney, *Studies in Theology* (London: Hodder & Stoughton, 1902), p. 244.

(3) Mysteriously once more, God maintains in all developed human beings the power of self-determining moral choice, and respects their choices, while yet, paradoxically, all who choose to trust God's mercy find themselves constrained to say that it was not their own intelligence or will-power, but the illuminating and drawing action of God himself that brought them to faith. Both aspects of this situation are glorious, and call for praise.

(4) Mysteriously, too, God sanctifies all believers' sufferings, through their faith-experience of the power of the risen Christ, as a means of furthering that character conformity to Christ that is their destiny. None of the pains they endure are simply retributive and penal; none of their experiences of frustration and disappointment are mere wastages of good potential; all, in the final analysis, serve God's soverign, forward-looking, transforming purpose for them, and so are true tokens of his wisdom. This also is glorious, and calls for praise.

(5) Mysteriously yet once more, God sends his people to publish the gospel throughout the human community, promising that as they plead with people to trust God through Christ and plead with God to touch people through grace, others will enter that new life that is being proclaimed. Here, again, is a glorious fact that calls for praise.

My use of 'mysteriously' is meant as a reminder that in each of these purposes and works of God there is much that is beyond us to grasp, and moreover that many of our questions about them are left unanswered by the Word of God. But my contention here is that despite this ignorance we have in the awareness, which my five points encompass, that all who are saved are saved by grace through faith, while all who perish do so through the fault of their own choice and impenitence, a magnificent overall theodicy that for time and eternity must prompt undying praise.

One final point. A British lay theologian, Sir Norman Anderson, poses an often-asked question as follows:

> Might it not be true of the follower of some other religion that the God of all mercy had worked in his heart by his Spirit, bringing him in some measure to realize his sin and need for forgiveness, and enabling him, in his twilight as it were, to throw himself on God's mercy?[11]

The answer surely is: yes, it might be true, as it seems to have been true for some non-Israelites in Old Testament times: think of Melchizedek, Job, Naaman, Cyrus, Nebuchadnezzar, the sailors in Jonah's boat, and the Ninevites to whom he preached, for starters. In heaven, any such penitents will learn that they were saved by Christ's death and their hearts were renewed by the Holy Spirit, and they will worship God accordingly.

---

[11] Sir Norman Anderson, *Christianity and World Religions* (Leicester and Downers Grove: Inter-Varsity Press, 1984), pp. 148f.

Christians since the second century have voiced the hope that there are still such people, and we may properly voice the same hope today. But – and this is the point to consider – we have no warrant from Scripture to expect that God will act thus in any single specific case where the gospel is not yet known. To cherish this hope, therefore, is not to diminish in the slightest our urgent and never-ending missionary obligation, any more than it is to embrace universalism as a basis for personal and communal living. Living by the Bible means assuming that no one will be saved apart from faith in Christ, and acting accordingly.

V

Now we turn to the second proposed revision of historic evangelical soteriology, the view that the question of salvation is less agonizing than we thought because after judgment day the unsaved will not exist. This is universalism in reverse: like universalism, it envisages a final state in which all are saved; unlike universalism, it anticipates, not post-mortem conversion, but annihilation and non-being for those who leave this world in unbelief. The exponents of this view, which for our purposes may be called either annihilationism or conditionalism, [12] are all Protestants or cultists. [13]

Having been condemned at the Fifth Lateran Council in 1513, it is not an option for Roman Catholics. Among the Protestants are some distinguished evangelicals, [14] including recently my fellow Anglicans John

---

[12] Annihilationism is the version of this view that assumes the natural immortality of created human beings, conditionalism the version that denies it. Since no creature has life at any level, or existence in any form, for a single moment apart from God's active upholding, this is a verbal distinction that corresponds to no theological difference. Only within a deistic frame of reference would the distinction mean anything.

[13] Jehovah's Witnesses, Seventh-day Adventists, and some continuing fragments of Herbert W. Armstrong's World-Wide Church of God are committed to conditionalism.

[14] 'In conservative circles there is a seeming reluctance to espouse publicly a doctrine of hell, and where it is held there is a seeming tendency towards a doctrine of hell as annihilation . . . Our interest here is with conditional immortality, which appears to be gaining acceptance in evangelical orthodox circles' (Peter Toon, *Heaven and Hell* [Nashville: Thomas Nelson, 1986] pp. 174,176). In *The Conditionalist Faith of our Fathers* (Washington, DC: Review and Herald, 1966) Leroy Edwin Froom, a Seventh-day Adventist, highlighted the conditionalism of Basil F. C. Atkinson, an able lay theologian of Cambridge, England (II. 881–88), who seems to have influenced many gifted evangelical students to embrace this view. H. E. Guilleband, author of *The Righteous Judge:*

Stott[15] and Philip Edgcumbe Hughes,[16] and I think it is currently gaining more evangelical adherents.[17] But the question whether an opinion is true is not resolved by asking who holds it.

Conditionalism is never advocated as expressing the obvious meaning of Scripture, for this it does not do. Its advocates back into it, rather, in horrified recoil from the thought of billions in endless torment – a thought to which the memory of Hitler's holocaust, and the modern statistical mind-set, no doubt add vividness. The arguments for conditionalism, however, are far from convincing. They boil down to four, which I state as Bible-believing conditionalists state them.

First, it is said that the New Testament terms for the fate of the lost – destruction and death, corruption and punishment, the worm and the fire – might mean annihilation. So they might, but this possible meaning is not the natural meaning. In all the contexts cited, the natural meaning of the phrases in which these words appear is ruin and distress, not entry upon non-existence. Conditionalism can be read into these passages, but not read out of them. And in all Bible study it is the natural meaning that should be sought.

Second, it is said that everlasting punishment is not required by God's justice, and would in fact be needless cruelty. But, leaving aside the question of how the conditionalists can know this, I would point out that this argument, if it proves anything, proves too much: for if it is needlessly cruel, and not required by justice, for God to keep the lost in being after judgement, no reason can be given why it is not needlessly cruel for him to keep the lost in the conscious misery of the intermediate state (on which see Jesus' story of Dives, Luke 16:23ff.), and then to raise them

---

[14] *(continued) A Study of the Biblical Doctrine of Everlasting Punishment* (Taunton: Goodman, 1964), a careful conditionalist statement, was close to Atkinson. Atkinson's own conditionalism, already explicit in his *Pocket Commentary on Genesis*, was later spelt out in *Life and Immortality: An Examination of the Meaning of Life and Death as they are Revealed in the Scriptures* (Taunton: E. Goodman, n.d.).

[15] David Edwards and John Stott, *Essentials* (London: Hodder & Stoughton. Also published as *Evangelical Essentials*, Downers Grove: Inter-Varsity Press, 1988), pp. 312–20.

[16] Philip Edgcumbe Hughes, *The True Image: The Origin and Destiny of Man in Christ* (Grand Rapids: Eerdmans, 1989), pp. 398–407.

[17] Among recent evangelical writers of distinction who incline more or less explicitly towards conditionalism are Edward William Fudge, *The Fire That Consumes* with (dissenting) preface by F. F. Bruce (Houston: Providential Press, 1982; originally published in the UK, Carlisle: Paternoster, 1982); John W. Wenham, *The Goodness of God* (Leicester and Downers Grove: Inter-Varsity Press, 1974), chapter 2, pp. 27–41; Stephen H. Travis, who declares 'If pressed, I must myself opt for' conditional immortality, *I Believe in the Second Coming of Jesus* (Grand Rapids: Eerdmans, 1982), p. 198.

bodily in what Jesus calls 'the resurrection of judgement' (NIV, they 'rise to be condemned'; John 5:28). What God ought to do, on conditionalist principles, is annihilate unbelievers at death, but Scripture shows that he does not do this. So the conditionalist argument, which sought to clear God of the suspicion of needless cruelty, actually puts him under it.

Third, it is said that the harmony of the new heaven and earth will be marred if somewhere the lost continue to exist in impenitence and distress. But again it must be asked how the conditionalists know this. The argument is pure speculation.

Fourth, it is said that the joy of heaven will be marred by knowledge that some continue under punitive suffering. But this cannot be said of God, as if the expressing of his holiness in retribution hurts him more than it hurts the offenders; and since in heaven Christians will be like God in character, there is no reason to think that their joy will be impaired in this way either.

What troubles me most here, I confess, is the assumption of superior sensitivity by the conditionalists. Their assumption appears in the adjec - tives (awful, dreadful, terrible, fearful, intolerable, etc.) that they apply to the concept of eternal punishment, as if to suggest that holders of the historic view have never thought about the meaning of what they have been saying. John Stott records his belief 'that the ultimate annihilation of the wicked should be accepted as a legitimate, biblically founded alternative to their eternal conscious torment.'[18]

Respectfully, I disagree, for the biblical arguments are to my mind flimsy special pleading[19] and the feelings that make people want condi - tionalism to be true seem to me to reflect, not superior spiritual sensitivity, but secular sentimentalism which assumes that in heaven our feelings about others will be as at present, and our joy in the manifesting of God's justice will be no greater than it is now. It is certainly agonizing now to live with the thought of people going to an eternal hell, but it is not right to reduce the agony by evading the facts; and in heaven, we may be sure, the agony will be a thing of the past.

VI

The third and fourth of the proposed revisions concern the central tenet of the Reformation and of the older forms of evangelicalism, namely the doctrine of justification by grace through faith on the ground of Christ's vicarious obedience to death. This doctrine has been somewhat in eclipse in recent years. For liberal and radical Protestantism, which denies the

---

[18] Stott, op. cit., p 320.

[19] For detailed argument confirming this verdict, see Robert A. Morey, *Death and the Afterlife* (Minneapolis: Bethany House, 1984), ch. 8, pp. 199–222; Robert A. Peterson, *Hell on Trial* (Phillipsburg: Presbyterian & Reformed, 1995).

realities of judgement and atonement, the assertion of justification in the evangelical sense has been an impossibility; and conservative evangelicalism has in recent years tended to stop short at proclaiming present forgiveness of sins and a personal relationship with Jesus, as modern Roman Catholicism also does, and to neglect the larger implications about the believer's relationship with God that the doctrine of justification carries. Recently the Anglican-Roman Catholic International Commission was given the topic of justification by faith to explore; they extended their terms of reference unilaterally and came up with a report titled *Salvation and the Church*, in which the key issues of the Reformation debate, namely the formal cause of justification and the content of Christian assurance, were ignored entirely; and few noticed the omission.[20]

As for the proposed revisions at which we shall now briefly look, it can be said at once that acceptance of them would virtually guarantee that justification by faith, as the Reformers understood it, would never be back on the Christian map again. So I make no apology for arguing polemically against them.

First question, then: 'Should we agree with Wrede, and Albert Schweitzer, and many exegetes and theologians since their time, that Paul's doctrine of justification was no more than a controversial device developed for use against Jews and Judaizers, and so need not greatly concern us?' No, for at least these reasons:

(1) Paul's letter to the Romans is by design a full-dress statement of his gospel, and the doctrine of justification is its backbone.

(2) In all the places where Paul writes in the first person singular of the convictions that made him the man and the missionary that he was, he couches his testimony in terms of justification by faith (Gal. 2:15–21; 2 Cor. 5:16–21; Phil. 3:4–14; cf. 1 Tim. 1:12–16). The terms in which the man gives his testimony indicate what is nearest his heart.

---

[20] Among those who did notice it, and comment on it, were Alister McGrath (*ARCIC II and Justification: an Evangelical Anglican Assessment of Salvation and the Church* (Oxford: Latimer House, 1987); 'Justification: the New Ecumenical Debate,' in *Themelios* 13, 2, (Jan–Feb, 1988), pp. 43–48; Christopher J. L. Bennen, 'Justification and ARCIC I,' in *The Banner of Truth* 297, (June 1988), pp. 6–11, 32; and, with profound pastoral insight matching theological acumen, Christopher Fitzsimons Allison, 'The Pastoral and Political Implications of Trent on Justification: A Response to the ARCIC Agreed Statement, Salvation and the Church' in *Churchman*, 103, 1, (1989), p. 15–31; reprinted from *St. Luke's Journal of Theology* (Sewanee, p. XXXL. 3, 1988). Bishop Allison's book *The Rise of Moralism: The Proclamation of the Gospel from Hooker to Baxter* (Milton: Morehouse Barlow, 1986) is the authoritative account of Anglican responses to the Tridentine teaching on justification in the sixteenth and seventeenth centuries. See also McGrath *Justitia Dei: A History of the Christian Doctrine of Justification* (Cambridge: Cambridge University Press, 1986), II. 1–134.

(3) Present justification, God's declaration that the believer is in the right with him, is for Paul God's basic act of blessing, which both saves from the past by remitting guilt and assures for the future by its guarantee of continuing acceptance. For justification is the judgment of the last day brought forward; a final, irrevocable verdict bringing peace and hope to sinners who previously had neither. The centrality of final judgement in Paul's view of life is plain, and justification is part of that central reality.

(4) Paul's total account of salvation has justification in and through Christ as its central reference point. It is in terms of justification that Paul explains grace (Romans 3:24; 4:4f.); the reconciling, redemptive, and revelatory significance of Christ's death (2 Cor. 5:18f.; Romans 3:24; 5:5–11; Gal. 3:13); the covenant relationship (Gal. 3:15ff.); faith (Romans 4:23ff.; 10:8ff.); adoption and the gift of the Spirit (Gal. 4:6–8); and Christian assurance (Romans 5:1–11; 8:1–39) – to look no further. Justification is thus seen to be at the heart of Paul's soteriology.

(5) The question that Paul deployed his doctrine of justification to answer in debate with Jews and Judaizers, namely, 'Who are the true children of Abraham?', was for him central to the gospel. For God's salvation is for Abraham's seed, and the mediatorial significance of Christ is that in union with him Jewish and Gentile believers become Abraham's seed for salvation (Gal. 3:6–29).[21]

The threefold claim, drawn mainly from Paul, that justification is a status, given now, and that the formal cause of its being given is the righteousness of Christ, and that the result of its being given is that sinners know themselves to be permanently right with God in a way that daily stumbling into sin cannot affect, revolutionized spiritual life in the sixteenth century, turning Christianity at a stroke from an affair of apprehensive aspiration into a joyful experience of assurance. That experience cannot survive, however, if its doctrinal foundation gets obscured or sidelined.

Luther is said to have predicted that after his death the devil would counter-attack with this sidelining as his objective, and that appears to be something that he is still doing today. Surely Scripture requires us to restore the often neglected emphasis on a coming personal judgment for each of us at the hands of a holy God, and against that background to reinstate the precious truth of justification[22] – the wonderful exchange, as Luther called it, whereby Christ took our sin on himself and

---

[21] For development of this point, see the brilliant chapter by Tom Wright, 'Justification: the Biblical Basis and its Relevance for Contemporary Evangelicalism,' in *The Great Acquittal: Justification by Faith and Current Christian Thought* , ed. Gavin Reid (London: Fount, 1980), pp. 13–37.

[22] Alister McGrath's otherwise admirable presentation, *Justification by Faith: What it Means for Us Today* (Grand Rapids: Zondervan, 1988), fails us here; amazingly, it makes no mention whatever of judgment to come.

set righteousness upon us in its place. (Never forget that penal substitu -
tionary atonement and the righteous justification of sinners are the two
sides of a single coin, the two elements in the one saving transaction
whereby God rescues us from hell.) It would be ruinously enfeebling
for us to be allured away at any stage from a central emphasis on
justification by faith.[23]

So we move to the fourth revisionary suggestion, which we shall
consider in the form in which it is made by an evangelical school of
thought which, ironically, has done more than most over the past
half-century to keep the doctrine of justification by faith at the centre.[24]
The suggestion is that saving faith is an assent to the truth about the
atonement, and a formalized receiving of Jesus as Saviour, without any
necessity of turning from sin to become his disciple and, in the relational
sense, follower, and that to ask for more than this as a response to the
gospel is a legalistic lapse into justification by works, and an unwarranted
restriction of God's free grace. To this suggestion I make a threefold
response.

(1) Faith must be defined, just as it must be exercised, in terms of its
object. But the Christ who is the object of saving faith is the Christ of the
New Testament, he who is prophet and king no less than he is priest.
More particularly it is the Christ of the gospels, who constantly called for
a life of active discipleship as the means of benefiting from his ministry,
who is our only basis of salvation.

Surely it is undeniable that God has joined faith and repentance, in
the sense of change of life, as the two facets of response to Christ, and has
made it clear that turning to Christ means turning from sin and letting
ungodliness go. Surely it is undeniable that in the New Testament true
faith is not only knowing facts about Jesus, but coming to him in personal
trust to worship, love, and serve him. Surely it is undeniable that if we
put asunder these things that God has joined together, our Christianity
will be seriously distorted.

(2) There is an evident confusion here between faith as a psychological
act, that is, something that you do (in this case, 'closing with Christ' as
the Puritans used to put it), and faith as a meritorious work, that is, a

---

[23] I develop some of these points in my introduction to James Buchanan, *The
Doctrine of Justification* (London: Banner of Truth, 1961), reprinted in this volume,
pp. 137–144, and my chapter 'Justification in Protestant Theology', in J. I.
Packer and others *Here We Stand: Justification by Faith Today* (London: Hodder
& Stoughton, 1986), pp. 101–102, reprinted in Vol. 4 of this collection.

[24] See John MacArthur, Jr., *The Gospel According to Jesus* (Grand Rapids: Zondervan and Panorama City: Word of Grace, 1988), citing and interacting with
relevant works by Zane Hodges, Charles Ryrie, Lewis Sperry Chafer, and
G. Michael Cocori. Darrell L. Bock wrote a judicious review of the interaction
in *Bibliotheca Sacra* (Jan–March, 1989), pp. 21–40. The debate continues.

means of earning God's favour and inducing his acceptance. When it is argued that to call for active commitment to discipleship as a response to the gospel is to teach works-righteousness, the confusion is clear. The truth is that every act of faith, psychologically regarded, is a matter of doing something (knowing, receiving, and trusting are as much acts in the psychological sense as is resolving to obey); yet no act of faith ever presents itself to its doer as other than a means of receiving undeserved mercy in some shape or form. This is as true of a trustful commitment to follow Christ as it is of a trustful resting on the Saviour's promise of pardon. There is no need to restrict faith to passive reliance without active devotion in order to keep works righteousness and legalism out of the picture.

(3) The pastoral effect of this teaching, if taken seriously, can only be to produce what the Puritans called 'gospel hypocrites' – persons who have been told, or who have told themselves, that they are Christians, eternally secure in Christ, because they believe that he died for them, when their hearts are unchanged and they have no inward commitment to Christ at all. I know what I am talking about, for I was just such a gospel hypocrite for two years in my teens before God mercifully made me aware of my unconverted state. If I seem harshly critical when I categorize this proposed redefinition of faith as a barren intellectual formalism, you must remember that I was once myself burned by teaching of this type, and a burned child dreads the fire.

VII

'Stand at the crossroads and look; ask for the ancient paths, ask where the good way is, and walk in it, and you will find rest for your souls' (Jer. 6:16). The only recommendation to which my survey leads me is that in relation to all the proposed revisions of evangelical faith that we have discussed, we should take these words to heart.

Some sources for the paper '*Evangelicals and the Way of Salvation*' by J. I. Packer.

1. On universalism:
   John Hick, *Evil and the God of Love*
   J. A. T. Robinson, *In the End God*
   M. Rissi, *The Future of the World*
   D. P. Walker, *The Decline of Hell*
   J. H. Leckie, *The World to Come and Final Destiny*
   H. H. Farmer, *The World and God*
   J. Baillie, *And the Life Everlasting*
   G. Rowell, *Hell and the Victorians*
   G. C. Berkouwer, *The Return of Christ*
   N. Ferré, *The Christian Understanding of God*
   Articles in *Themelios* 4:2, Jan. 1979

2. On conditionalism:
   J. W. Wenham, *The Goodness of God*
   John Stott, *Essentials* (with David Edwards)
   Philip E. Hughes, *The True Image*
   O. C. Quick, *Doctrines of the Creed*
   L. E. Froom, *The Conditionalist Faith of Our Fathers*
   S. H. Travis, *Christian Hope and the Future*
   A. A. Hoekema, *The Four Major Cults*

3. On justification:
   Tom Wright in *The Great Acquittal* (ed., G. Reid)
   H. N. Ridderbos, *Paul: An Outline of His Theology*
   J. Buchanan, *The Doctrine of Justification*
   H. Küng, *Justification*
   A. E. McGrath, *Justitia Dei: A History of the Christian Doctrine of Justification* (vol. 2)

ARCIC II report: 'Salvation and the Church': text and responses in *Evangel* 5:2, Summer 1987; responses also by A. E. McGrath in *Themelios* 13:2, Jan. 1988, and *Latimer Studies* 26 (1987), *ARCIC II and Justification*.
C. F. Allison, *The Rise of Moralism*

4. On saving faith:
   J. MacArthur, *The Gospel According to Jesus*
   Z. Hodges, *The Gospel Under Siege*
   Dictionary articles on 'universalism,' 'annihilation,' 'conditionalism,' 'justification,' 'faith'.

Chapter 15

An Agenda for Theology

Theology is a complex of disciplines – exegesis, biblical theology, historical theology, systematics, symbolics, ethics, apologetics, liturgics, missiology, spirituality, pastoral theology, and more – but in essence it is one threefold activity throughout: listening to God's utterances in scrip - ture, testifying to what one has heard, and testing all human utterances and behavior, past and present, in and outside the church, by what the Bible says. Theology is meant to function in the church as both disinfec - tant and nutrient, sterilizing and fertilizing our minds, guiding our wills and desires, stirring our imaginations, calling forth our praises, informing our pastoral care, and focusing our message to the world. Theology thus has a vital contribution to make to the church's life.

Because theology's task is to reinterpret the unchanging gospel in such a way that every generation may understand its substance and perceive its relevance, the church's theologians must have their mental windows open not only to the warm rays of Christian tradition but also to the cold blasts of secular thought. Yet in their listening and responding to the world they must not let go their Christian identity nor forget their churchly function. A theologian who gets swamped by the secularity with which they interact is someone whom the church can do without. 'The place for the ship is in the sea,' said D. L. Moody, speaking of the church in the world, 'but God help the ship if the sea gets into it.' Sadly, however, much academic theology has in recent years gotten swamped and waterlogged in this way, and large segments of the church have been weakened as a result.

To understand this situation, one must take account not only of the resurgence of that post-Enlightenment relativism and skepticism which by the turn of this century had spawned both Protestant liberalism and Catholic modernism, but also of the sociology of the present day theologian's trade. To achieve a career as a theological academic one has to find employment in a teaching or research institution, and to do that

AN AGENDA FOR THEOLOGY was originally published as the appendix in *Summons to Faith and Renewal: Christian Renewal in a Post-Christian World* eds, Peter Williamson and Kevin Perrotta (Ann Arbor, Mich: Servant Press, 1983), pp. 151–155. Reprinted by permission.

one has to impress potential employers as being likely to make a significant contribution in one's own field, and to do that one has to have a point of view of which they can approve. If one viewpoint comes to dominate the minds of those who manage academic institutions, it immediately becomes harder for scholars who do not share that point of view to get jobs. This fact soon creates the optical illusion that most significant scholars are on the one side! Again, academics who have got their feet on the ladder and want to climb professionally (and there is nothing wrong with such a purpose) must publish in approved journals and with approved publishers, be seen and if possible heard at conferences of learned societies, and join in the ongoing debates among their peers. In such circumstances it is the easiest thing in the world to forget one's churchly identity and responsibilities and simply think along with generally accepted opinion, concerning oneself only with keeping in the swim. In this, of course, theology does not differ from any other academic field, and I do not mention these things in order to censure them. I mention them only to explain how it was possible for the current landslide into theological relativism among Catholics, and the parallel landslides among Protestants into such things as Bultmannism and situation ethics, to take place.

In academic theology today we face an extraordinary diversity of specific opinions held together by an equally extraordinary consensus as to what academically worthwhile opinions will be like. Most of the time it is simply taken for granted that any views which merit academic consideration will be tentative and concessive, opposed to the categories of heresy and blasphemy as being invalid, tolerant of pluralism as being stimulating, intolerant of orthodoxies as being hostile to intellectual enterprise, and observably different in some way from the received wisdom. Novelty is at a premium, as once it was at Athens, and reassertions of traditional views evoke little enthusiasm within our theo - logical establishments. The restless, skeptical spirit of our age has deeply infected the theological world, and the result is that in many Christian minds the outlines of historic Christian faith have crumbled, and the content of that faith has been obscured, in just the same way as the features of weathering statues grow increasingly indistinct, to the point where they are quite unrecognizable. In this bleak milieu all significant theological study and debate takes place today, for this is the mainstream. There are backwaters, to be sure, where theologians of particular conservative traditions meet together, but such meetings make little difference to what goes on in the mainstream. And out in that stream there are few points of classical Christian theology which have not become matters of struggle and dispute.

Thus, there is struggle over *the Bible*. Should we trust its history? How far may we pick and choose among its varied theological contents? Should we give up the idea of biblical teaching as revealed truth in favor of a theology of story, or of existential encounter with God through the evocative impact of Bible words? How, from what scripture meant historically, should we determine what it means for us? How, in the light of its doctrine, should we make ethical decisions? And so on.

Then there is a struggle over the doctrine of *God* and of *Jesus Christ*. Is God finite? evolving? impassible? Is he intrinsically and eternally triune, or does the doctrine of the Trinity just express three aspects of our experience of God who in himself is unipersonal? Can one distinguish God as he is in himself from God in relation to his creatures? Is there validity in the doctrine of the Incarnation, which states that the eternal Son took humanness without his deity being diminished, or should we see this as myth and the Jesus of history as just a particularly godly man? When and how should God the Father and Jesus the Son be recognized in non-Christian religions (for it is nowadays axiomatic that they should be)? Et cetera, et cetera.

Also there is struggle over the doctrine of *salvation*. Are the Anselmic, transactional ideas of the atonement, according to which the Son offered himself in death to the Father as a satisfaction for sin, believable? Should not all atonement language be interpreted subjectively, of the Christian's changed relationship to God, rather than objectively, of the divine act that was the basis of that change? How should believers view the cross of Christ? Should not universal salvation through the cross be asserted? Is it conceivable that anyone can be eternally lost, and that hell will have permanent residents? Are not all mankind in a state of grace by virtue of the cross? Is it a matter of priority in our service of others to lead them, if we can, to conversion, or are other forms of service more important? The debates continue.

It has long been taken for granted that the deepest theological differences, at least in the West, are those dividing Protestants from Roman Catholics. The assumption is that all Protestants are closer to each other in thought than any of them are to Roman Catholics, and vice versa. Perhaps it once was so, but the sample questions just cited make us aware that it is not so today. They are all quite fundamental to one's view of Christianity, and they are agitated with equal vehemence on both sides of the Reformation divide. The truth is that the deepest contemporary cleavage in theology is between those who may be labelled traditionalists and radicals respectively – 'trads' and 'rads'; that is, between those for whom the God-givenness of all biblical teaching, and of the historic faith as therein set forth are fixed points, and those for whom they are not. This division cuts across the Roman Catholic Church, just as it does across all the older Protestant church families. On the one side are those who still affirm the ontological Trinity, the divine sovereignty, the incarnation of the Son of God, the transactional atonement, faith in Jesus as the way of eternal life, the divine–human mediator as the focus of devotion, the primacy of evangelism in mission, the absoluteness of biblical moral teaching, and the need of orthodoxy as a basis for right living (orthopraxy).

On the other side are those who think that they may and must treat all these historic affirmations as culturally conditioned symbols, open to any form of reinterpretation which strikes the theologian as meaningful for today. It is obvious that these attitudes reflect different and incompatible views of the nature of the divine realities to which theological statements made in the church refer, and this is a more fundamental division than that over any particular doctrine.

It is a recognized principle of Christian ecumenism, and also of common sense, that we should not do separately what we can better do together. It seems clear from what has been said that maintaining the basic ingredients of the historic faith against their opponents in and outside the church is something that can better be done by Catholics and Protestants working together than by either battalion of 'trads' working separately. So I conclude that our times call for an overt alliance of conservative theologians from both stables, an axis relationship finding expression in a joint academic strategy, whereby more effective breakwaters against the erosive and distorting effect of the pounding waves of modernity in Christian minds may be set up.

Such an alignment would helpfully clarify what is actually going on in our churches. It would strengthen the hands of those who at an academic level are currently laboring to keep open the old paths, and finding themselves isolated as they do so. It would give layfolk resources for assessing what their official theological leaders say. And its long-term ecumenical and pastoral potential is beyond our power to calculate. For Protestant and Catholic theological conservatives thus to cooperate, in these areas where they are in fact fundamentally agreed, would certainly enrich both sides (no one who has had experience of joint Protestant–Catholic theological work will doubt that), and should equally certainly further the cause of God and truth in all our churches. New associational structures and conference patterns will be called for, but these should not be hard to mount, given the vision and the will. The project is surely a practical one. This is a venture that we badly need. Shall I see it made in my lifetime? God knows – but I hope so.

Chapter 16

Shy Sovereign

He shaped creation; he gave revelation and caused the Bible to be written, he renews hearts and transforms lives; he assures Christians of their eternal salvation: and he equips them to sense their Saviour. Who? The Holy Spirit; who else?

You noticed, I hope, that I said 'he.' The Spirit, who in the Old Testament represented himself merely as a divine force, appears in the New Testament as a Helper and Counsellor who can be grieved and lied to, and who intercedes for Christians on a regular basis. These are ministries that only a person could fulfil. The Spirit is the third person of the Godhead: that is why he is called 'Holy.' He is the executive agent of the Father and the Son in both providence and grace. He must be honoured as such, and it is never right to do as is so often done and speak of him as 'it.'

Have you ever been asked, from the pulpit or in conversation, whether you know the Holy Spirit? In renewal circles this question is often put, and with reason, for versions of Christianity, even orthodox Bible-based Christianity, are current in which the Spirit's ministry is for practical purposes ignored. But the question is not biblically angled, for it is the Spirit's way to keep out of direct view, like a shy child hiding behind the door. So Christians never know the Spirit in the way they know the Son, and we can be led astray by questioning that suggests we do.

The New Testament leads us to picture our relation to the Spirit like this. Christ stands before us, addressing us, while the Spirit stands behind us, with access to our innermost being. The Spirit shines light over our shoulder so that we see Christ and know him to be real, and with that whispers into the ear of our heart the words that Christ speaks to us. 'Do you hear him saying, "Come to Me . . . learn of Me . . . you shall find rest . . ." Go to him; he is saying those things to you.' This is the formula, not only for conversion, but for our entire Christian life: beholding, approaching, trusting, loving, adoring, and serving the Lord Jesus is the essence of it.

SHY SOVEREIGN was originally published in *Tabletalk*, Ligonier Ministries, Lake Mary, Florida, June, 1988. p. 4. Reprinted by permission.

So the Spirit is the floodlight, illuminating the Lord Jesus; he is the contact lens that enables us to see him clearly; he is the match-maker, leading us to Christ for a permanent union; he is the intercom, making constant communication between Christ and us a reality of our experi - ence; and he is the channel through which Christ pours his life and power into us for worship, sanctity, and service. But in all this, though he abides with us and indwells us and by his sovereign grace transforms us into Jesus' moral likeness, he keeps himself out of sight. When the Spirit works in us. Christ himself, and not the Spirit, is the focus of our attention. 'Spiritual' experience that leads away from Christ, or bypasses him, is not from the Holy Spirit at all.

Is that a rule by which to judge the New Age mysticism? The meditative disciplines of Asian gurus? The pantheistic euphoria of Shirley MacLaine? Yes, it is: and theosophy, and anthroposophy, and Christian Science, and scientology, and all other man-made alternatives to faith in the Christ of the Scriptures.

Religious muddle around us is frantic and furious. How urgently we need, in these days, to get clear about the Holy Spirit!

on their oars, churches settle on their lees. Ecclesiastical formalism sets in, and the Spirit is institutionalized with disastrous consequences.

For the Holy Spirit's true work is to lead sinners to Christ and through Christ to God; to make individual believers Christ-like in love, humility, righteousness, and patience; and to animate the church corporately to offer praise to God, service and help to each other, and compassionate outreach to the world. Institutionalizing the Spirit in the way described makes for apathy and indifference to spiritual quality so long as the ecclesiastical machine rolls on. This obstructs church growth in Paul's sense of the phrase – that is, corporate advance toward the fullness of Christ (Eph. 4:15–16; Col. 2:19) and thus quenches the Spirit by not taking him seriously. Complacency is the cause, and Laodicean lukewarmness the consequence.

The third thing to say is that taking the Holy Spirit seriously means that Christians must rediscover the naturalness of three things that modern believers in the West rarely see as natural – namely, worship, evangelism, and suffering. With regard to worship, A. W. Tozer wrote in 1948, 'There are today many millions of people who hold "right opinions," probably more than ever before in the history of the Church. Yet I wonder if there was ever a time when true spiritual worship was at a lower ebb. To great sections of the Church the art of worship has been lost entirely, and in its place has come that strange and foreign thing called the "program." This word has been borrowed from the stage and applied with sad wisdom to the type of public service which now passes for worship among us.'

This is arguably truer now than it was when Tozer wrote about it. Worship – in the sense of telling God his worth by speech and song and celebrating his worth in his presence by proclamation and meditation – has been largely replaced, at least in the West, by a form of entertainment calculated to give worshipers the equivalent of a sauna or Jacuzzi experi-ence and send them away feeling relaxed and tuned up at the same time. Certainly true worship invigorates, but to plan invigoration is not necessarily to order worship. As all that glitters is not gold, so all that makes us feel happy and strong is not worship. The question is not whether a particular liturgical form is used, but whether a God-centred as distinct from a man-centred perspective is maintained – whether, in other words, the sense that man exists for God rather than God for man is cherished or lost. We need to discover all over again that worship is natural to the Christian heart, as it was to the godly Israelites who wrote the psalms, and that the habit of celebrating the greatness and graciousness of God yields an endless flow of thankfulness, joy, and zeal.

Neither stylized charismatic exuberance nor Anglican Prayer Book correctness nor conventional music-sandwich Sunday-morning programs provide any magic formula for this rediscovery. It can occur only when the Holy Spirit is taken seriously as the One who through the written word of Scripture shows us the love and glory of the Son and the Father and draws us into personal communion with both.

Harry S. Boer wrote tellingly of the naturalness of evangelism in *Pentecost and Missions* (Grand Rapids: Eerdmans, 1961). There he showed that the view of evangelism as first and foremost a Christian duty required by the Great Commission of Matthew 28:19–20 is no older than the last century, prior to which the mainspring of evangelism among lay Christians was the naturalness of sharing Christ with one's neighbour out of sheer inner excitement over the new life of hope one had found.

Thus it was in Jerusalem after Pentecost. Thus it was for three centuries after that, during which Christianity, though it was legally proscribed and its adherents were often killed, became the strongest religion in the Roman Empire – so strong that it can truly be said to have won the Western world. Thus it was in the day of the Reformers, in the time of the Puritans, and during the evangelical awakenings that revived faith on both sides of the Atlantic in the eighteenth century. In those eras the gospel spread like a prairie fire, not primarily because of the quality of the preachers but because lay Christians kept gossiping the gospel to their neighbours. And they did so spontaneously, simply because they had been thrilled to the marrow by their own experience of God's salvation, which had made them into conscious lovers of Christ and heirs of heaven, no longer victims and prisoners of the pains and pressures – physical and mental, secular and religious – that threatened them on earth.

But during the past century Christians have become unbiblically and indeed pathetically earthbound, concentrating their hopes of happiness on the here rather than the hereafter. And as the glow of the hope of glory has faded, credibility has diminished, and zeal for sharing Christ has waned.

Meantime, evangelism has been institutionalized in various forms and programs of organized mission activity, thus becoming a duty rather than a delight. Paul prayed for the Romans, 'May the God of hope fill you with all joy and peace as you trust in him, so that you may overflow with hope by the power of the Holy Spirit' (15:13). Only as the Holy Spirit is taken seriously enough for this overflowing to become a reality in our own lives will the naturalness of evangelism be discovered again.

As for suffering, by which I mean all forms of pain, frustration, and disappointment – 'losses and crosses,' as the Puritans used to put it – the New Testament is consistent and emphatic in viewing this as the natural condition of Christians and churches as long as they are in this world. We follow Christ through humiliation here, sharing his sufferings, and thus arrive at glorification with him hereafter. Afflictions achieve 'an eternal glory that far outweighs them all,' Paul tells us (2 Cor. 4:17), while the alternative, in William Penn's haunting phrase, is 'no cross, no crown' (see Heb. 12:7–14). Suffering is the Christian's road home; no other road leads there. But the twentieth-century West has come to think of a life free from pain and trouble as virtually a natural human right, and Christian minds have been so swamped by this thinking that nowadays any pain and loss in a Christian's life is felt to cast doubt on God's goodness. It is perhaps no wonder that our age has produced the gospel of health and wealth, promising that God will give us right now whatever we name and claim under either heading; no wonder, either, that the triumphs of the 'power encounter' between the Christ of the Gospels and the secular and satanic forces that he faces should be equated by some with supernatural healings of the physical body rather than with supernatural transformations of the moral character. But if we can learn to take the Holy Spirit seriously once more, he will convince us afresh of the naturalness of suffering in the Christian life, probably by leading us into a higher degree of it than we have yet had to face.

It seems that at this point in history the burden of evangelizing and planting churches worldwide, wherever doors remain open, rests upon the shoulders of evangelicals who recognize in the Lausanne Covenant God's marching orders for mission. Other Christian constituencies seem for practical purposes to have abandoned this task. Humankind's need and evangelical responsibility are both great, and the call to take the Holy Spirit seriously, as the renewer of God's people and the empowerer of their witness, was never more urgent. The Consultation that produced this book and the book itself should be seen as pointers in the direction in which, please God, we shall all soon find ourselves moving. For the word that bears on our unfinished task, as on Zerubbabel's long ago, is ' "Not by might nor by power, but by my Spirit," says the Lord Almighty' (Zech. 4:6). God help us to hear it!

Chapter 18

The Holy Spirit and His Work

Fifty years ago when I was a student, the person and work of the Holy Spirit were neglected themes in the world church, so much so that witty folk would from time to time speak of the Spirit as the displaced person of the Godhead and the Cinderella of theology. Apart from popular evangelical exposition of what was then called holiness teaching in its two main forms, Wesleyan (entire sanctification) and Keswick (victorious life),[1] plus the Pentecostal emphasis (at that time thought eccentric) on tongues and healing as the Spirit's gifts, no sustained speaking or writing about the Paraclete went on anywhere. Potent factors operated across the Christian board to preclude any serious attention to pneumatology.

In most of the Protestant world theological initiative remained in liberal hands. But liberalism was hamstrung and hobbled in its pneumatology, as where it survives it still is, by its Unitarian or, at best, Binitarian thought-forms.[2] The liberal habit since Schleiermacher has always been to reduce the Trinity to a threefoldness in our perception of God – God above, beside, and within us; to explain or explain away the Incarnation as a special case of divine influence in a human life; and to treat the Spirit as another name either for the unipersonal God in action or for the continuing influence, however conceived, of the historical Jesus. In either case, liberals would conceive of the Spirit as the personal, relational dimension of divine life on the analogy of the human spirit as known to us by our own introspection; and this movement of thought effectively turned pneumatology into a department of natural theology. Within this frame of reference New Testament teaching about the Spirit's personhood and ministry could

THE HOLY SPIRIT AND HIS WORK was originally published in *Applying the Scriptures: Papers from the Third ICBI Summit*, ed. Kenneth S. Kantzer (Grand Rapids: Zondervan, Academie Books, 1987), pp. 51–76. Reprinted by permission.
[1] I have discussed these positions in *Keep in Step with the Spirit* (Old Tappan, N.J.: Revell and Leicester: IVP, 1984), pp. 121–69.
[2] As, for instance, in G. W. H. Lampe, *God as Spirit* (Oxford: Oxford University Press, 1977) (Unitarian), or C. F. D. Moule, *The Holy Spirit* (London: Mowbrays, 1978) (Binitarian).

hardly be given proper weight and, in fact, it was not. As now, so then, liberals said little about new birth and the moral and dispositional transfor - mation of the believer; and when they spoke of the work in the world of the divine Spirit, what they envisioned was large-scale cultural change, evolutionary or revolutionary, to be brought in by some form of political action and to be identified as the coming of God's kingdom on earth. Reflected here was liberalism's characteristic confidence in the power of latter-day Christian reason to understand Christianity better than its own founders did: this was liberalism's Pelagianism of the intellect, matching the Pelagianism of the complacent liberal certainty that the new order could be brought in by the power of education and politics. Christian interest will only ever focus on the doctrine of the Holy Spirit where the inadequacy of all human effort is acknowledged; inevitably, therefore, in the liberal world of thought pneumatology was neglected to a scandalous degree.

Moreover, traditional Trinitarianism, where it still held sway, was itself a hindrance to sustained pneumatological thought, for it fed into the main streams of both Roman Catholic and Protestant theology, with something approaching normative force, Augustine's image of the Trinity as the lover, the beloved, and the love that binds them together. But this formula fails to express, and so obscures, the Spirit's distinct personhood; and where this is played down, his ministry is bound to be played down, too. Evidence of this was the Roman Catholic habit of referring to gifts of internal grace rather than ministrations of the Spirit and the Protestant habit of calling the Spirit 'it' rather than 'he.' To be sure, in my student days it was possible to read in English the first half-volume of Barth's *Church Dogmatics*, which rejects Augustinian analogies altogether and argues that the truth of the Trinity is to be drawn from the reality of divine revelation: *God* reveals *God* through *God*.[3] But this argumentative *tour de force* had not in those days been widely read and weighed, and its one-is-three line of analysis, coupled with its sharp rejection of liberal ways of conceiving divine personality, had brought Barth under suspicion of teaching modalism in a refined form (that is, the idea that the Trinity is fully explained by saying that one divine agent acts three roles). Also, Barth's categorical rejection of natural theology in favour of biblical revelation was at that time thought to be overdone. The truth is that, among the relatively orthodox Trinitarians, thought was languishing every way, and no part of it languished more than the doctrine of the Third Person.

At the same time, more conservative outlooks in the Roman Catholic church and older Protestant bodies were stifling reflection on the Spirit by their institutionally minded triumphalism, by which I mean their ready assumption, without evidence, that the Spirit's beneficent presence was

---

[3] Karl Barth, *Church Dogmatics*, 1.i., trans. G. T. Thomson (Edinburgh: T. & T. Clark, 1936).

locked into their own current practice. Then, as now, Protestants would censure Roman Catholics for assuming this in relation to the sacramental ministrations of their priesthood, as if the apostolic succession of orders that Rome claims could guarantee such a thing. But great numbers of Protestant churches. Anglican and Presbyterian in particular, were at that time contentedly running on a basis of mere moralism divorced from any joy in worship, any zeal in witness, any incidence of conversions, or any meaningful expressions of informal Christian fellowship; and this made their censure of Roman Catholic institutionalism appear as a case of the pot calling the kettle black. For when churches trust their orthodoxy or their liturgy or their traditionalism or their up-to-dateness or anything else about themselves as guaranteeing the blessing of God, they quench the Spirit, just as they do if they regard good organization, stockpiled skills, and overall ecclesiastical expertise as evidences of that blessing. Here, too, is a sort of Pelagian self-sufficiency, which, now as then, has the effect of damping down concern about the Holy Spirit. Serious pneumatology is only ever sparked off by recognition of spiritual need, and there was little such recognition in those days.

By a combination of circumstances that the world would call chance and I call providence and divine mercy, I stumbled during my student days on what was then literally buried treasure, namely the classic teaching on the Holy Spirit given by Calvin, the English Puritans, and Jonathan Edwards. At that time all I was competent to say about it was that this was masterful wisdom that spoke profoundly and caused Scripture to speak profoundly to both my mind and my heart. Today I would maintain in any company that as Augustine was *the* theologian of grace and Luther *the* theologian of justification, both *par excellence*, so Calvin was and remains *the* theologian of the Holy Spirit in the post-apostolic Christian church, with the Puritans and Edwards in close support. No one has ever surpassed these men; few have come near them. There are amazingly pregnant declarations in Calvin's *Institutes* of knowledge of God through the Word and Spirit; of the Spirit's common grace in scholars, artists, rulers, and all architects of culture; of union with Christ through the Spirit as the principle of personal salvation and churchly identity; and of the Christian's faith and fortitude, the preacher's fruitfulness, and the efficacy of the sacraments, as flowing from the Spirit's work within us. Reading them convinced me that to call Calvin *the* theologian of the Holy Spirit, as B. B. Warfield first taught me to do,[4] was *prima facie* just. Puritan contributions, such as John Owen's massive *Pneumatologia*, along with his separate treatises, on life in the Spirit (*Indwelling Sin*; *Mortification of Sin*; *Temptation*; *Spiritual Mindedness*; *The Spirit As a Comforter*; *Communion with God*; *The Reason of Faith*; *Spiritual Gifts*; *The Work of the Spirit in Prayer*),

---

[4] B. B. Warfield. *Calvin and Augustine* (Philadelphia: Presbyterian and Reformed, 1956), pp. 484–87.

seemed to me to stand in relation to Calvin as does a massively enlarged photograph to its small but beautifully focused original. Of this body of literature on the Holy Spirit, together with Edwards' *Distinguishing Marks of a Work of the Spirit of God*; *Religious Affections*; and *Reflections on the Revival*, I find myself still constrained to say what David said of Goliath's sword: 'There is none like it; give it to me' (1 Sam. 21:9).

In addition to this, during my student years I came under influences that formed in my mind the Trinitarian vision of the church as the family of God, body of Christ, and community of the Holy Spirit that I still hold, or rather that still holds me, at this present time. The vision is of the church, both universal and local, as a supernatural, Christ-animated community in which every-heart adoration of the Father and the Son through the Spirit and every-member ministry to God and others through the same Spirit are the divine rules. The church takes the visible forms that it does, both local and connectional, in order to express and channel the life that by grace it has; its structures are secondary because its Lord and its life are primary; its organization is to be shaped by its organic life as a communion of saints in and with Christ, not vice versa. By the Spirit, Christ rules each congregation through the Scriptures, refining, reviving, and reforming as he wills according to local need, confronting his people continually as they commune with him via Word and sacrament, em - powering them to be salt and light to those outside, and giving them foretastes of heaven in their worship experience. The vision remains with me, and I continue to find myself restless in congregations that do not share it and are not consciously seeking fulfilment of it.

All of this was clear to me at least fifteen years before the charismatic movement began, and none of it, of course, was new; I had simply tapped into the tradition of thought stemming from Calvin in particular which, as I now know, had sustained men like George Whitefield, Charles Simeon, and J. C. Ryle in my own Anglican fold and, outside it, men like C. H. Spurgeon and Martyn Lloyd-Jones in Britain, Murray McCheyne in Scotland. Robert Haldane in Switzerland, Jonathan Go - forth in China, and Andrew Murray in South Africa. But when I was a student there was not much knowledge of this heritage nor much interest in it anywhere in the world as far as I could see, and the literature of it was not readily available as it is now.[5]

Today, however, it is a different story. Perhaps one should say that the Holy Spirit himself has stepped in and taken a hand! The pendulum has swung, and in many quarters the Spirit of God is now the subject, not of cool neglect, but of almost obsessive concentration and certainly of

---

[5] The difference is mainly due to the pioneer reprint program undertaken by the Banner of Truth Trust, which made available the works of John Owen, Richard Sibbes, John Flavel, Jonathan Edwards, John Newton and much more seventeenth- and eighteenth-century material.

passionate confusion. The work of such theologians as Leonard Hodgson; the later Barth; Eberhard Jüngel; Jürgen Moltmann; Thomas and James Torrance; Robert Jenson; and, most recently, David Brown and Colin Gunton has brought back a thorough-going Trinitarianism with full emphasis on the personal deity of the Holy Spirit and has done much to re-establish it as normative for thought. [6] Meanwhile, charismatic renewal has touched and challenged the whole Christian world, and Spirit-centred literature has emerged from this movement at different levels – academic, apologetic, homiletic – in large quantities. [7] We shall not be able to discuss in the present paper all the questions relating to the Spirit's work that the charismatic movement has thrown up for debate, but some of the more interesting and weighty ones may be listed at this point.

1. *In Spirituality* (the life of fellowship with God). Is Spirit baptism, in the sense of a felt enlargement of one's assurance, peace, and praise, sense of Christ's love and closeness, wholeheartedess of consecration, and uninhibitedness of Christian expression, divinely prescribed for all Chris - tian people at some point following their first believing and/or their reception of water baptism? Is it proper to direct all Christians to seek such an experience? Can it be had for the asking? Is one inevitably a deficient Christian without it? [8]

---

[6] See Leonard Hodgson. *The Doctrine of the Trinity* (London: Nisbet, 1943); Colin Gunton, *Becoming and Being* (Oxford: Oxford University Press, 1978), pp. 117–85 (on Karl Barth); ibid., *The One, the Three, and the Many* (Cambridge: Cambridge University Press, 1993); Eberhard Jüngel, *The Doctrine of the Trinity* (Grand Rapids: Eerdmans, 1976); Jürgen Moltmann, *The Trinity and the Kingdom of God* (London: SCM, 1981); Robert W. Jenson, *The Triune Identity* (Philadelphia: Fortress, 1982), D. M. MacKinnon, 'The Relation of the Doctrines of the Incarnation and the Trinity,' *Creation, Christ and Culture*, ed. R. W. A. McKinney (Edinburgh: T. & T. Clark, 1976); David Brown, *The Divine Trinity* (LaSalle, Ill.: Open Court, 1985); see also now *The Forgotten Trinity*, ed. Alistair I. C. Heron (London: BCC/CCBI, 1991) and Gordon Fee, *God's Empowering Presence* (Peabody MA.: Hendrickson, 1994).

[7] See J. R. Williams, 'Charismatic Movement,' with bibliography, in *Evangelical Dictionary of Theology*; ed. W. Elwell (Grand Rapids: Baker, 1984), J. I. Packer, 'Theological Reflections on the Charismatic Movement,' *Churchman* XCIV.1 (1980): pp. 7–25 especially 20ff (reprinted in Vol. 2, pp. 111–55 of this collection); F. D. Bruner, A *Theology of the Holy Spirit* (Grand Rapids: Eerdmans and London: Hodder & Stoughton, 1970); ed. Kilian McDonnell, *Presence, Power, Praise: Documents on the Charismatic Renewal in the Churches* , 3 vols. (Collegeville, Minn.: Liturgical, 1980).

[8] See James D. G. Dunn, *Baptism in the Holy Spirit* (London: SCM, 1970), John R. W. Stott, *Baptism and Fullness*, rev. ed. (Downers Grove: InterVarsity and London: IVP, 1976) Anthony A. Hoekema. *Holy Spirit Baptism* (Grand Rapids: Eerdmans and Exeter: Paternoster, 1972); F. D. Bruner, *Holy Spirit*.

What is Pentecostal–charismatic glossolalia? Does it always accompany Spirit baptism? Does it ever occur in persons who have not been Spirit baptized in the stated sense? In what ways is it spiritually beneficial? Is it always beneficial? Is it proper to encourage all Christians to seek glossolalic ability?[9]

What expectations should Christians have with regard to the healing of body and mind through the prayers of others? What constitutes a Christian's health in this world? Is supernatural, miraculous healing ever part of the will of God in these days? Is denial of requests for supernatural, miraculous healing ever part of the will of God in these days? Will God sanctify the enduring of pain and frustration through physical and mental disability? May possibilities of supernatural healing be forfeited through prayerless unbelief? In what terms should sick Christians be counselled? [10]

By what means and how specifically will God guide believers in their decision making? How does God guide from the Bible? Does he supplement biblical guidance by direct revelations through prophecies (understood as messages given for delivery to others) or through imme - diate disclosures to the decision-makers? Is it proper to direct all Christians to seek and expect such messages? Are there any other modes of communication whereby the Holy Spirit gives certainty that one option should be embraced rather than another? [11]

How is faith to be exercised in prayer? What may one 'name and claim' in the presence of God? In what respects must the exercise of faith exclude doubt and uncertainty as to the outcome? In what respects is the exercise of faith compatible with doubt and uncertainty as to the outcome? Does God's giving in answer to our prayers ever depend on our being

[9] See J. I. Packer, *Keep in Step*, pp. 177–78, 206ff., 224–25, 229–30, 280–81; W. J. Samarin, *Tongues of Men and Angels* (New York: Macmillan, 1972); J. P. Kildahl *The Psychology of Speaking in Tongues* (New York: Harper and Row and London: Hodder & Stoughton, 1972).

[10] See J. I. Packer, *Keep in Step*, pp. 194–95, 214–15; 'Poor Health May Be The Best Remedy,' *Christianity Today* (May 21, 1982), pp. 14–16; Francis MacNutt *Healing* (Notre Dame: Ave Maria, 1974); B. B. Warfield, *Miracles Yesterday and Today* (Grand Rapids: Eerdmans, 1953); Joni Eareckson with Steve Estes, *A Step Further* (Grand Rapids: Zondervan, 1978 and Glasgow: Pickering and Inglis, 1979), Don Dunkerley, *Healing Evangelism*, with Preface by J. I. Packer (Grand Rapids: Chosen Books [Baker], 1995).

[11] See G. Friesen with J. Robin Maxson, *Decision Making and the Will of God* (Portland: Multnomah, 1980): Elisabeth Elliot, *A Slow and Certain Light* (Waco: Word, 1976); Sinclair B. Ferguson, *Discovering God's Will* (Edinburgh: Banner of Truth, 1981); M. Blaine Smith, *Knowing God's Will* (Downers Grove: InterVarsity, 1979); Dallas Willard, *In Search of Guidance* (Ventura: Regal, 1984); J. I. Packer 'Wisdom Along the Way,' 'Paths of Righteousness,' 'True Guidance,' *Eternity* April–June, 1986.

subjectively certain that we shall receive exactly what we ask for? Does divine action against evil depend at all on verbal and attitudinal techniques of 'binding Satan' and 'taking authority' as we pray? Does faith require us to thank God for evil things, telling ourselves they are good things because they come from God?[12]

2. *In Christology.* Is it proper to see Jesus as the archetypal Charismatic and to view his water baptism as the occasion of his Spirit baptism? Does this idea reduce the incarnation of the pre-existent Son of God to a special case of God indwelling a man as liberal christology does?[13]

3. *In Ecclesiology.* Are charismatic manifestations (tongues, prophecy, claimed miracles, claimed healings, claimed interpretation of tongues) a restoring or renewing of the 'sign-gifts' that authenticated the apostles?

Since gifts for ministry are given to all Christians, what is the right place for women in the church's ministering structures?

Does God give revelations today that should have canonical status for the future?

What pastoral authority structures in and over charismatic communi - ties are appropriate? How should the relation between these and local churches be understood and managed?

Are house churches (an increasingly common charismatic structure) in any sense schismatic?

How far should the confessional differences between Roman Catholi - cism and Protestantism be regarded as overcome, or transcended, through sharing charismatic experience?

As was said, we cannot discuss all these questions here (in any case, I have dealt with several of them elsewhere);[14] I list them simply to indicate the range of thought about the Spirit that over a generation the charismatic movement has opened up.

Nor is the charismatic movement the only focus of contemporary Christian thought about the Holy Spirit. A small but vigorous group of evangelical speakers and writers (J. Edwin Orr, D. Martyn Lloyd-Jones, Iain Murray, Leonard Ravenhill, Richard Lovelace, et al.) have sought to promote an Edwardsean concept of revival as the outpouring of the Spirit, viewing this as involving significantly more than is found in charismatic renewal.[15] The sense of the nearness of a holy God, the

---

[12] See Merlin Carothers, *Prison to Praise* (Plainfield: Logos, 1970); *Power in Praise* (Plainfield: Logos, n.d.); *Answers to Praise* (Plainfield: Logos, 1972).

[13] See on this the shrewd tightrope walk of Thomas A. Smail, *Reflected Glory* (London: Hodder and Stoughton, 1975 and Vancouver: Regent College, 1995), pp. 61–88.

[14] *Keep in Step*, pp. 121–69; articles in *Christianity Today* and *Eternity*, as above.

[15] The case is put in J. I. Packer, *Keep in Step*, pp. 235–62; 'Steps to the Renewal of the Christian People.' *Summons to Faith and Renewal*, ed. Peter S. Williamson and Kevin Perrotta (Ann Arbor: Servant, 1983), pp. 107–27. See also Richard Lovelace. *Dynamics of Spiritual Life* (Downers Grove: InterVarsity, 1979).

intense anxiety and humbling for sin and the violent energy of repen -
tance, leading to rapid, deep maturing in Christ, that have characterized
earlier revival movements seem to have no counterpart in the current
charismatic movement, which in consequence appears to Edwardseans
to be somewhat shallow. The relation between renewal and revival,
both conceptually and experientially, thus becomes a talking point for
them.[16]

In the world of ecumenical Protestantism it is often nowadays claimed
that the Holy Spirit is currently prompting (1) involvement in various
forms of revolutionary violence and (2) convergence and coalescence of
the world's great ethnic religions. That these are two potent trends is true,
but the suggestion that the Holy Spirit of God is behind them looks in
the light of Scripture too ludicrous to merit detailed treatment in this
paper.

Mention of Scripture introduces the next question. What will evan -
gelical inerrantists bring to the discussion of the renewal-revival theme?
Three things, I suggest.

First, inerrantists will bring *support for the robust supernaturalism* of these
two viewpoints. The mark of inerrantists in theology is their intense
concern that everything taught in Scripture be treated with full seriousness;
this is the other side of their refusal to allow that anything taught in Scripture
might need to be discounted as erroneous. Inerrantists know that the effect
of such discounting, when it occurs, is regularly to erode aspects of biblical
supernaturalism, reducing the Trinity to some sort of Unitarianism; or the
Incarnation to a case of God indwelling a man; or the penal, substitutionary
sacrifice of Christ to an example of faithfulness till death; or Jesus' bodily
resurrection to the continuing impact of his personality; or Jesus' miracles
to honorific myths; or the Second Coming to a hope that God will triumph
in the end; or the personal Holy Spirit to a pervasive uplifting influence; or
the imparting of a new life by regeneration to the turning over of a new
leaf by repentance; or the church from an awesome divine creation to a
venerable human club. As, like tracking dogs, inerrantists sniff out half-
truths and untruths in theology, barking at them incessantly and trying to
bite them to pieces lest they ruin souls, so they applaud movements of
Christian thought that restore biblical supernaturalism to its rightful place,
and this the viewpoints under discussion clearly do.

Second, inerrantists will also bring *watchfulness against supersupernatu -
ralism and subjectivism* among charismatic people. The charismatic desire,
very proper in itself, to maximize awareness of the supernatural in daily
life, starts to go over the edge into what I call 'supersupernaturalism' when
the ordinary is depreciated as a field of divine action, and God is looked
to to act habitually against the nature of things, producing fairy-tale
miracles, cures, manifestations, and providences. The charismatic belief

---

[16] See J. I. Packer, 'Renewal and Revival,' *Channels* Spring (1984), pp. 7–9.

in revelatory prophecy constantly exposes the movement to the danger of following in good faith someone's subjective impressions which cannot in fact be from God because they run contrary to Scripture. Seeing these possibilities as occupational hazards of the charismatic movement, iner - rantists will think of themselves as required when they relate to the charismatic constituency to keep a sharp lookout for them and to blow the whistle the moment they spot them.

Third, inerrantists will in addition bring *a concept of divine communication that correlates the Spirit and the Word*. They will affirm the *coherence* of the sixty-six books of Scripture against any form of the fashionable idea that the substance of one Bible writer's teaching is inconsistent with the substance of another's (a contention, be it said that is often declared but has never yet been demonstrated); they will affirm their God-given *sufficiency* as a guide for faith and life and a judge of any proposed supplementary guide, like *Science and Health* or *The Book of Mormon*; and they will affirm their *clarity*, in the sense that everything essential to salvation is stated in them so fully, in so many mutually illuminating ways, that every serious reader will see it, without any need of a supposedly infallible church to interpret it.

With this they will affirm the ministry of the Holy Spirit, the divine author of the books, who authenticates them to us as the Word of God; interprets them to us so that we see what they mean and know that the divine realities spoken of truly exist; applies to us the principles of believing and living that the Scriptures teach and illustrate; and animates us to respond to what we know in faith, worship, and obedience. They will underline again and again the incapacity of the fallen human mind to think rightly of God apart from the guidance of Scripture, and they will constantly emphasize that it is only as each one is the beneficiary of the Spirit's illuminating and interpreting ministry that they have any knowledge of divine things to share with others. Anything that looks to them like reliance on self-generated human speculation (going beyond Scripture) or supposed private revelation (going against Scripture) or uncriticized church tradition (overlaying and obscuring Scripture) will earn their special hostility.

When Willem Mengelberg told Arturo Toscanini that he got his way of playing Beethoven's overture *Coriolan* from the true German tradition, going back to Beethoven himself, Toscanini replied that his way of playing it came to him from Beethoven directly – through the score! ('You play it your way, and I'll play it Beethoven's way.') Toscanini would have been similarly scathing with anyone who added bars and notes to, or subtracted them from, what Beethoven had written, and for the same reason: disrespect for the composer was to Toscanini the supreme musical sin. So, too, inerrantists, led by the Spirit himself to regard Holy Scripture as God's score for human faith and life, will insist that what is written must have full and decisive authority over everything else.

What overall view of the Holy Spirit's person and work will inerran -
tists deploy in their treatment of the renewal-revival theme? I now give
some space to setting out one inerrantist's answer to that question. [17]

First, we glance at the Old Testament, for the New Testament builds
on the Old, proclaiming the fulfilment in Christ of its principles, prophe -
cies, types and hopes, using it as what the late Alan Stibbs called 'a divine
dictionary and phrasebook' for articulating the truth of Christ, and
claiming it as Christian Scripture – Scripture, that is, written to instruct
Christians in the knowledge and service of God and yielding up its deepest
meaning only to them (Rom. 15:4; 1 Cor. 10:11; 2 Cor. 3:14–18; 2 Tim.
3:15–17; 1 Peter 1:10–12; 2 Peter 1:19–21; 3:16; cf. Heb. 10:15). To
generalize, there are just under a hundred explicit references in the Old
Testament to the Spirit of God. 'Spirit' each time is *ruach*, a word also
denoting 'breath' and 'wind' and signifying power let loose, or energy in
exercise. Always the reference is to God himself, present and at work.
Though the distinct personhood of the Spirit can and, according to the
New Testament, should be read into the Old Testament, it cannot be
read out of it. The eternal fact of God's triunity was not known to or
expressed by the Old Testament writers. In the course of the hundred
references, the Spirit of God is said to:

1. Mould *creation* into shape and animate created beings (Gen. 1:2; cf.
2:7; Ps. 33:6; Job 26:13; 33:4).

2. Control the course of *nature and history* (Ps. 104:29–30; Isa. 34:16;
40:7).

3. Reveal *God's truth and will* to his messengers by both direct
communication and/or distilled insight (Num. 24:2; 2 Sam. 23:2;
2 Chron. 12:18; 15:1; Neh. 9:30; Job 32:8; Isa. 61:1–4; Ezek. 2:2; 11:24;
37:1; Mic. 3:8; Zech. 7:12).

4. Teach God's people through these revelations *the way of faithfulness
and fruitfulness* (Neh. 9:20; Ps. 143:10; Isa. 48:16; 63:10–14).

5. *Elicit personal response to God* in the form of faith, repentance,
obedience, righteousness, openness to God's instruction, and fellowship
with him through praise and prayer (Ps. 51:10–12; Isa. 11:2; 44:3; Ezek.
11:19; 36:25–27; 37:14; 39:29; Joel 2:28–29; Zech. 12:10).

6. Equip individuals for *leadership* (Gen. 41:38 [Joseph]; Num. 11:17
[Moses]; 11:16–29 [seventy elders]; 27:18, Deut. 34:9 [Joshua]; Judg. 3:10
[Othniel]; 6:34 [Gideon]; 11:29 [Jephthah]; 13:25, 14:19, 15:14 [Samson];
1 Sam. 10:10, 11:6, cf. 19:20–23 [Saul]; 16:13 [David]; 2 Kings 2:9–15
[Elijah and Elisha]; Isa. 11:1–5, 42:1–4 [the Messiah]).

7. Equip individuals with *skill and strength* for creative work (Exod.
31:1–11 [Bezalel and Oholiab]; cf. 1 Kings 7:14 [Hiram]; Hag. 2:5, Zech.
4:6 [temple builders]).

---

[17] Much of what follows was originally presented at the Consultation on the
Work of the Holy Spirit and Evangelization, Oslo, May 1985.

In short, the Spirit of God in the Old Testament is God active as creator, controller, revealer, and enabler, making himself present to humankind in order that he and they might deal with each other (Ps. 139:7). But there is no clear suggestion as yet of a plurality of persons within the unity of God.

In the New Testament, however, the case is altered. All that the Old Testament says of God's Spirit is evidently taken for granted, and the Holy Spirit sent at Pentecost is identified explicitly with the Old Testament Spirit of God (Acts 2:16–21; 4:25; 28:25; Heb. 3:7–11; 10:15; 1 Peter 1:11; 2 Peter 1:19–21), but the divine Spirit is now unambiguously spoken of as a distinct person acting in defined relation to two other distinct persons, God the Father and Jesus Christ the Son. The Spirit's personhood appears from the verbs of personal action – hear, speak, witness, convince, show, lead, guide, teach, command, forbid, desire, give speech, help, intercede with groans – that are used to tell us what he does (John 14:26; 15:26; 16:7–15; Acts 2:4; 8:29; 13:2; 16:6–7; 21:11; Rom. 8:14, 16, 26, 27; Gal. 4:6; 5:17–18; Heb. 3:7; 10:15; 1 Peter 1:11; Rev. 2:7, 11, 17, 19, et al.). It appears also from the fact that he can be lied to and grieved (Acts 5:3; Eph. 4:30; cf. Isa. 63:10). It appears with supreme clarity when Jesus in John's Gospel introduces him as 'the Paraclete' (14:16, 25; 15:26; 16:7); for this rich word, which means by turns counsellor, helper, strengthener, supporter, adviser, advocate, ally, signifies a role which only a personal agent could fulfil. Jesus confirms this by calling the Spirit 'another' Paraclete, second in line to himself and continuing his ministry after his departure (14:16); that is a way of informing us that the Spirit is as truly a person as he is himself. This point John clinches by using the masculine pronoun (*ekeinos,* 'he') to render Jesus' references to the Spirit, when Greek grammar required the neuter *ekeino* ('it'), to agree with the neuter noun *pneuma* ('Spirit,' the Greek equivalent of *ruach*). This masculine pronoun, which appears in 14:26; 15:26; 16:8, 13–14, is the more striking because in 14:17, where the Spirit is first introduced, John had used the grammatically correct neuter pronouns (*ho* and *auto*), thus ensuring that his subsequent shift to the masculine would be perceived not as incompetent Galilean Greek but as magisterial apostolic theology.

To understand what is said about the Spirit and the Son tritheistically, however, would be a Mormon mistake. No apostolic writer thinks of the Father, Son, and Spirit tritheistically. In the New Testament the distinct personhood of the Spirit, along with that of the Son, is only ever thought or spoken of as part of the revealed reality of the one God of Israel in action. Decisive for this way of thinking was the recognition of the risen, ascended, and enthroned Jesus as a person to be worshipped and prayed to alongside, yet in distinction from, the one whom he called Father, so that it was right to say to Jesus what Thomas said to him – 'My Lord and my God!' (John 20:28) – just as it was and is right to address those words to the Father. And from this recognition of Jesus' divinity the apostolic writers go on to link the Holy Spirit with him in what is effectively a parity relationship, one that combined solidarity in redemptive action with coequal divine dignity. This is in direct line with Jesus' declaration that in the Holy Spirit's post-Pentecostal ministry as, specifically, the Spirit of Christ, he would be the Second Paraclete, replacing Jesus permanently in order to mediate to Christians constantly the presence – not physical, but yet real and beneficent – of both the Son and the Father (John 14:16–23). Many New Testament passages speak of the Son and the Spirit side by side, correlating and co-ordinating them in a way that is clearly deliberate: see, for instance, Acts 9:31 (divine communion); Romans 8:9–11 (divine indwelling); 8:27, 34 (divine intercession); 15:30 (Chris - tian motivation; cf. Phil. 2:1); 1 Corinthians 6:11 (justification); Hebrews 10:29 (apostasy); Revelation 2:1, 7, 8 and 11; et al. (divine revelation). More striking still are the triadic passages linking Father, Son, and Spirit as collaborators in a single plan of grace: see John 14:16–16:15; Romans 8; 1 Corinthians 12:4–6; 2 Corinthians 13:14; Ephesians 1:3–13; 2:18; 3:14–19; 4:4–6; 2 Thessalonians 2:13–14; 1 Peter 1:2. These testimonies show that as in terms of role the Spirit acts as agent – colleague, we might say – of the Father and the Son, so in terms of deity he is on a par with them, and in our doxology he should be honoured with them and praised alongside them.

Nor is this all. Though the Spirit is nowhere explicitly called God, the New Testament writers intimate his deity in ways clearer than any yet mentioned. Thus, 'holy,' like 'Lord,' is an Old Testament designation of God, 'the Holy One'; and as the New Testament writers use 'Lord' of Jesus over and over, so they call the Spirit 'holy' no less than eighty-nine times. Again, 'glory' in the Old Testament means deity in manifestation, Yahweh being 'the God of glory' (Ps. 29:3); in the New Testament, as the Father is 'the Father of glory' (Eph. 1:17) and Jesus is 'the Lord of glory' (1 Cor. 2:8; James 2:1), so the Spirit is 'the Spirit of glory' (1 Peter 4:14). Similarly, as the Father and the Son give 'life' (a relationship of conscious response to God's grace in love, peace, and joy – spiritual *joie de vivre!*), so the Spirit gives 'life' (see John 5:21, 26; 6:32–33, 63; Rom. 8:2; 2 Cor. 3:6). Ontologically and functionally, all three persons are thus identified with Yahweh in the Old Testament, the Spirit as directly as the two others.

And there is more. Lying to the Holy Spirit is diagnosed as lying 'not . . . to men *but* to God' (Acts 5:3–4). Also, Jesus declares that the name of God, into which his disciples are to be baptized, is a tripersonal name: 'the name of the Father and of the Son and of the Holy Spirit' (Matt. 28:19). 'The name' means the designated party; 'name' is singular here, for there is only one God; but God's 'name' – his 'Christian name,' as Barth sweetly called it – is tripersonal. Again, John starts his letters to the churches by wishing them grace and peace 'from him who is, and who was, and who is to come, and from the seven spirits before his throne, and from Jesus Christ' (Rev. 1:4–5). The 'seven spirits' according to the number symbolism of the book signify the Holy Spirit in the perfection of his power (the NIV margin, exegeting rather than translating, actually says 'the sevenfold Spirit'), and when the Spirit is set between the Father and the Son as the second of the three personal sources of divine blessing, no room remains for doubt as to his coequal deity.

Whether one finds a doctrine of the Trinity in the New Testament depends on what one means by 'doctrine.' As Arthur Wainwright says: 'In so far as a doctrine is an answer, however fragmentary, to a problem, there is a doctrine of the Trinity in the New Testament. In so far as it is a formal statement of a position, there is no doctrine of the Trinity in the New Testament.'[18] But if it is proper to give the name of 'doctrine' to a position that is explicit and defined, it cannot be improper to give the same name to that which is basic and presuppositional to, and in that sense explicit in, positions that are explicit and defined; and since the Trinitarian way of thinking about God is in fact basic and presuppositional to all the New Testament's explicit soteriology, being the answer to the problem about the unity of God which the fact of Christ, the event of Pentecost, and the shape of subsequent Christian experience, had raised, it is far more accurate, profound, and enlightening to affirm that the New Testament writers teach the doctrine of the Trinity than to do as is fashionable today and deny it. Though innocent of later Trinitarian formulations, these writers do in fact think of God in the tripersonal way that the later formulations were devised to safeguard and reject other conceptions as anti-Christian (cf. 1 Tim. 3:16–4:5; 2 Tim. 3:1–9; 2 Peter 2:1; 1 John 2:18–27; 4:1–6). The true path is to affirm this and thereby negate all forms, old and new, of the idea that the Spirit is a creature of or a function of or a title for a unipersonal God. No version of this Unitarian idea can express what the New Testament writers mean when they speak of the Spirit – or of Christ and the Father, for that matter – so we shall say no more about it.

The statement that post-Pentecostal Christian experience raised a problem about the unity of God no doubt requires explanation. The problem was posed by the fact that that experience, the experience of being 'in the Spirit' and 'in the Lord,' involved awareness of a dual relationship, to God as Father and to Jesus as Saviour and Master, which relationship was seen as dependent on the personally indwelling Holy Spirit (Rom. 8:9). Thus, as James D. G. Dunn puts it: 'Christians became aware that they stood at the base of *a triangular relationship* – in the Spirit, in sonship to the Father, in service to the Lord.'[19] This awareness prompted the question whether

---

[18] Arthur Wainwright, *The Trinity in the New Testament* (London: SPCK, 1962), p. 4.
[19] James D. G. Dunn, *Jesus and the Spirit* (Philadelphia: Westminster, 1975), p. 326.

God is tripersonal in himself. While knowledge of the triangular relation - ship would not have come without some instruction (and the gospel shows clearly who the first instructor was), it is hard to doubt that experience within the relationship shaped some of the New Testament expositions of it, Paul's in particular, and so became a means of establishing the way of thinking about God that underlies it.

Here it is appropriate to characterize the New Testament sense of God with some exactness. It is uniformly Trinitarian; more particularly, it is Christ-centred and Spirit-generated to the core. It is true to say that the Christian awareness is of God above, beside, and within, but for the New Testament that is not true enough; we need to be more precise. The authentic Christian awareness of God, as the New Testament writers exhibit it, is:

(1) a sense that God in heaven, this world's maker and judge, is our Father, who sent his Son to redeem us; who adopted us into his family; who loves us, watches over us, listens to us, cares for us, showers gifts upon us; who preserves us for the inheritance of glory that he keeps in store for us; and to whom we have access through Christ, by the Spirit (Matt. 6:1–18, 24–33; Luke 11:1–13; John 14:21; 16:27; 20:17; Rom. 8:15–17; Gal. 4:4–7, Eph. 2:18);

(2) a sense that Jesus Christ, who is now personally in heaven, nonetheless makes himself present to us by the Spirit to stand by us, to love, lead, assure, quicken, uphold, and encourage us, and to use us in his work as in weakness we trust him (Matt. 28:20; John 15:1–8; Rom. 15:18; 1 Cor. 6:17; 15:45; 2 Cor. 12:9; Eph. 3:14–19; 2 Tim. 4:17);

(3) a sense that the Holy Spirit indwells us (a) to sustain in us what nowadays is called a personal and existential understanding of gospel truth (1 Cor. 2:14–16; 12:3; 1 John 2:20–27; 5:7–8, 20); (b) to maintain in consciousness our fellowship with the Father and the Son, and to assure us that this love relationship is permanent and that glorification lies at the end of it (John 14:18–23; Rom. 8:14–25; Gal. 4:4–7; 1 John 1:3; 3:1–2, 24), (c) to reshape us in ethical correspondence to Christ (2 Cor. 3:18; Gal. 5:22–24; Eph. 5:1–2) as he induces us to accept suffering with Christ which is the road to final glory (Rom. 8:12–17; 2 Cor. 1:5; 4:7–5:5; Phil. 3:7–10, 20–21); (d) to equip us with abilities for loving personal worship of God in praise and prayer (John 4:23–24; 1 Cor. 13:1; 14:2, 26–32; Eph. 6:18; Phil. 3:1; Jude 20) and loving personal ministry to others, expressing Christ to them (Rom. 12:4–21; 1 Cor. 12:4–13; 1 Peter 4:10–11); (e) to engender realization of our present moral weakness and inadequacy of achievement (Rom. 7:14–25; 8:22–27; Gal. 5:16–17), and to make us long for the future life of bodily resurrection and renewal, the life of which the Spirit's present ministry to us is the first fruits (Rom. 8:23) and the initial instalment, guaranteeing the rest (2 Cor. 1:22; 5:5; Eph. 1:14).

This structured tripersonal sense of God is literally constitutive of New Testament Christianity, and the awareness that 'the Spirit of your Father'

(Matt. 10:20) in his role as 'the Spirit of truth' (John 14:17, where the Greek construction is a hendiadys), the Spirit of wisdom (Acts 6:3, 10), 'the Spirit of Jesus' (16:7), 'the Spirit of life' (Rom. 8:2), 'the Spirit of Christ' (v.9), 'the Spirit of adoption' (v.15 KJV), 'the Spirit of [God's] Son' (Gal. 4:6), and 'the Spirit of grace' (Heb. 10:29), is now given to abide with all Christians is the central constituent of this sense of God. Interpreting Paul, Dunn has written:

> The risen Jesus may not be experienced independently of the Spirit, and any religious experience which is not character and effect and experience of Jesus Paul would not regard as a manifestation of the life-giving Spirit . . . At the same time the identification of Spirit and risen Jesus in experience means that Paul can clearly mark out the limits of charismatic experience; only that experience which embodies the character of Christ is experience of Spirit. If Christ is now experienced as Spirit, Spirit is now experienced as Christ . . . the distinctive mark of the Christian is experience of the Spirit as the life of Christ.[20]

Dunn goes on to claim that on at least twenty-one occasions the phrase 'in Christ' denotes religious experience (or a particular religious experi - ence) as experience of Christ – deriving from Christ as to both its source and character, so that it 'expresses . . . a consciousness of Christ.'[21] In a word, the New Testament is witness that as believers know God in and through Jesus Christ, so they know Jesus Christ in and through the Holy Spirit. This makes Christian experience – that is, the Christian's affective awareness of the divine – radically and categorically different from its Jewish and Gentile counterparts.

It seems clear that the apostles' convictions and formulations concern - ing the Spirit are the product – the intellectual precipitate, we might say – of living in the Spirit and directly experiencing Christ in the manner described, though passion for abstract orthodoxy has sometimes betrayed Evangelicals into overlooking this fact. That the apostles' convictions are divinely revealed truths, and as such are matters of doctrine and norms of faith, is a fixed point for the present writer, as it is for all Evangelicals. But that does not necessarily mean that they popped into apostolic minds ready-made. It is more natural to suppose that they crystallized out of the experiential-ethical transformation that those who received the Spirit, the apostles among them, underwent. The insights of the New Testament writers concerning the Spirit took their rise, no doubt, from the words of Jesus but were distilled into their mature form via experiential response to experienced deity. The idea that because apostolic teaching is revealed truth it must have come to the apostles by some means other than noting,

---

[20] Ibid., p. 323.
[21] Ibid., p. 324.

describing, and reflecting on their own experience of God appears groundless. The apostles' evident view is that experience of the Spirit comes spontaneously and directly but reveals its authenticity by creating an immediate awareness of the presence of the Christ of the gospel in love and power and by evoking a heartfelt response of confession, celebration, repentance, obedience, and praise. Those who share this experience, so they assume, will know that they have received the Spirit (cf. Acts 2:13–21; Rom. 8:23, 26–27; Gal. 3:2; Eph. 1:14; 1 John 3:24; 4:13; Rev. 1:10). The apostles recognized that some claims to be experiencing the life of the Spirit had to be challenged, for major error concerning Christ's person, place, authority, and law would show those claims to be false (see 1 Cor. 12:3; 14:37–38; 1 John 3:24–4:13), and what looked like such error was sometimes found among the supposedly Spirit-led. But the essential 'unambiguity' (Alasdair Heron's word) of the Spirit's action in Christ's professed disciples is taken for granted throughout the New Testament. The apostles do not think it difficult to judge when the Spirit is at work, nor do they doubt their own participation in the Spirit's ministry. So there is no reason to doubt and every reason to suppose that their theology of the Spirit reached its mature form in and through this participation rather than being given in revelatory experiences distinct from it.

Against this background of shared conviction and experience we shall now review what is special in each of the various strands of apostolic witness to the Spirit and his work.

We start with the Gospels. Written, as P. T. Forsyth somewhere points out, for readers who had already embraced the theology of the Epistles, these are four selective accounts of Jesus' words and deeds in his public ministry, each climaxing in the Crucifixion and Resurrection, and each comprising in its totality a proclamation of the gospel (the good news about Jesus) from one particular angle. Each evangelist is an artist, writing with thought and skill in order to get his planned effect. Mark, who may have been the inventor of this new literary form, presents Jesus as the authoritative, wonder-working, disciple-gathering Son of God who became the Suffering Servant of Isaiah's prophecy. Matthew expands Mark's outline (so, at least, I think) to depict Jesus in addition as the Davidic king who is also the new Moses reformulating God's law for the new age of the kingdom. Both evangelists leave their readers facing the fact that Jesus is now risen, alive, sovereign, and at large, Mark ending his story (so, again, I think) with the emptiness of Jesus' tomb (Mark 16:8) and Matthew ending his with the Great Commission (Matt. 28:18–20). Neither highlights the Holy Spirit; their few references to him make just two simple points.

The first point is that the Spirit was upon Jesus throughout: as a divine source of his conception and birth (Matt. 1:18–21), as the divine anointing at his baptism (Matt. 3:16; Mark 1:10), as the divine guide who led him to his temptation (Matt. 4:1; Mark 1:12), and as the divine agent of his exorcisms, which, therefore, it was blasphemous and ruinous to ascribe to Satan (Matt. 12:18, 24–32; Mark 3:22–30).

The second point is that Jesus will baptize with the Holy Spirit ('and with fire' Matthew adds) for the purging and transforming of human lives (Matt. 3:11–12; Mark 1:8). How this will happen, and what the results in experience will be, we are not told. (No doubt John the Baptist himself did not know and so could not say.) Jesus later specifies one consequence: his disciples would be supplied with things to say when under pressure (Matt. 10:20; Mark 13:11). This foreshadows the realized *parrhasia* (boldness) of Acts.

The indication that the enabling Spirit with which Jesus is to baptize his followers is the same enabling Spirit with which the Father first anointed him is confirmed by the rest of the New Testament (see John 1:32–33; Acts 2:33; 10:38 with 44–48; 11:15–17; Gal. 4:4–6).

Luke's Gospel is another version of Mark's, expanded differently from Matthew's. It is the first volume of a two-part work which Michael Ramsey well describes as 'the drama of the Holy Spirit.' He states its plot thus:

> In the story of the conception and birth of the Messiah the work of the Holy Spirit is presented as the creation of a new era in history . . . Filled with Holy Spirit, the Messiah teaches and heals with authority and power. . . . On the day of Pentecost the exalted Jesus pours the Holy Spirit upon the Church, and the subsequent story sees the Church working in the power of the Spirit at every stage of the progress of the gospel from Jerusalem to Rome.[22]

Writing as a historian, modelling his vocabulary and style on the historical literature of both secular and Septuagintal Greek, Luke offers factual descriptions rather than theological analyses, but his interest in the Holy Spirit's ministry and his sense of its significance are plain to see.

Luke's interest in the Spirit, like that of Matthew and Mark insofar as any interest at all can be read out of what they write, is historical and eschatological rather than subjective and charismatic – it focuses, that is, on the coming of the kingdom of God rather than on the supernatural - izing of individual experience. Norms for experience are no part of Luke's concern, a fact to be remembered when we study the variety of Pente - costal happenings that he records (2:1–13; 8:14–17; 10:44–48; 19:1–6). But Luke's interest in the Spirit as leader and Lord of the church's mission is strong; indeed, the Spirit is the chief agent throughout his volume two, which might well have been called 'Acts of the Holy Spirit' rather than, as in the traditional Greek title, 'Acts of the Holy Apostles.' So we find that Luke highlights the renewal of prophecy through the Spirit (Luke

---

[22] Michael Ramsey, *Holy Spirit* (London: SPCK, 1977), p. 33.

1:15–17, 41–42, 67; 2:25–28, 36–38; Acts 2:18; 11:27–28; 13:1; 21:4, 10–11); that he speaks constantly of individuals, from John and Jesus on, as 'filled with the Spirit' for faithful and fruitful service (Luke 1:15, 41, 67; 4:1, 14; Acts 2:4; 4:8, 31; 6:3, 10; 7:55; 9:17; 11:24; 13:9; et al.); and that he makes much of the Spirit as a divine gift (Luke 11:13; Acts 2:38; 5:32; 11:17) for encouragement (8:31), joy (Luke 10:21; Acts 13:52), guidance and decision-making (15:28; 16:6–10), and ability to witness to Christ with clarity and boldness (4:31). His point in all this plainly is that the Holy Spirit is the supreme resource for the church's life and mission. Only as the Spirit is poured out will there be convincing speech and convinced hearts; only so will there be power, advance, and fruit, and only through the Spirit's power are such outpourings effectively sought (Luke 3:21; Acts 1:14; 4:24–31).

John's Gospel, with which we may bracket his letters, has personal communion with God, for which the Johannine name is 'eternal life,' or 'life' simply (John 17:3), as a main concern. Hence John's interest in the Spirit who rested on the incarnate Son (1:32–33; 3:34) centres on the fact that following Jesus' departure (death, resurrection, ascension) the Father and the Son would send him to the disciples to be the Second Paraclete (helper, advocate, adviser, ally, supporter, encourager, as was said earlier) in Jesus' place. His ministry as paraclete would take the form of making Jesus, and with and through him the Father, consciously present to the disciples (14:16–24), and also of making the full truth about Jesus clear to them, partly by causing them to remember and understand what he had said while he was with them, partly by additional revelation (16:13; 14:26). Thus 'He will glorify me; for he will take what is mine and declare it to you' (16:14) – and the disciples will find that it was to their advantage that Jesus left them, by reason of the richness of this new relational experience (16:7). The Spirit's paraclete ministry would have an evangel - istic significance, too, for he would convince the world of the truth about Jesus. In 16:8–11 Jesus speaks of this ministry in relation to Jewish unbelief in the first instance and promises that the Spirit will convince of sin, righteousness, and judgement. In 1 John 2:20–27; 4:1–6; and 5:6–10a, the apostle looks to the Spirit to attest the truth of the Incarnation against gnostic docetism, with its consequent denial of sacrificial atonement and propitiation by blood. In both cases, the Spirit acts as the Spirit of truth, vindicating the reality of the incarnate Son as our mediator, sin-bearer, and source of life against all forms of misbelief and denial. This is his work as *witness* (John 15:26; 1 John 5:78).

Correlative to the Spirit's bestowal of revelation and understanding is his inward work of drawing us to Christ in faith and keeping us in the knowledge and worship of God (John 4:23–24; 17:3). It is in this sense that the Spirit 'gives life' (6:63). The life belongs to those who see and enter the kingdom of God by putting faith in Jesus (3:14–18), and the seeing and entering occur only through being born again 'of water and

the Spirit' (3:3–7). The fact that Jesus censures Nicodemus, 'a teacher of
Israel', and therefore presumably a biblical expert, for not knowing how
new birth could take place (3:10) indicates the interpretation: new birth
is a two-word parable of the totally new start that the prophesied cleansing
and renewing of the heart by the Spirit according to Ezekiel 37:25–27
will effect (cf. also Ps. 51:10–12). In 1 John the parable has become a
theological doctrine in its own right: birth from God, which makes us his
children, produces true belief in Christ, righteousness of life, and a loving
disposition, and makes habitual sin a thing of the past, since sinning is
now contrary to our renewed moral nature (2:29–3:10; 4:7; 5:1, 4, 18).
Though the epistle does not explicitly link birth from God and being 'of
God' (4:6; 3 John 11) with the Spirit's inward work, clearly it is the new
birth of Jesus' speech to Nicodemus, whereby one is 'born of the Spirit'
(John 3:6), that is being talked about.

The Spirit as witness to Christ, maintaining the believer's communion
with him so that 'rivers of living water' (the life-giving, health-giving
influences of a transformed life) flow from him (John 7:37–39; cf. Ezek.
47:1–12), 'was not yet [Gk.] . . . because Jesus was not yet glorified' during
his earthly ministry. Not until he had been glorified on the cross
(13:31–32) and by return to the Father's side (17:25) would the Spirit in
his paraclete role begin work. This had to be so, in the nature of the case;
the Spirit could not glorify Christ to the disciples by showing them
Christ's glory until Christ had entered into that glory so that it became a
reality to be shown (16:14). After the Resurrection, Jesus breathes on the
disciples and says, 'Receive the Holy Spirit' (20:22); but since at that
moment Jesus had not yet ascended (20:17) to be glorified in the full
Johannine sense, it is better to treat this as an acted promise of what would
very soon happen (at Pentecost, about which it cannot be thought that
John's intended readers were ignorant, any more than John was himself)
than to suppose that John means us to gather that the Pentecostal Spirit,
the Spirit as paraclete, was actually bestowed in that moment by Jesus'
action.

Finally, we look at Paul. As he is the widest-ranging, tautest-reasoning,
deepest-analyzing theologian in the New Testament, so his account of
the Holy Spirit is in many ways the richest, and if we were to attempt to
draw out all the implications of the great Holy Spirit statements and
episodes in his letters (Rom. 7–8; 14:17; 15:7–21; 1 Cor. 2; 3:16–17;
6:9–20, 12–14; 2 Cor. 3; Gal. 3:14; 4:6, 21–6:10; Eph. 1:13–20; 2:18–22;
3:14–19; 4:1–16, 30; 5:15–33; 6:10–20; 1 Thess. 1:2–10; 5:16–20; 2 Tim.
1:6–14; Titus 3:3–7), we should be composing a book rather than
concluding a paper. The outlines of Paul's thought about the Spirit,
however, as distinct from its wealth and depth, can be stated in a brief
and simple way.

Salvation through Christ – Christ crucified, risen, enthroned, reigning,
and coming again; Christ known, loved, and adored as our path and our

prize, our deliverer and our destiny – is Paul's constant theme. Salvation is the life of the new and eternal order, the life of heaven begun for us on earth through the coming of Christ and his Spirit. As Heron puts it:

> Paul regularly speaks of two realms of reality, two modes of existence. The contrast is formulated in many ways – light and darkness, faith and works, life and death, righteousness and sin, sonship and slavery, divine foolishness and human wisdom, Isaac and Ishmael, Jerusalem above and Jerusalem below, Second and First Adam, the new age and the old. All these antitheses pivot upon Jesus Christ himself . . . in him the new age has broken in and our present life is set in the tension between it and the old. But the old is doomed, standing under the judgement of the cross, while our sharing in the new is the promise of salvation through him.[23]

As 'flesh' in Paul is always some aspect of life under the old order, so 'spirit' – always when used of God's Spirit and almost always when used of the human spirit, the self to which the divine Spirit ministers – points to the life of the new order. When Paul speaks of the God-sent Holy Spirit, his perspective is always eschatological, looking forward to the end of which our present experience of redemption and life in the Spirit is the beginning. The Spirit is the gift of the new age, the guarantee and foretaste, pledge and first instalment, (*arrhabon, aparche*) of what is to come when the fullness of salvation is revealed at Christ's return (Rom. 8:23; Eph. 1:13–14).

Within this broad perspective Paul has two focal centres of interest: the individual Christian and the church, the Israel of God which is the body of Christ. In relation to the individual Christian, the Spirit's ministry is fourfold. He *enlightens*, giving understanding of the gospel so that the 'spiritual' man has 'the mind of Christ' (1 Cor. 2:14–16; 2 Cor. 3:14–17). He *indwells* as the seal and guarantee that henceforth the Christian belongs to God (Rom. 8:9–11; 1 Cor. 3:16–17; 6:19). He *transforms*, producing in us the ethical fruit of Christlikeness (2 Cor. 3:18; Gal. 5:22–24): love, joy, peace, patience, kindness, goodness, faithfulness, gentleness, self-control, plus (we may add, from Rom. 8:26–27; 15:13) prayerfulness and hope. And he *assures*, witnessing to our adoption by God, our eternal acceptance, and our future inheritance (Rom. 8:15–25, 31–39, which is a transcript of the Spirit's witness; Gal. 4:6).

'So the Christians are called to holiness and to sonship,' writes Michael Ramsey.

> They do not, however, find sin once for all overcome, for their life is one of conflict and growth. In this conflict and growth the Spirit is their guide, and the apostle often exhorts them to yield to His promptings and to let Him

---

[23] Alasdair Heron, *The Holy Spirit* (Philadelphia: Westminster, 1983), p. 45.

complete what He has begun in them. They must be led by the Spirit, let the Spirit rule in their hearts, not quench the Spirit, not grieve the Spirit, and endeavour to guard the unity of the Spirit in the bond of peace. The conflict is variously described. It is a conflict with sin *flesh and spirit* . . . Here is the issue. 'To live according to the flesh' is to live by the world's standards, by the lower impulses (it would be clearer without the 'lower') of unredeemed human nature, as if Christ had not died and risen again and bestowed His Spirit and as if we were not living within the new order. But 'to live according to the Spirit' is to live with the awareness of the new order into which we, as Christians, have been brought.[24]

Excellently said! Would that all bishops and archbishops were such good biblical theologians.

In short, as the Christian's whole life is life in Christ in terms of its meaning, centre, and direction, so the Christian's whole life is life in the Spirit from the standpoint of his knowledge, disposition, and ability to love and serve. Putting off the old man and putting on the new man, which God renews (Eph. 4:20–24; Col. 3:9–10), and being new created in Christ (2 Cor. 5:17) corresponds in Paul to new birth in John, and though Paul nowhere says this explicitly, it is plain that the initial inward renewal is the Spirit's work, as is the living that expresses it. All that we ever contribute to our own Christian lives, according to Paul, is folly, inability, and need. Everything that is good, right, positive, and valuable, comes from Christ through the Spirit.

As for the church, Paul's basic idea that the community of believers, both universal and local (the latter being an outcrop and microcosm of the former) are the body of Christ (1 Cor. 12:12–31; Eph. 4:1–16) is evidently an extension of his thought that every believer is covenantally, vitally, and experientially 'in Christ.' That thought is extended into this metaphor in order to make the two points that Paul does make by his use of it. The first is that unity must be acknowledged and expressed by love and mutual care within the diversity of Christian individuals (1 Cor. 12:14–26; cf. Phil. 2:1–4). The second is that the diversity of *charismata-diakoniai-energemara* (gifts-ministries-operations: 1 Cor. 12:4–6) in which the Spirit is manifested (v.7) must be acknowledged and put to full use within the unity of the fellowship (vv.4–11). To be a manifestation of the Spirit, a gift would have to be an expression of Christ in some form, and this seems to be precisely Paul's idea: a gift is an ability to express Christ by following the instincts of one's renewed nature in acts of worship and service. By this criterion gifts are to be distinguished from other sorts of performance. The Spirit creates and sustains the unity of the body (Eph. 4:3), gives the gifts, and builds up the church through their exercise (1 Cor. 14:3–4, 26; Eph. 2:22; cf. 4:16). When gifts are used, it is Christ

---

[24] Ramsey, *Holy Spirit*, pp. 67–68.

ministering to his body through his body. The gifts themselves are diverse, some relating to speech, others to practical Samaritanship, and there is no reason to regard any of Paul's lists as exhaustive (see Rom. 12:4–13; 1 Cor. 12:8–11, 28–30; cf. Eph. 4:11, where the 'gifts' are gifted functionaries and 2 Tim. 1:6–14, where Timothy is reminded that he is a specially anointed functionary). The references to love in each gifts context (Rom. 12:9–10; 1 Cor. 13; Eph. 4:16) remind us that, whether or not love be classified as a gift of the Spirit or as a fruit of the Spirit or as both, abilities to serve cannot be exercised in a way that will edify the church and please God without it. Using four of Paul's key words, we may say that the pattern of life in the church must always be *agape* (love) expressed in *diakonia* (service, ministry) by means of *charismata* (gifts) for *oikodome* (edifying, literally the erecting of a building). Since the gifts are meant to be used for edifying, any neglect or restraint of them will quench the life of the Spirit in the church inescapably and drastically: every-member ministry in the body of Christ is meant to be the rule and is the only healthy way.

It should be said explicitly that in all this Paul is thinking in terms of relational dynamics and functions, not of organization of offices or demarcation of status. How these principles are best translated into local church order is a question which each congregation must think through for itself. First Corinthians 14 reflects one pattern, and there are others.

Our survey has now embraced all the main thoughts about the Holy Spirit that the New Testament contains, and we need not take it further. (In fact, the non-Pauline epistles and Revelation do not develop the doctrine of the Spirit very broadly at all.) If it were asked why this paper has not, as is fashionable, made much of signs and wonders (Rom. 15:19; Heb. 2:4) and tongues (Acts 2:4; 1 Cor. 14), the answer would be that these authenticating manifestations which accompanied the apostles' ministry were evidently regarded by the apostles themselves as peripheral to life in the Spirit for the Christians and churches whom their letters instruct, and it seems desirable to maintain an apostolic perspective in these matters. I repeat: in my view, all the main things have now been dealt with.

I think evangelical inerrantists in the Protestant churches will all accept the above analysis of the biblical witness, so far as it goes. (If not, tell me at once; I need to know!) But if this is so, then our range of agreement in pneumatology is revealed as impressively wide. We shall all be found as one on the fact of the Spirit's personal deity; on the fact that Jesus and the Father give the Spirit to all believers; on the fact that the Spirit within us works through our minds and wills and not apart from them (that is, he does not move us by physical force without persuasion, as one would move a stick or rock or robot); on the fact that faith and assurance, new birth and spiritual growth, spiritual gifts and ministry, holy habits and Christlike character, particularly love, humility, hope, and patience, along with boldness and usefulness in witness and Samaritanship, all flow from his work in our hearts; and on the fact that sanctification is progressive: We shall all be at one in acknowledging that faith and repentance, holiness and service, become realities through our cooperation, although not by our power; and in recognizing our obtrusive sense of present spiritual imperfection (that is, of reach exceeding grasp) as itself a reminder from the Spirit that his work in us here is no more than – just as it is no less than – a pledge, beginning, and foretaste of glory hereafter. We shall also be at one in seeing the church as God's charismatic movement, in which every-member ministry, both Godward and humanward, through the use of spiritual gifts universally given, is an abiding clause in the divine rule of life. We shall all agree that the church must see itself as the agent of God's mission, with the whole company of Christians labouring to fulfil their role as Christ's hands and feet and mouthpiece. And we shall all be as one in recognizing that as the creating of the church by regeneration is the Spirit's sovereign work, so is the renewing, reviving, and reforming of it when the fires of spiritual life have burned low. These are significant and far-reaching agreements, and the fact that they will form the frame - work within which continuing differences will be discussed shows at once that such differences, however passionately debated, cannot be of major importance.

The most acute tensions between inerrantists today, as has been said, concern the credentials and claims of the charismatic movement in the mainline churches. I have written about this movement in two books. In the first (*The Spirit Within You*, 1961, jointly with the late Alan Stibbs) it was maintained that Spirit baptism as Charismatics conceive it and the 'sensational' manifestations which I have here referred to as 'sign-gifts' are no necessary part of full Christian experience. In the second (*Keep in Step with the Spirit*, 1984) it was argued that though charismatic theology in its usual forms is not viable, charismatic experience could and should be accounted for theologically in other terms and on that basis accepted as from God, and therefore valuable. I argued there that Spirit baptism, along with other 'second-blessing' experiences (Wesley's 'entire sanctifi - cation' and the 'Keswick experience' of 'Spirit-filling'), ought to be understood in terms of the Spirit witnessing to our adoption and medi - ating to us Jesus' presence and love (John 14:21–24; Rom. 5:5; 8:15–17). I am loath to repeat either argument here, and, in any case, space does not allow it. So let me simply say that I stand by the double purpose for which *Keep in Step with the Spirit* was written: first to lay a basis for mutual trust, acceptance, and cooperation between those Protestant Evangelicals who profess a charismatic experience and those who do not, and second to call both sorts to seek revival in what we may call Edwardsean terms, that is, a restoration through the Spirit of the exalted quality of Christian communion with God to which most of the New Testament letters testify, and of which the charismatic renewal has given us only a small part as yet. Here, I believe, are two lines of action on which all inerrantists ought to be embarking today.

I will make two final points now, both about breadth and balance. First, *just as the Word is insufficient without the Spirit, so the Spirit is insufficient without the Word*. Well may Charismatics and others censure those who seem in practice to embrace the idea that biblical orthodoxy is all that matters and biblical teaching alone produces a healthy church. The critics are right to point out that idolizing orthodoxy is not the same as worshipping God and that complacent 'orthodoxism,' by inflating pride, actually quenches the Spirit. But pneumatic preoccupation can slow down maturity, too. Many Charismatics appear anti-intellectual in basic attitude, impatient with biblical and theological study, insistent that their movement is about experience rather than truth, content with a tiny handful of biblical teachings and positively zany in their unwillingness to reason out guidance for life from the Scriptures. Endless possibilities of self-deception and Satanic befoolment open up the moment we lay aside the Word to follow supposedly direct instruction from the Spirit in vision, dream, prophecy, or inward impression. The history of fanaticism is gruesome; I do not want to see it return among my charismatic friends. But this is always a danger when the formation of the mind by the Word is in any way neglected. What is needed across the board is constant instruction in biblical truth with constant prayer that the Spirit will make it take fire in human hearts, regenerating, redirecting, and transforming into Christ's likeness at character level. Whatever agenda others have, the fulfilling of Christ's prayer that his people would be sanctified by the Spirit through God's Word of truth should be the inerrantist's first concern.

Second, *just as the Spirit must not be forgotten when we focus on the Father and the Son, so the Father and the Son must not be forgotten when we focus on the Spirit*. A full-blown, thorough-going Trinitarianism is the needed basis for devotion and discipleship, just as it is for theology. As some branches of Bible-believing Christendom seem clear and sound on the saving love of the Father and the Son in the covenant of grace, yet devotionally dry because of unconcern about the enlivening Spirit, so some parts of charismatic Christendom, for all their stylized exuberance, seem stunted and immature, running out of steam and stuck in their own mud because they have centred their concern on the Spirit more than on the Son and have virtually ignored the Father.[25] Exclusive concentration on any one person of the Godhead always narrows and cramps one's spiritual style. It did so in the 'Jesusolatry' of older evangelical pietism, which confined its concern to the Redeemer and the redeemed life and had no adequate

---

[25] This is the contention of Thomas A. Smail in *The Forgotten Father* (London: Hodder & Stoughton, 1979; Grand Rapids: Eerdmans, 1981 and Vancouver: Regent College, 1995); see especially pp. 9–20. Smail was for a time secretary of the Fountain Trust, Britain's leading charismatic organization.

appreciation of creation and the created order, so that natural beauty, human creativity, the cultural mandate of Genesis 1:28, the arts, higher education, and political and social responsibilities, were neglected and the supposedly spiritual Manichean mentality, the occupational disease of pre-Reformation monasticism, was cultivated afresh in a Protestant frame.

In the same way, exclusive concentration on the Spirit and the emotional side of the Christian life (the two go together) produces its own crop of neglects, first and foremost in the realm of thought, where the primacy of the mind is forgotten and much of the revealed purpose of God is forgotten too. To focus on the Father is to remember that this is God's world despite the demons; that its history is 'his story' because the Creator is never unseated from his throne, that he is transcendently high and holy ('Our Father *in heaven*'), so that our proper passion for intimacy with him must never be allowed to banish awe and reverence for him; and that the immaturity of spiritual self-absorption must give way to an all-embracing God-centredness ('Hallowed be *Thy name*' – 'glory to God *alone*'). To remember these things is as necessary as it is to remember the Holy Spirit and to do justice to the experiential side of communion with God through Jesus Christ. As 'Jesusolatry' is lopsided and deficient, so is 'Spiritolatry'; comprehensive Trinitarian devotion founded on comprehensive Trinitarian doctrine is essential if today's church is to find the fullness of the renewing and reviving that it needs.